TWICE AROUND THE WORLD

TWICE AROUND THE WORLD

Some memoirs of diplomatic life
in North Vietnam and
Outer Mongolia

by
JOHN COLVIN

LEO COOPER
LONDON

First published in Great Britain in 1991 by
LEO COOPER
190 Shaftesbury Avenue, London WC2H 8JL
an imprint of Pen & Sword Books Ltd.,
47 Church Street, Barnsley, S. Yorks S70 2AS

A CIP catalogue for this book is available
from The British Library

ISBN: 0 85052 289-7

Printed in Great Britain by
Redwood Press Limited, Melksham, Wiltshire

To the memory
of
My Mother and Father

CONTENTS

'When the ship returns to harbour
with the hull battered and the rigging
torn, before we assess the blame of the
pilot, before we award the verdict of
posterity, let us pause to inquire whether
the voyage has been twice around the world
or to Ramsgate and The Isle of Dogs.'

Thomas Carlyle

'If we don't put our foot on the egg,
we shall have to chase the chicken 'round
the world's farmyard.'

Winston Churchill in 1919,
defending Allied intervention
in the Russian Civil War

FOREWORD

This work, as has been said within, is a personal memoir of daily life as head of British diplomatic and Consular Missions in two Communist countries, the first as Consul-General during the war years at Hanoi in North Vietnam, concurrently representative of the Co-Chairman of the 1954 Geneva Conference, and the second as Ambassador at Ulan Bator, the capital of Mongolia.

The first describes a time of intense political excitement focused on a single issue, the attempt by South Vietnam, aided by the United States of America and her allies, to defeat the subversion and, ultimately, the invasion of the South by the Democratic Republic of Vietnam and her Marxist-Leninist armourers. That attempt, unsuccessful and ending in Vietnamese Communist hegemony over the whole of Vietnam, Cambodia and Laos, led, however, to the reconciliation of China and the United States, the most significant political *renversement* in the two generations since the end of the Second World War.

And the economic development, indeed the survival in sometimes authoritarian but never totalitarian circumstances, of the other countries of South-East, and even North-East Asia, is owed to the courage and endurance of Americans, Vietnamese and other Asians through long years of struggle. Their terrible, often unnecessary losses stain the consciences of men alive in Washington today, but were not in vain: the line of freedom held.

They were grim days. The restrictions of war, privation, confinement almost to a single town, ideology and its consequences — dislike, perhaps hatred, and harassment — the frustrations of an observer's status, produced occasionally in one a rigidity comparable to one's hosts. Not so in the People's Republic of Mongolia.

There, the absence of war, the amplitude of that enormous landscape, the ancient, gentle, but robust character of the Mongols, above all 'space', while not masking the incompetence and brutality of the collectivist system, balanced it in one's considerations. For what little harm Mongolia did to the world, it did, unlike Vietnam, because it had no choice.

This is a work of record, if not of history. It recounts events of the past - 1971 to 1975 - at a time when Mongolia was still under Soviet and Marxist influence, if not control. That influence ran grossly counter to Mongol ways and culture.

Many countries, in this terrible century, have been liberated, Mongolia among the most recent to embrace political pluralism and the free markets. These concepts, although not precisely native to Mongolia, are welcome to her inhabitants. In celebrating their arrival, however, nothing but advantage can be gained by recounting the background to the leap that this extraordinary and lovable Central Asian people is about to make.

Mongols only lack control of their destinies, they are not evil. They were our friends and perhaps, one day, they may become our permanent friends. Until then, we were happy there; too happy to return.

PART ONE

NORTH VIETNAM

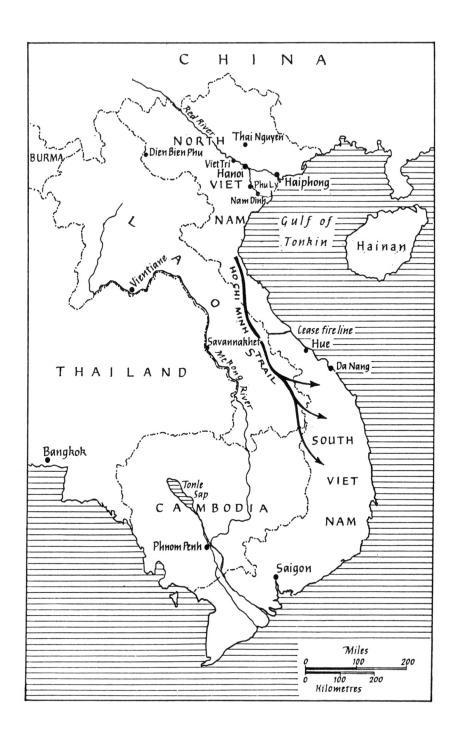

C H I N A

Red River

NORTH
Dien Bien Phu   Thai Nguyen

BURMA

Viet Tri
Hanoi
VIET   Phu Ly   Haiphong
              Nam Dinh

NAM   Gulf of
             Tonkin   Hainan

L

Vientiane   A

O

Savannakhet   Cease fire line
                     Hue

Mekong River   HO CHI MINH STRAIL   Da Nang

THAILAND

                                    SOUTH

Bangkok   VIET

              Tonle
              Sap   NAM

C A M B O D I A

Phnom Penh

              Saigon

                              Miles
                    0   100   200
                    ━━━━━━━━━━━━━━━━━
                    0   100   200
                              Kilometres

I

APPOINTMENT TO HANOI

MY FIRST RECORD, of the British Mission at Hanoi, capital of the Democratic Republic of Vietnam then in the flood of war against Britain's principal ally, the United States of America, covers the years 1966-1967. Since no Americans, other than prisoners of war in camps outside the cities, lived in North Vietnam during those years, I have tried to present a picture of the enemy citadel, the dark side of the moon, unknown then to any Westerners other than the few diplomats also resident there: the story of those days, and the conclusions to be drawn, may provide a missing piece or two in the jigsaw of the Indo-China War.

If the account has a theme, other than the observations or anecdotes which it contains of political and domestic life under bombardment at Hanoi, it is that of deception, courage, ignorance, even treasonable ignorance, but above all of the ultimate, still unrecognized triumph of the United States, not yet acknowledged by even the best of that country's inhabitants.

In 1945, as a member of the Royal Naval port party for Saigon, I had taken part in the liberation of French Indo-China from the Japanese. Since the outbreak of war in 1939, in a succession of warships and a variety of foreign or colonial waters and ports, I had tried to engage in war and to grow up. The aims had seemed irreconcilable. But on 14 August, 1945, there was no more war; instead, peacetime in a French provincial town in the tropics, where to grow up was agreeable and easy. (There *was* a war of sorts but not, it seemed, mine.) Exposure to France, for some English, at some ages, civilizes, enriches, opens the windows of the spirit: later contact with French bureaucracy or other republican manifestations may sensibly reduce but never destroy the gentle weakness, in excess categorized as 'French flu'. What are engendered are pride in self, elegance, sense of theatre, conversation directed by reason, respect for body as for mind, reserve, urban use of light and shade, trees in streets, *venétiennes*, an environment created to human requirements, the discretion of love.

Twenty-one years later, when the Diplomatic Service invited me to become Head of the British Mission and Consul-General at Hanoi, nostalgia for 1945 as well as less unrealistic considerations prompted rapid acceptance. There was, I knew, no jostling queue of place-seekers for the post: American bombing grew more intense as the weeks went by, Western amenities were minimal, and indeed, the survival even of French influence seemed improbable. But Hanoi was a point of adventure, even of history, perhaps the fulcrum on which might turn the future of more than Asia. The naked confrontation of what then seemed to be only two and not the three worlds that actually faced one another in Vietnam was not to be rejected in favour of continued occupancy of a Chelsea apartment and an Economic desk at the Foreign Office. Here was the chance to break with compromise, to discard the chic ennui of London life, to play a part in or at least directly to observe the main battle of the epoch. To return to Indo-China was also, of course, as in every foreign posting, an escape from routine, from the known, from dull care, toward a concept of the exotic that has as one purpose an evasion, however temporary, of 'reality'. And as usual, 'with the first turn of the screw, all debts are paid', the sailor's adage here referring less to financial than to sentimental dues, to commitments joylessly and for too long endured.

The incumbent of the Hanoi post was appointed as:

Consul-General for North Vietnam and those parts of Central Vietnam lying north of the line of the Song Ben Hai River between its mouth and the village of Bo Hu Su and thence due west to the Laos-Vietnam frontier.

But the post was not accredited to anyone. Even the Mayor of Hanoi would refuse to receive me if I attempted to arrange a meeting; my predecessor had never had official dealings with him during his stay in Hanoi. The authorities of the Democratic Republic of Vietnam (DRV) controlled our activities through the so-called External Affairs Bureau of the Administrative Committee of Hanoi, theoretically responsible to the Mayor. When corresponding with the Consulate-General on administrative matters, the subsidiary offices of this committee would always be careful to address my office not by title, but by the use of my name and street address. At the DRV National Day celebrations, we were customarily accorded the status of foreign journalists, in parallel with that of the two DRV journalists in London, although included with ambassadors, Ho Chi Minh and the Politburo at the top table. In their request for visas, the DRV authorities simply used the office as a post box. The office was therefore, if not unique, of unusual status.

The posting began, as it were, in a Swedish restaurant in Wigmore Street to which, in the spring of 1965, I had been invited for lunch by a member of Personnel Department with some experience in South-East Asia. Since I had recently returned from a visit to Washington, where the American effort had been much discussed, I gratuitously thrust upon him my views on Indo-China. I noticed that reference to previous residence in Saigon aroused interest in a manner which I did not then identify. But as we travelled on the 53 bus back to the Foreign Office, my colleague showed an unaccustomed distraction, the chance of placing some sort of peg into so curiously sided a hole seen as worth the cost of smorgasbord and aquavit.

When approached later that week to accept the appointment, I hesitated for no more than 24 hours: the factors described earlier and some regard for married colleagues − British wives and families were excluded from Hanoi − made agreement inevitable. The decision became a liberating one.

First appointment as Head of Mission affords independence and the sort of emotional charge provided, say, by first command in the Royal Navy. It has, however, its subversive aspects in inflating the self-importance of the individual, swelling like Mr. Toad's until return to reality at Heathrow.

'Looking eastward, as I do, toward Asia,' one victim observed from Beirut, 'and westward to the Mediterranean,' ignoring the mountains of the anti-Lebanon obscuring the view to the east and, to the west, the apartment block opposite. Such eccentricities rarely achieve the bizarre heights reached by an Ambassador at Washington given to expressing displeasure at incorrect placement by turning his plate upside down. (One of his compatriots, dutiful but anti-social, at a reception in Buenos Aires from which egress had seemed impossible, took French leave through the kitchens disguised in a chef's hat and apron.) Others underline whole paragraphs of their despatches, compose forty-page annual reviews from obscure People's Republics, or transmute rare encounters with Prime Ministers into intimate friendship. 'Monsieur Tel et Tel, by his own fireside, assured me ....'

It is when nations, not people, are involved that nations are brought

face to face. During the Cultural Revolution, when the mob was burning our Embassy in Peking, the Red Guard chargé d'affaires of the
Chinese Mission at Hanoi spat in my face at a reception in that city,
but accompanied the gesture not with any *official* salutation but with the
phrase 'Mr English journalist.' To have replied, in these circumstances,
with a backhander across the chops would have carried no national consequences. The chargé was, however, surrounded by five beefy colleagues, and retaliation would also have led to unsuccessful brawling,
even less thinkable had the Crown been involved.

By all accounts, however, the atmosphere at Hanoi seemed unlikely
to be congenial to official pomposity or other manifestations of the ego.
This was a revolutionary régime in the hands of a single Marxist-Leninist Party, the Lao Dong, concerned with the consolidation within its
own borders of a totalitarian system and outside those borders with the
conquest ('reunification') of the non-communist Republic of Vietnam
(RVN) and ultimate hegemony over the entire Indo-Chinese peninsula,
including Laos and Cambodia. (It may be that even the subversion of
Thailand was not excluded from the DRV's eventual political
ambitions.) Not only de Gaulle correctly perceived Tonkin as the Java
of the Peninsula, but in the West only de Gaulle advocated acquiescence
in Tonkin's irredentism.

But the summer of 1966 before my departure was, and not only at
this distance, a summer of bright joy, much of it spent with Mark and
Zoë, my elder children, in Christopher and Marcianne Wren's house in
the Algarve. The prospect ahead occupied most of my mind, and
without foreboding. One English evening, after dinner, my cousin
Ursula Rayleigh, looking out at the great park at twilight, said that the
loss of such things must make for a sad departure. I found that the padi-
fields of Asia, the rain forests, the people of village and city had at least
as strong a call on emotion as the landscape of home which, anyway,
would still be there when the adventure was done.

II

VIETNAM IN HISTORY

ELLEN HAMMER, in her major work *Vietnam, Yesterday and Today* (1964), observed that 'the Vietnamese are an ancient people, with a complex society, who were building temples and writing works of poetry and prose more than 15 centuries ago. They were profoundly influenced by Chinese civilization, but their struggle against the imperialism of China is almost as old as the Vietnamese nation itself. In the 19th century, the country became part of another empire — that of France. The French opened Vietnam to the West. Although they occupied the country for less than a century, they too left their imprint on it, although to a lesser extent than China.' That imprint was difficult to trace in 1966, whether in Saigon or collectivist Hanoi.

'Nationalism and Communism made common cause to achieve independence for Vietnam in 1954. But that uneasy alliance was never a complete one, for if some Nationalists were also Communists, many were not. The breach between these two groups led to civil war and the direct cause of the division of the country into separate and opposing states.'

After the fall of Metropolitan France in 1940, Indo-China became both part of the 'Greater East Asia Co-Prosperity Sphere' and an indispensable link in the Japanese drive in 1941 toward Singapore and Burma.

After the Japanese defeat in August, 1945, the occupation of Vietnam and disarmament of the Japanese had been allocated, north of the 16th Parallel, to the Chinese, and south of the Parallel to the British. The French meanwhile maintained their determination to resume rule over Indo-China and dispatched troops under General Leclerc to Saigon. That town had been governed since 23 August by the Provisional Executive Committee for the South, a mainly Vietminh body similar to the Vietminh authorities already in place in Hanoi and Hué. (The Vietminh was the executive organ of the Communist Party of Vietnam under Ho Chi Minh.) On 29 August in Hanoi, Ho Chi Minh had formed the Provisional Government of the Republic of Vietnam, claiming non-Vietminh as well as Vietminh representation, and with Emperor Bao Dai as Supreme Adviser. 'This government,' in the words of one observer, 'could claim to be the legal successor of the Vietnamese empire.'

It was, however, also a communist-dominated 'People's' government on the lines of its East European siblings, as Ngo Dinh Diem later recognized when refusing office from Ho in February, 1946. And Emperor Bao Dai left the country and abandoned Ho one month later, to return only in 1949 and then to Hué, the southern capital.

When, in August, the British liberation troops landed in Saigon, the city was therefore under the control of the Vietminh, their flag, yellow star on red ground, flying from balcony and rooftop. Soviet interests in Europe and, hence, Soviet Communist Party instructions at that time, dictated tactical cooperation by the Vietminh with General de Gaulle's aim of sovereignty in Indo-China through federation within the French union.

The Vietminh did not therefore refuse collaboration with either the British or the French. But, on the one hand, the non-Communist Nationalists demanded immediate independence from France, and on the other, the local French authorities refused any cooperation with the Executive Committee. Law and order could thus only be maintained by the employment, humiliating to the victors, of surrendered Japanese troops.

British responsibilities in French Indo-China were restricted to the surrender and the repatriation to Japan of Imperial troops; our tasks were not intended to include, indeed precluded, assistance in the reimposition of French rule.

British local policy was not changed or weakened. But events, including Vietnamese atrocities against European women and children, the consequent release from barracks of the Colonial Infantry, the arrival of Metropolitan troops, the Communist ideology of the Vietminh, and French reluctance to cede power, all led to the long Franco-Vietnamese war, ending only in 1954 at Dien Bien Phu. They culminated in the eventual emergence of collectivist régimes embodying various degrees of squalid barbarity throughout the peninsula but not, thanks to French and American courage in Vietnam, throughout South-East Asia.

Meanwhile, in 1946, Chinese troops withdrew from the north at the same time as the British left the south. A Franco-Vietnamese Treaty provided for French recognition of Vietnam as a 'Free State with its own government, parliament, army and finances,' and for Vietnamese agreement that Vietnam should form part of 'the Indo-Chinese Federation of the French Union'.

The incompatibility of these objectives was made plain at a series of subsequent conferences at Dalat, Paris and Fontainebleau between the two Governments, while such efforts to reconcile them as were made by the French government at Paris were consistently obstructed by the High Commissioner, Admiral Thierry d'Argenlieu, in Saigon.

Ho Chi Minh had by then determined that war was inevitable and that preparations for war demanded the elimination of all opposition to the Vietminh from the non-communist parties and the southern sects. 'Coalition' was roughly discarded. Murder, judicial murders by 'People's Courts', Vietminh warfare against the sects, drew many Nationalists away from the Vietminh, sometimes to the French side. The independence movement, hitherto supported by Nationalist parties of non-ideological character, became solely a vehicle for Communist and totalitarian aims. It is to be feared that the defection of the moderates and, as the French saw it, the consequent isolation of the Communist Party of Vietnam, was as welcome to France as to the Vietminh authorities. Intransigence in colonial as in other spheres seems to lead to a polarization disadvantageous to nearly all concerned.

After eight years of the ensuing war, and as a result of General Navarre's decision to defend Laos, France met final defeat at Dien Bien Phu on the day before discussions on Indo-China began at the Geneva Conference of 1954.

At that conference the Vietminh, under Chinese and Soviet pressure, accepted partition of Vietnam at the 17th Parallel and agreed that Pan-Vietnamese elections be held in two years; the cease-fire agreement merely provided for the regroupment of French Union and Vietminh forces. No one signed anything (other than the cease-fire agreements), and the conclusions of the conference were opposed by the United States and the new Republic of South Vietnam. The Americans would, from now on, assume the burden.

South Vietnam after 1954, unlike North Vietnam, was no monolithic state, rather a collection of heterogeneous elements without a unifying factor or even a coherent civil service or National Army. Parts of the territory south of the 17th Parallel forming the southern Republic of

Vietnam (RVN) were in the hands of outlandish sects, Cao Dai, Hoa Hao and Binh Xuyen, while the mass of Catholics, mostly Tonkinese or other northern refugees, lived in their own communities isolated from the rest of the population and hostile to the Buddhist majority.

But few sought communism, although few believed that the new state could be consolidated solely on the basis of a policy of anti-communism. The solution should surely have been one of collaboration between those native officials who had participated in the Bao Dai and French administrations, and the non-communist, anti-French, Colonial resistance, composed of the great majority of the southerners.

Ngo Dinh Diem, appointed Prime Minister on French advice in 1954 by Emperor Bao Dai, a Catholic but like most of his constituents 'a profound believer in the theory of Confucianist monarchy,' was uncompromised in Vietnamese eyes by 'puppet' associations. But, obliged by the weakness of his country to retain United States assistance during Washington's most active period of militant anti-communism, Diem rejected the policy of reconciliation in favour of support for irreconcilable northern refugees upon whom he initially constructed his régime. The State was thus at first deprived of popular participation or broad nationalist appeal and was, after Diem's later repressive measures against political opponents, vulnerable to subversion and terror within South Vietnam by Viet Cong agents left in place by Hanoi in 1954 or subsequently infiltrated across the 17th Parallel.

By 1955, however, Diem had at least defeated the sects and, through the deposition of Emperor Bao Dai, secured personal power as president of the Republic of Vietnam. His refusal, on the valid grounds that 'free' elections in the communist DRV could only be a contradiction in terms, to meet the Geneva requirement for north-south consultations on pan-Vietnamese elections may have deprived his régime of 'presentational' successes abroad. It did not appear to have substantially weakened his own internal position.

The constitution of 1956, a foreign policy seen throughout the larger part of even the non-aligned world as independent of the United States, the relative success by 1963 of the British-inspired strategic hamlets programme, Diem's progress toward a national conduct by Vietnamese of Vietnamese political and military affairs, although in conflict with the views of many American advisers, had laid the foundations of an indigenous national republic. The new state was potentially able, given friendly and non-intrusive aid, which North Vietnam, for its part, did not reject from Soviets or Chinese, to defend and support itself.

Buddhist unrest, provoked not so much by the government but by Catholic clergy, including the president's brother (Ngo Dinh Nhu), had, however, led to demonstrations in the summer of 1963 followed by raids on the pagodas and by arrests of bonzes (monks), students and other Buddhist militants. As a partial consequence of United Nations mediation, tension between the communities then subsided and an eventual compromise seemed certain. But Diem's insistence on 'national control of national policies' and on indirect contacts with Hanoi led Washington to fear a catastrophic *renversement des alliances* and thus to American acquiescence in the military coup which toppled and murdered Diem in November, 1963.

'The overthrow of the Diem government marked the end of nine years of stability and relative calm .... His administration, in spite of its mistakes and its failure to promote healthy political life in the country, had finally evolved into a coherent nationalist régime. And Diem's overthrow was considered by his formidable opponents, Ho Chi Minh and Mao Tse Tung, as marking the end of the attempt to create an independent state in South Vietnam free of communist interference.'*

The Mandate of Heaven had, with Diem's fall, expired. In this still-Confucian land, this led not to democracy — since the political parties lacked grassroots support and new elections were not held until 1966 — but to a series of coups and counter-coups, at length respectably culminating in a junta led by General Nguyen Van Thieu and the flamboyant but gallant and patriotic Tonkinese, Vice-Marshall Nguyen Cao Ky. (The latter's wife expressed her views on nationalism by a cosmetic operation to eliminate the Mongoloid fold.) Although elections, fairly conducted, did take place in 1966, and more or less representative institutions were established, neither the Buddhists nor the Cochin-Chinese lent cohesive support to a régime which they opposed as, respectively, pro-Catholic and without regional balance.

But although it could not be claimed that either trade, or agriculture, or security, or the economy in general, or village life, or even regional equilibrium were yet adequate to the demands of the people, evolutionary improvement within a national democratic framework — not then disturbed by armed DRV intervention with Soviet and Chinese support — was a more probable, if distant, outcome to South Vietnamese problems than the elitist panaceas of the Lao Dong (Communist) Party of North Vietnam.

From assassinations of officials and attacks on army posts, the DRV

* Hammer, op. cit

in 1960 had moved to the establishment in the south of an Executive Committee exactly paralleling the Politburo of the Lao Dong in Hanoi, and the creation of the National Front for the Liberation of South Vietnam (NLF) with its own army, 'the Viet Cong', under strategic and often tactical control from Hanoi. Non-Communist officials participated in the Front and, in the earlier stages, the Front advocated 'a zone of neutrality and peace' with Cambodia and Laos, while openly demanding no more than a provisional independent and sovereign status for South Vietnam. But the presence of the Communist Party and of North Vietnamese marionettes within the Front demonstrated the nature and the unreality of these claims.

In response to Hanoi's escalating intervention in South Vietnam, the United States under President Johnson moved, in March, 1965, from the policy established by President Kennedy (largely confined to American advice and material aid for the army of the Republic of Vietnam (ARVN)) to intervention in the southern war by her own land armies and those of certain of her allies, Australia, South Korea and Thailand.★ At no time, however, were any of the ground forces employed in South Vietnam permitted to breach the 17th Parallel, to enter, still less invade, the territory of the DRV. The war on land thus remained a defensive reaction to external intervention and therefore not one capable of victory in terms acceptable to the American people.

In 1965 the Americans took the war to the north in the form of aerial bombardment of military and industrial targets, supply dumps, factories, communications, troop concentrations, power supplies, docks, anti-aircraft sites, etc. The strategic objective of these attacks, as of those on communications and other targets in Laos and, eventually, Cambodia, was to deprive North Vietnam — politically inaccessible to conventional military pressure — of the resources necessary to prosecute the campaign of terror and subversion in the south. The strategy was sound but, until mid-1967, improperly implemented.

When the attacks in the north-east in 1967 at last began around the clock against the logistic entry points to Vietnam — road, rail and river — they were immediately effective. By the autumn, as we shall see, the objective and its corollary, the reduction of the aggressor to economic collapse within its own borders had been accomplished. The major war

★ But President Kennedy, in March, 1963, had already warned that a communist capture of South Vietnam might result in communist 'control of all South-East Asia with the inevitable effect that this would have on the security of India and therefore really beginning to run perhaps all the way to the Middle East.'

was over, in the sense that a game of chess conducted by Capablanca could actually be over in two minutes, but might, with a stubborn or less intelligent opponent, drag on for hours without changing the final decision.

Capablanca, alas, for reasons upon which we shall speculate, then left the board.

Failure of will, aided by a *trahison des clercs*, has since been interpreted as 'military defeat'. But victory, humane and with the technology appropriate to the purpose, was at hand in 1967. Few noticed, fewer believed; 'there are none so blind as those that will not see.'

We suffer the consequences now.

III

SAIGON AND THE SOUTH

THE UNITED KINGDOM was in a balance-of-payments crisis. Since no seats were available on any BOAC aircraft to South-East Asia, the Prime Minister's authority, as in Amin's Uganda, was required for reservations on foreign carriers, in this case Swissair to Bangkok. The impression of centralized penury, familiar in Marxist and other indigent states, was not only new but cast doubt on the purpose of the mission. A bankrupt country, as Sukarno demonstrated in Indonesia, may own a foreign policy, but the aims of the policy then require examination. The influence on Vietnamese events of a power apparently lacking economic and thus political strength was likely to seem, in Hanoi, Moscow or Washington, questionable.

But Britain was, of course, not bankrupt, only misgoverned. One hoped that such distinctions were as well recognized by the countries involved in Indo-China as by Britain's citizens. And one might hope for acknowledgement of her authority in Asia, rooted not only in history but in a continuing commercial and military presence. If not, and if the role of honest broker, whether as British Government representative or as that, with the Soviet Ambassador, of the Co-Chairman of the 1954 Geneva Agreements, was truly unplayable, the reporting function remained.

In September Moranna Cazenove, with whom from 1967 I was to live happily ever after, drove me in her Mini to Heathrow. As dinner jackets, uniforms, or any dress more substantial than tropical suits were unknown at Hanoi, my personal effects for twelve months' residence in that city were fewer than those demanded by weekends in the English countryside. I left London, indeed, with one suitcase, a tennis racket and a wireless receiver, returning fourteen months later with, apart from additions to a collection of Chinese ceramics, rather less baggage, most of the clothes threadbare, the tennis racket presented to the Indian Consul-General and the receiver to my successor.

Laurens Van Der Post and countless others agree that British Airlines' competence, calm and good manners set standards not equalled by other lines. But the excellence of Swissair's cuisine on this flight caused patriotic unease; the Swiss produced a largesse equal to the most luxurious restaurant. The experience was improper. Although this part of the journey ended at Bangkok, one felt that passengers for so rigorous a destination as Hanoi should not be fattened like Strasburg geese, rather, submitted to a diet appropriate to warriors or, more aptly, camp followers. But that diet would follow soon enough.

At Bangkok sound advice was offered by the Ambassador, Anthony Rumbold, whose family had once owned the great Palladian bulk of Pyt House where I had spent much of my adolescence before the war. The residence at Bangkok was also palatial, its fame not confined to the last foot-driven punka in any British establishment in Asia, albeit installed in an air-conditioned dining room. But here in Bangkok, Pyt in England, with its columns, shaded rooms, loggias and pavilions folded into the Wiltshire hills, was far away, the country pursuits of 'before the war' a thing of woods at morning, of *jeunes filles en fleur*, Paradise Lost, not to be regained.

Than Son Nhut, reached the following afternoon by Cathay Pacific, was the commercial and main military airport of Saigon and the site of the largest U.S. Air Force base in Indo-China, its perimeter crowded with fighters, bombers and enormous transport aircraft dispersed or, more unwisely, ranged in long lines abreast. Although I had seen large concentrations of Thai or American aircraft at Bangkok, the surrounding defences at Saigon seemed, from the air at least, inadequate for threat of guerrilla infiltration. As the aircraft descended over the flat landscape, cratered for miles around by heavy explosive, smoke from new bombing raids could be seen rising at several points in bush and padi to the north of the city. The Viet Cong, it was apparent, had been driven by 1966 no farther from Saigon than in 1945, although in receipt of counter-action different in kind and degree.

One wondered, for the first time, not so much whether the means were in proportion to the ends, but whether the ends could be reached by any means. Fire-power, whether from ground or air, certainly seemed to be an alternative, if not the only alternative, in the absence of that effective counter-guerrilla action in which the South Vietnamese Army (ARVN) had not, until recently, been trained. But if the Viet

Cong, by dispersal or in underground redoubts, could evade fire-power...? Or if the revamped ARVN had no will to fight ...? But these were jejune comments, to be answered only as part of a longer political question.

The interior of Saigon airport dripped with heat, ceiling fans revolving in the torrid air over arriving, and joyously departing, American troops, small-boned Vietnamese infantrymen, and occasional groups of solid, menacing South Koreans, whose bearing authenticated their reputation for violent response. Chaos was apparent, not actual. The Movements Officers of the various armies cleared their charges with competent if noisy skill, while civilian travellers were dealt with by Vietnamese clerks abjuring the squeeze insouciantly demanded by their Siamese colleagues at Bangkok.

Luggage retrieved, I was driven to the British Ambassador's Residence on Phan Tan Gian, past gigantic U.S. earth-movers and the construction work in progress around Than Son Nhut, through the white or colour-washed colonial suburbs of the city, along roads battered beyond recognition since 1945 by military traffic, under Saigon's overcast skies and in her fierce, perpetual humidity. To the right, as we turned into Phan Tan Gian, and immediately opposite the Residence was the miniature house − once the love-nest of the Japanese Consul-General − which I had occupied during Liberation in 1945 and 1946. Memories of that careless past merged with the present's concerns and with the low rumble of war.

The post of Ambassador to South Vietnam, given Labour party sensibilities and pressures at home, was of a fairly acute, domestic delicacy. The Government, like any British Government since 1954, was committed to military non-intervention in Vietnam and, unlike her fellow (Soviet) Co-Chairman, obedient to that commitment.

But the Administration was vulnerable to charges, from an opportunist left, of complicity in American measures. ('Complicity', thus interpreted without reference to the Anglo/American alliance or to the framework of bilateral or multilateral agreements, meant failure to condemn any action taken by the United States or to support and advocate the invasion of South by North Vietnam.)

These were characterized with venom and disregard for the aims, leave aside the bestialities, of the Viet Cong, as 'War Crimes', institutionalized in the 'Bertrand Russell Tribunal', manned by such interested participants as Tariq Ali, Ralph Schoeneman and Laurence Daley.

Total objectivity, in regard to the host government at Saigon and the

American command, was therefore the first requirement on the British Embassy, not a unique task but one on which no compromise, especially compromise occasioned by natural sympathy, was advisable. The Ambassador, Peter Wilkinson, accomplished the task, nor did he indicate that the Hanoi post had not met the standard.

We dined alone after my arrival, two immaculate Vietnamese servants in attendance, in the gloomy residence, too small for large purposes, and on furniture supplied by a Ministry of Works not over-anxious to investigate the circumstances. Old friends joined us after dinner.

(Peter, among more pressing worries, was also concerned by a misprint from the Saigon English-language Press: Thomas Hobbes, in his reference to a constitution excluding monarchy, had been there misquoted by the phrase 'Nasty, British and short.' But this error could not, we agreed, have been improved by corrections such as 'For British, read brutish.')

Next day I allowed myself a nostalgic pilgrimage to the Continental, that great hotel as French as — before the Singapore management installed boutiques there and brought in blue-rinse package tours — the Raffles had been British. Here, after Liberation in 1945, despite fitful electricity, the management had transmuted Spam and other rations by a cuisine unknown to wartime British messes. In lofty rooms, mosquito nets covering vast mahogany beds, the more fortunate of the British staff had been accommodated, supporting with equanimity the irregularity of the water supply and other essential services in exchange for Gallic delights of restaurant and terrace.

Beside the Continental now, under the shadow of the Assembly (once Opera), rose the statue to the Army of the Republic, two gesticulating soldiers with weapons aimed toward the Lower House: elections notwithstanding, the representation seemed confirmed by the experience of the Diem régime and the nine military coups that had followed. Opposite, in modernist contrast to the old, verandahed provincial edifice, lay the new Caravelle Hotel with its shifting population of reporters and journalists. Round the corner ran Tu Do, once Rue Catinat, the Rue St. Honoré of Saigon. Up this long street, lined in 1945 with elegant shops, cafés, restaurants, coiffeurs and *hotels de passage,* had moved in solid mass the Foreign Legion and the Second Armoured Division, in white kepi or scarlet beret, from the Quai Francis Garnier to barracks and to eventual defeat in the mountains of the north-west.

But Tu Do was now abandoned to sleazy bars and their skinny cargo of teenage prostitutes, wearing not the Ao Dai, most erotic of national dress, but the shorts and halters preferred by lounging GI clientele. Only in the old Hotel Royale, among aged planters, Corsican Mafia and the more enterprising press, a sort of life still obtained: in those dilapidated surrounds — for even at the best of times the Royale had been little more than a *maison de passe* — information was exchanged, payments made, interests asserted, among the last cynical or desperate adherents of a vanished civilization and their attendant carrion.

Gavin Young, ex-Brigade of Guards and Foreign Office, returned as *Observer* correspondent from an arduous journey through Burma to Nagaland, also lived here, now in discussion with a Corsican planter. The latter's face, seamed like the Ganges Delta or tributaries of the Mekong, reflected 40 years of a broken country, a wife kidnapped and children massacred by the Viet Cong. Here were the smugglers, the black marketeers, the sources of CIA, SDECE* and the Republic's Security Services; here were profits calculated and speculation assessed, here contracts — whether food, drugs, gold or human lives — negotiated, here protection, alike from police and guerrillas, purchased. And here, certainly, were the agents of the Democratic Republic of Vietnam, like all the world venal or idealist, witting or duped, in search of victory or gain.

The 'boys' lit the lamps on the terrace of the Continental. Fines, vins blancs, St. Raphaels or, for infrequent colonels and other American customers, whisky and soda were dispensed. In the dusk liaisons began as they had before, the business of the day was reviewed, hands met, gossip exchanged and plans made. But the Continental was now, despite the machinery of efficient service, a place of transit between two worlds: the spirit of 1945 had gone and Europe hung here by its fingernails to an eroded cliff.

Elsewhere in the country, among the leafy streets of the banlieus, in villas still maintained in the old manner, in certain cafés and restaurants, in the evident growth of native entrepreneurship, in increased tolerance both political and religious, under flamboyants and bougainvillea, in the scent of frangipani, in a quickening economy, in a more coherent army and civil service, in land reform, in the Chinese market with its swinging carcasses, its pervading reek and the overflowing baskets of fruit and vegetables, in assessments of the war by men of reason and knowledge, it was possible to believe otherwise.

And to be persuaded was to believe that the Vietnamese, in city, hills or padi, did not seek to exchange Colonialism for Totalitarianism. Nor

* French Secret Service

was it incredible that Nationalism should not be synonymous with tyranny, that the Vietnamese did not want blindly to reject European technology, and that the West had the will and the ability to honour undertakings freely given, indeed positively urged by the Republic.

'Must a government,' said Lincoln, 'be too strong for the liberties of its own people or too weak to maintain its own existence?'

The central dilemma of Vietnam was that a Nationalist revolutionary movement, hijacked by a small totalitarian group with a regional (northern) base, without significant popular support — at least since the departure of the colonists — but with the means of compulsion and terror, attempted the forced unification of an entire nation hostile to its philosophy but disunited in its own objectives. This southern disunity, while it contained the antipathies illustrated by the Buddhist/Catholic troubles, the sullen resentment of the Cochin-Chinese towards exiled northern interlopers, and a divisive system of land tenure, was not ideological. It did not embody collectivist and other Marxist criteria, rather a confused demand for internal reconciliation and decent administration.

While Diem, despite grave misjudgments, had begun not only to recognize the domestic diagnosis but to achieve the cure, the difficulties in meeting this demand, common and difficult enough in any newly independent country, were further compounded by Communist propaganda, terror, subversion and, finally, armed intervention. These, perhaps manageable in countries with ancient institutions, both required an unanticipated military and counter-subversive effort from the young state and infinitely complicated any solution to domestic problems.

To build a viable pluralist state, from as various regional, religious and sectarian elements as South Vietnam contained would have been task enough. To do so *unaided* under the pressures of an external aggression trained and supplied by China, the Soviet Union and the East European Communist countries was an impossibility.

The United States, with South Vietnam not a signatory of the 1954 Geneva Agreements, began to help the Republic with technical, economic and military assistance as soon as the settlement was complete. This assistance, even before President Johnson chose to intervene in 1965 with U.S. combat troops, eventually included up to 20,000 American military advisers. The U.S. had provided an essential support to the stability, slowly and painfully achieved under President Diem of South Vietnam.

But Diem's overthrow, the political vacuum which followed and the consequent intensification of NLF infiltration had to lead, unless to

American withdrawal and loss of confidence throughout South-East Asia, only to direct U.S. military intervention appropriate to protect an underdeveloped country with the desire but not yet the strength to protect itself. Precedents for the salvation of liberty in weak and struggling countries had, after all, been set by great powers throughout Europe in the 19th century, whether in Greece, Italy, Spain, Portugal, Holland or, in the 20th, in two world wars.

Every decision taken by the West in Vietnam since 1945 had been taken in the light of considerations which, although concerned with Vietnam, did not exclude others of wider scope. France's return to Indo-China in 1945 was approved by the U.S.S.R., and because the restoration of French confidence was vital to the renaissance of Western Europe, neither was it resisted by the United Kingdom, the occupying power, if only because Vietminh atrocities against French civilians made such resistance impossible.

Franco/Vietnamese negotiations thereafter were conducted with lack of candour by either party. But although until 1954 no French government showed much courage or determination, neither could any French government have convinced its electorate that independence for French Indo-China under a régime led by Ho Chi Minh represented anything but another dishonourable surrender, shameful as well as economically catastrophic. Even the cease-fire, as late as 1954, and the Geneva Agreements were to have consequences for French politics in Algeria and in France itself which are evident but not, even today, measurable.

Political decisions in this world are made, alas, not *sub specie aeternitatis,* nor with hindsight. The prophets of hindsight, however, assuming the attributes of eternity, and none more so than those with the least excuse for ignorance of their own history, condemn without regard for time and circumstance nearly all such decisions and, above all, the U.S. decision to maintain in 1954 the coherence of South Vietnam and with it South-East Asia.

Time and circumstance, thereafter, certainly did not excuse connivance in the fall of Diem, 'worse than a crime: a mistake,' but they more than excused, they explained, the military decisions of 1965. In 1966, only time would tell whether those decisions would be ratified by time. In the autumn of that year the steady escalation of American ground-force strength and the failure of American air power to reduce DRV intervention in the south did not seem encouraging.

But as to *principle,* Great Britain herself, in the 18th, 19th or 20th centuries, had not hesitated to bring force to bear in the pursuit of liberty and an end to despotism.

Meanwhile, since my route to Hanoi lay through Vientiane, where floods had put that airport out of action, departure for the north had been delayed. The additional 48 hours thus available in Saigon enabled extended calls on the Canadian, Indian and Polish delegations to the International Control Commission. The Commission, composed of representatives of those three countries, had been established in 1954 to supervise the cease-fire agreement and, after Diem's decision in 1956 not to join the DRV in nationwide elections, had remained in existence until the present time. Its military observer teams had been stationed at strategic points throughout the country, both in the south and the north, with the function of preventing breaches of the Agreements such as 'imports of war material, introduction of foreign military personnel and hostile acts between North and South Vietnam.'

Since neither of the two governments under surveillance intended to regulate their actions to the requirements of the commission, and since ideological contradictions within the commission precluded unanimity and, therefore, effective action on any incident or complaint by either side, its protests, rarely unanimous and seldom strongly worded, were largely ignored. The body was effectively without authority. Impotence had, indeed, been admitted in the 1962 Indian and Canadian report (from which the Poles had dissented), declaring the DRV guilty of aggression and subversion against the Republic of Vietnam, and the RVN in breach of the Geneva Agreements through the receipt of U.S. military aid and tacit military alliance with the U.S.A.

By 1966 the ICC was represented only in the Demilitarized Zone (DMZ), at a reducing number of points in the south, at headquarters (with three ambassadors) at Saigon, and by static teams at Hanoi. It remained, however, responsible for the sole air link between Hanoi and Saigon, and its individual Heads of Mission sometimes acted as intermediaries in attempts to bring the parties to the negotiating table. Since, furthermore, the commission *was* represented at Hanoi, formal visits to the Headquarters and separate Delegations at Saigon were essential preliminaries to professional relationships with their representatives in the northern capital. Colleagues, of any colour, were thin on the ground at Hanoi, and therefore to be pursued with vigour in Saigon.

My reception by the three delegations varied in predictable mode: warm, relaxed and friendly by the Canadians; the Indians genial but detached, if not wary; the Polish attitude, if neither hostile nor suspicious, didactic and without chiaroscuro.

In fact, the then Polish Ambassador was engaged on an initiative, at the behest of the Soviet government, to bring about a cease-fire and negotiations, to which the United States had given at least tacit approval. According to subsequent Bloc propaganda surviving in Washington at least as late as 1979, the initiative was nullified by a USAF raid on Hanoi mounted by the Saigon command in defiance or ignorance of the political discussions in progress.

The duties of these ambassadors, at least those of Canada and India, barely tolerated by the Saigon régime and, at best, regarded by Hanoi as no more than potential instruments to manipulate as occasion offered, were not enviable. Even the Poles, less objective participants, found the role periodically distasteful and, in particular, the Asian climate, habits and conditions, to which they were unaccustomed, disagreeable.

IV

THE JOURNEY TO HANOI

ALTHOUGH VIENTIANE AIRFIELD IN LAOS remained out of action, the necessity for contact between the two main centres of the Commission made an early flight imperative: replacements for the teams were overdue, food and drink stocks at Hanoi needed replenishing, and not all correspondence could be telegraphed. The Commission decided to dispatch an aircraft some days after my arrival at Saigon which would, it was hoped, be able to fill these gaps and at the same time re-establish touch with the commission for Laos at Vientiane.

The ICC's air communications between Saigon and Hanoi were provided by three propeller-driven Stratoliners contracted from the French airline UTA and flown by UTA air crews with, as cabin staff, handsome Saigon *métisses,* recruited locally and often married to air crew members. The aircraft, prototype of the magnificent Stratocruisers (although lacking curtained beds) on the 1950s Trans-Atlantic run, were all that remained of a programme of six built in the United States as long ago as 1935. North Vietnamese gunners had shot down one 'in error' some years before in mountainous country between Vientiane and Hanoi with total loss of life; another had crashed elsewhere, and a third served as no more than a reserve of spare parts (cannibalization) for the surviving trinity. Despite skilled French manpower and remarkable maintenance by Vietnamese mechanics, the age and earlier history of these aircraft sometimes gave cause for alarm; but although a replacement fleet was frequently proposed by one or more members of the Commission, the necessary funds were never, in my time, available.

In any case, the mere fact of the line's existence and the admittedly irregular egress that it provided from Hanoi or, indeed, from the often demoralizing atmosphere of Saigon, were advantages outweighing possible dangers. Danger there was, as much from weather, terrain, anti-aircraft defences and failure by the USAF strictly to obey the 'rules', as from metal or engine fatigue. But the experience in Vietnam of these air crews, their refusal to take chances, although frequently leading to lengthy interruption to schedules and consequent frustration, at least discounted those risks that lay within their control. (Similarly, after a hair-raising flight through the Hangayn Mountains, I asked the Mongolian pilot whether there had been much danger: 'Had there been, I wouldn't have flown,' he replied. That is the kind of man one likes.)

Cleared through Immigration and after a sojourn among discarded Seven-Up bottles in the airport restaurant, the ICC passengers, Indian, French, Canadian, Polish and British, moved through the gate to the faded Stratoliner on the tarmac. The noise around us while we boarded the aircraft from the jet engines of the U.S. Air Force as they prepared for the morning's bombing, patrol or escort missions precluded speech, while the temperature and humidity in the Stratoliner were even more intense than the vile, shimmering heat on the ground.

Although travel was one-class only, a class which would have been, had the line been managed on commercial principles, categorized as 'Economy', the passengers took their places on white linen seats hierarchically, heads of delegation forward, other ranks and auxiliaries aft. On this occasion the voyagers included the pretty wife, placed forward, of a newly appointed Third Secretary to the French Delegation-General, and an enormous goose named Alice tethered aft under the care of a Canadian corporal, the beast's escort on the journey toward its Christmas nemesis. 'Human interest' stories were rare enough for an *Agence France Presse* story on the subject of Alice to be carried in the French Metropolitan dailies.

The route ordinarily included a stop at Phnom Penh as well as Vientiane, its duration dependent on a number of factors, including the weather ahead, the competence of that airport's employees, etc. On this, my first flight, because the expected improvement in conditions and, above all, the proper functioning of the beacon, had not materialized at Vientiane, all passengers were disembarked at Phnom Penh for an indefinite period. In the duty-free shop we examined spoons, cigarette tin holders, ashtrays and Cambodian silver objects of Indo-Buddhist design, worked in soft, deep relief. Around us the flat brown plain stretched south to the Vietnam border and east toward the Mekong and the Tonle Sap.

An Embassy car took me to the Phnom Penh Hotel Royale, one in the chain established throughout Indo-China of massive, even palatial

French hotels. The Royale, because of austerity and anti-foreign restrictions imposed by Monseigneur (Prince Norodom Sihanouk), now lacked the plenitude, even some of the services, of happier days. But in the nearby garden pool, surrounded by bougainvillea, the families of French technicians and advisers pursued, under palm trees, aquatic contests, brisk exchange of beach balls, formal flirtations and more clandestine arrangements with the energy devoted by that people to its relaxation.

The British Embassy at Phnom Penh, after the withdrawal of the Ambassador, was in the hands of a chargé d'affaires, Leslie Fielding, then a young First Secretary with an unusual empathy for Asian, in particular Cambodian, realities. But, in the light of the 1975 massacres, he might have agreed with Frederic Prokosch on Cambodia in 1935; 'And as for love, which is the real thing that makes us think of time and fear time, there's no trace of it anywhere. Look in the eyes of the women or the idle young men, and there will be no softness visible, no tenderness at all.'

As official functions occupied Fielding and his staff that evening, I took a rickshaw into town from among those ranged, shafts resting on the gravel, in a great fan around the columned portico of the Royale. The driver was an articulate guide to the restaurants, bars and bordellos of the flower-hung city, the most beautiful city, with Penang and Malacca, then remaining in Asia, small, proportioned to the country's size and its divisions, half Khmer, half French, its red and gold pagodas coexisting with European gardens and broad streets, beside the wide Mekong.

This driver, occasionally wiping off with a rag jauntily placed round his neck the sweat that poured down his body, maintained a stream of suggestions about the evening's entertainment. This, he supposed, should begin in the Chinese quarter with its shadowed shophouses and customary sharp odours, smoked fish predominant. Redirected through the area occupied by detested Vietnamese, where the reek was of nuoc mam, fish sauce as delicious and universal as its smell is abhorrent, he deposited me at a French restaurant near more illuminated avenues. In the empty dining room, hung with out-of-date posters for local events and with written guidance from Sihanouk on moral questions, the dinner was mediocre and consumed in silence.

But in the street the rickshaw waited unbidden. Studies, even theses, have been written about the various types of rickshaw plying in South-East Asia, their size, design, colour, decoration, seat covering, number of seats, canopied or otherwise, quality and general design, bell-tone, speed and shelter provided, their method of progress, whether gin (man or foot-drawn) or pedalled from front or back. I cannot recall the mode current at Phnom Penh although I believe it to have been *cyclo-pousse,* or bicycle astern. The vivacious spirit of my emaciated driver that night remains, however, clear: on the sidewalk at departure from each bar and café recommended by himself, his main concern seemed my eventual return to the Royale.

The most agreeable of these bars, although like the others barely lit, small, smoke-filled, its clients resentful Cambodian youths, an antiquated jukebox playing at full volume harmonies forgotten elsewhere, was managed by a *métisse* of aquiline distinction and flexible mind. Uninterested in external events and certainly not in the Vietnam war, her philosophy seemed Hobbesian, even Calvinistic. She expressed, after gratuitous warnings of the risks of intercourse with the sullen black and contemptuous prostitutes at her tables, chief displeasure at interference recently initiated by the Ruler in her own profession and in other beneficial European customs. 'Monseigneur will not let you take these dirty girls back to your hotel. You certainly could not go to *their* homes, and I have no accommodations here. Why can he not leave you alone if that is the sort of filthy thing men want?'

At her own apartment, a half-naked Chinese watchman, roused by sharp kicks, slept across the threshold. The salon, so described by Madame, contained under the screen windows a double bed in which snored her grandmother and another, much disarranged, occupied by one of the bar girls. In the middle of the room, the black eyes of an infant Cambodian boy for whom my hostess disclaimed parentage gazed smilingly from between the bars of his cot. Accommodation being thus limited, the heat saturating, and my hostess' conversation not inexhaustible, after a dilute cognac or two I took myself off to the Royale, duty-rickshaw in continued attendance, through early morning air nearly as hot and moisture-laden as full noon.

Next morning, positioned on the hotel steps to await Fielding's arrival, I heard among the cries of *'Vous voulez un rickshaw?',* or *'Vous voulez une fille?'* from the crescent of *cyclo-pousses,* the jovial but incorrect response of *'Non, c'est le Consul-Générale à Hanoi: il en veut trois'.*

At a party that evening in the European quarter, two Australians, married to other partners, were discovered under a shower in the act of love: the incident caused jollity but few recriminations.

When the following afternoon the Stratoliner took off once more, our immediate destination was the Lao provincial capital of Savannakhet, Vientiane still suffering from flood or the effects of flood.

Savannakhet lay on the Mekong in a part of Laos disputed between the Royal Government and the Pathet Lao, guerrilla troops allegedly active on the outskirts, the town itself invisible to us from air or ground.

The purpose of the stage, no Commission activities or representatives being present on the ground, was solely to take on the fuel which conditions had rendered unobtainable at Vientiane. The passengers, once disembarked and dispersed on the grass beside the aircraft or, to avoid direct sunlight, under the wings, a local official informed the captain that right-wing Lao General Ma had mounted a coup d'état in the neighbourhood, in the course of which he had impounded all the available gasoline.

Vientiane airport was unserviceable, fuel was permanently unobtainable to the Commission at Hanoi, Phnom Penh airport was closed, and the passengers were without visas for Bangkok or Saigon. The General's demand that the aircraft quit Savannakhet in three hours presented a problem to which, as the French Third Secretary's wife observed, there was no logical solution. And should we by some means acquire an alternative local source, we should still approach Hanoi off schedule. The air crew, gallant but hysterical, reminded their audience of occasions on which they had been forced to land at Hanoi in the middle of American air raids or subjected to direct DRV surface-to-air missiles or, once, forced down by United States aircraft, dangers now increased by the temporary restriction of the beacon to three, not fifteen minutes. One would have preferred, as so often, ignorance, but the audience was captive.

As we lolled among the bushes ten yards from the aircraft, a co-passenger, elegant in white silk suit, pointed in immaculate French to the dangers of our position:

'We should sit in the airport building.'

'What airport building?'

'There, of course,' he replied, indicating a rattan hut gaping with holes and leaning to one side.

'But what dangers do you fear?'

'Dangers! My dear, there are *communists*,' the word spoken with fear and loathing, 'on the other side of that hedge.' My interlocutor was, it emerged, a senior Polish delegate of the commission, his instinct for self-preservation more acute than his political persuasion, a phenomenon often thereafter encountered among Soviet and East European colleagues and adding to the savour of life in Indo-China.

A reservoir of fuel, as the hours ticked by, had fortunately been discovered in barges on the Mekong below the airstrip, and permission for use obtained from General Ma. A bowser was dispatched, returned, disappeared behind groves to the eastward. The darkness was immediately thereafter illuminated by a violent explosion, smoke and flame rising above the treetops. Despair seized the onlookers.

'What has happened, Captain?'

'Doubtless,' with a shrug, 'they are refining it.'

It seemed probable that, in the process of filtering as opposed to refining, some of the gasoline had caught fire. But the loss was not substantial; we departed for Hanoi without further delay at 7.50 p.m., only a few minutes past the General's deadline. The coup, we subsequently learned, although incorporating air action, had been put down by Prime Minister Souvanna Phouma's forces without difficulty, but in Hanoi nothing was known of the fate of General Ma. The Lao rulers, in those days, did not exact draconian retribution on competitors of anti-Vietnamese or anti-Communist complexion. And Savannakhet, one of the larger French-built towns in Laos, was also capital of the fiefdom of Prince Boun Oum, a magnate in whose territories Central Government moved with care.

The night sky over the Hanoi area, as the Stratoliner approached, was ablaze with anti-aircraft fire. To the east I could see the lights of ground fires and little pinpoints of flame as the Vietnamese guns opened up. An Indian officer insisted that we ourselves were under, doubtless inadvertent, 'rocket' attack. The rumour, aided by gratuitous warnings from the cockpit, produced alarm in the cabin, Alice the Goose alone maintaining sangfroid. The aircraft banked, turning westward for some fifteen minutes before resuming the approach to the city and a successful landing for the final halt opposite the square white airport building and control tower. I recalled for the first time James Cameron's book *Witness,* written after an earlier visit to Hanoi, and his inscription on the flyleaf: 'On the edge of the abyss'.

The door of the aircraft opened and two Vietnamese officers, one in soiled white ducks and a solar topee, the other in jungle green with on his cap the five-pointed star of the Republic, entered the cabin, sprayed it conscientiously and thereafter collected passports, immigration cards and the countless documents required by the Communist administration. These officials seemed unsurprised by the goose, their narrow faces tense under the habitual strain imposed by the suspicion necessary for junior cadres and reinforced by a thousand political harangues. Thin smiles, excluding hard eyes with Mongoloid fold, responded to pleasantries from the crew.

But our Captain, after questioning the officer in jungle green, claimed confirmation of an American attack on targets in the country-side to the east of the city and, more improbably, of rocket attacks on the Stratoliner. Under comprehensible stress, he uttered general threats of refusal to undertake further flights unless the USAF, to allow for delays like that at Savannakhet, stood down within wider time scales during the aircraft's passage over DRV territory.

We disembarked and, crossing an apron wet with rain, entered the high, columned halls of the airport. Tubular sofas of Soviet design, covered in a shiny maroon material resembling oilcloth, were regimentally disposed under the tall windows. A small bar, dispensing soft drinks, gaseous and orange only in colour, was set in a corner of the lounge. A few Tonkinese civilians tightly buttoned into gray two-piece suits of meagre cut observed us morosely, while a wooden counter occupying four sides of a large square, within which two or three uniformed officials were stationed, constituted the Customs and Immigration services.

The Vietnamese made no attempt on this occasion, although my diplomatic status was a matter of logical dispute, to investigate my slender baggage. The officer in charge of the Customs, speaking passable French, was an agreeable, even jovial functionary with whom joking was permissible. ('Immigration' were, and remained, intransigent.) Regulations, however, required completion of a long green questionnaire in which I was instructed to answer questions on life, residency, status, experience, as well as detailed inquiries on the portage of machine-guns, pistols, revolvers, explosives, wireless receivers, transmitters, etc.

Owing to the complexity of this form, I mistakenly stated that I was *not* carrying a wireless receiver in the shape of a small commercial portable, but that I *was* in possession of a transmitter, an instrument denoting illicit communications, probably for espionage. This unfortunate statement, although an innocent error, confused the smiling official, indeed myself, until I could explain my mistake; but the exchange was polite and without menace or hostility. (Perhaps, as with the process of criminal interrogation, the Customs man had been chosen to provide confidence, to soften up the suspect, and indeed, I did not see him again subsequently.) I began to feel that the abyss might not be so precipitous.

But like every Communist public building, this airport was a spare place, sanitized of humanity's muddle, officials and passengers marching to an inner rhythm, compounded, it seemed, of discipline, gratitude for privilege, and fear — among other fears — for its removal; silent, purposeful and secret. The contrast with Saigon, not only because troop movements in totalitarian countries do not take place in full view, was sharp. It was that between the Marxist revolutionary, with the revolutionary's undeclared but rigid intentions and constraints and the spirit of free men striving for purpose through the acknowledged imperfections of humanity.

Behind the communist order lay a horrible idea, the conviction that mankind, God's creatures, should be bent to a single, disproven economic theory, to whose requirements all nature, love, frivolity, laughter, decency, truth itself should be subdued, to which indeed the virtues as well as the defects of humanity were irrelevant, even hostile. To dedicate the spirit to a cause, even a wrongheaded cause, was one thing. To submerge the spirit to the exclusion of everything but the mechanics of the cause was another. In these distempered anterooms, inhabited only by suspicious functionaries or groups of apparatchiks bearing gladioli, the skull beneath the skin was all too evident.

Nor was it, in the months ahead, difficult to understand why that order, that power, evil but power, that purpose, evil but purpose, the single answer to the pluralist questions of mislaid belief should seduce the riffraff of the 'intellectual' West, nor why, in their rootless and unstable considerations empty of historical perspective, truth should be willingly discounted. Truth for a Communist, of course, coincides, or is distorted to coincide, with whatever current aspect of Marxism-Leninism is under review. Truth for the anti-war activists was also subordinate to more personal criteria: advancement, power, hatred of country, publicity and self-preservation.

My predecessor, Brian Shepherd, outward-bound later that night, met me after I had safely negotiated Customs and Immigration. We walked through the humid, familiar, tropical night to a small blue Ford Escort, sole vehicle owned by the Consulate-General, with its dispirited Tonkinese chauffeur, 'Monsieur' Tien, an honorific obligatory for all servants employed by capitalist envoys. Tien, in the grip of hypochondria, sniffed resentfully as he lifted light suitcase, radio and portable icebox into the trunk. Nothing could be expected of this *fainéant,* his preferred location during daylight, at temperatures up to 120 degrees, within the stationary and blazing metal box of the motor-car.

V

ARRIVAL AT HANOI

AT LOW SPEED, with dimmed lights, in inappropriate gear-ratio, we jolted along pot-holed roads through padi, village and forest toward the east bank of the Red River. On either side of the two-lane 'highway', buildings loomed intermittently, wooden, unpainted and dilapidated for the most part, a rare kerosene lamp glimmering through a window slid askew by age, neglect or blast. Huge cylindrical gasoline drums, painted black, were dispersed at the edges of the trees: the forest had spread unchecked to the verges of the road, closing on the half-abandoned houses and on the damaged railway marshalling yards. Small workshops, acetylene lamps flaring in the darkness, functioned industriously through the night.

Pedestrians, soldiers of the People's Army of Vietnam (PAVN), militiamen or black-pyjamaed civilians, women and men laden with pots and baskets on yoke or head, carrying or leading the liquid-eyed infants of Vietnam, straggled hesitantly along the ditches. Bicyclists on French machines of formidable solidity looped and curvetted up the gradients in wild parabolas among trucks and vans of Soviet and Chinese provenance, gray-green, dusty or mud-caked, silent troops hunched expressionless within the unlit vehicles. From these conveyances, some powered by gasoline and others — as in wartime France, with excrescent chimneys — by coal gas, the pinched Tonkinese faces regarded us dispassionately. The eyes of the northern Vietnamese male resemble, after childhood, those of dedicated torturers.

At the eastern approach to the Paul Doumer Bridge, that miraculously beautiful work of French engineering which, with its massive spans, links by railroad the east and west banks of the Red River, stood the penultimate checkpoint before arrival at Hanoi itself. At such frequent controls, the militia examined, noted and telephoned forward details of the passports, permits, driving licences and other bits of paper demanded by régimes everywhere in the communist world, even on the Mongolian steppe. Smiling officials with red badges and grubby topees also closely inspected the passengers themselves, examined the contents of the trunk, flashed torches under seat or dashboard. The search inward-bound was presumably for contraband or sabotage materials, while outward for malcontents escaping Utopia.

Waved peremptorily forward, we inched behind heavy traffic on to the bridge, wheeled transport proceeding in the outer lanes, the central track bearing the rail and sleepers of the rickety and overcrowded trains which still connected the city with Haiphong and with the Eastern provinces. Narrow catwalks against the guardrails of the bridge carried those walking or, under laden yokes, swaying in the pendulum half-walk, half-run of Asia.

Before us, shrouded in night, lay Hanoi; below lay the wide river, lights flickering on its banks, little boats moored until dawn or poling slowly on the stream, the dyke walls of the river just visible through the interstices of the pyramidal steel spans of the Paul Doumer and, beyond the dyke, rice fields, go-downs and those few installations of the port that Socialism had managed to maintain. (As the moon rose, the first of many unexplained *rafales* of rifle fire broke out in the city.) We turned off the bridge and cleared the final militia checkpoint into town.

Last seen under French rule twenty years before, the streets of once colour-washed houses were now unrecognizable, shutters broken or hanging from a rusted nail, paint peeling or, more usually, vanished from the facades, water in stagnant pools on the roadways, rubbish and ordure in stinking heaps, doors fallen in, slats off the roofs, collapsed cornices, glassless windows, bricks missing from the walls, a decay beyond remedy, the degradation of one of the most noble cities in Asia. (This phenomenon was no consequence of U.S. bombardment, which had expressly spared Hanoi, but the deliberate choice of President Ho Chi Minh's government. The town, because 'built by colonialists', had been allowed to die. One wondered, not for the last time on this and kindred excesses, why 'Uncle' Ho did not ask the inhabitants for *their* views.) Nor was collapse only aesthetic or architectural, comprising also water, electricity and sewage services.

Hanoi, apart from a few streets devoted by the leadership to embassies and to one hospital, was a catchment area for fatal disease, a town expertly reduced by its own rulers to the Stone Age, sweltering helpless in the summer, drenched and shivering under the winter rains.

33

The British residence, a square box-like structure, cream and brown with blue shutters, stood in a garden off a quiet, tree-lined road running, at one extremity, to the Red River, and at the other, into the relative bustle of downtown Hanoi. Under the covered entrance, Monsieur Dong, butler, 'boy', factotum and genial incompetent, lightly clad in singlet and white ducks, shifted nervously from foot to foot before, with an uncertain smile of welcome, opening the car door and, head bowed, seizing my hand in both of his.

The pillared hall, although partially illuminated in daylight from a 'lantern' on the top of the pitched roof, was dark brown, gloomy and obscure, the white columns themselves painted in Chinese characters, not then explicable. On the left lay a small blue drawing-room furnished with sofas and armchairs appropriate to a Bromley parlour and hung with sub-Medici reproductions of British water-colourists. Ahead was the dining-room, chocolate wainscots, green walls and fumed-oak table, sideboard and chairs, heavy and inelegant. The joviality of lunch parties in this room owed little to its surroundings, nor were my solitary repasts ceremonious, an informality as much due to sombre appointments as to Monsieur Nguyen's cuisine.

The staircase, in matching sepia, doubled on itself to the upper floor. One bedroom, containing only a metal bedstead, was not in use. The other, or 'Master' bedroom repeated the uninspiring cream and brown chosen by the Department of the Environment. It held an enormous double bed, a wardrobe of similar proportions, two bedside tables, and a dressing table, all of stripped pine; both this and the drawing-room were equipped with box (window) air conditioners, at least until the machine in the bedroom was destroyed in my successor's time by an American rocket. My photographs, and local ceramics gradually acquired, eventually made this and the other rooms tolerable, if by no means representational.

The living-room across the landing, however, with its French windows opening on to the long, galleried terrace hung with convolvulus and other climbers and scattered with potted shrubs and orange trees, was the centre of my small life. It was in this room that I read, thought, wrote, drank and listened to the radio, to the sounds of bombing and air defence, to the noises of the city. In that room I watched the sunset, saw the great bombers coming in over the Red River, scrutinized the passers-by, discussed the day's events with Soviet and East European callers, sifted the lies, or sought to, and tried to predict the future. It was on the terrace at dusk, or in the heat of the day, that visi tors from the West were happy to unburden themselves of impressions, to seek — the best of them — a balance to the loaded presentations of the DRV's Department of Information.

Here Bishop Reeves of Chichester spoke in throbbing tones of liberal principles. Here, under a wicker table during a raid, cowered an Australian Communist journalist of professed derring-do. Here sat Signor Trombadori, member of the Central Committee of the Italian Party, discoursing with wit and sangfroid among the crack of surface-to-air missiles and the thud of high explosive. Here pontificated Harrison Salisbury. Here Felix Greene spoke of journeys in China and interpreted Mao's reasons for the Cultural Revolution. Here Wilfred Burchett analysed the motives of Pham Van Dong. Here Swiss, Yugoslav and Swedish ambassadors resident at Peking pieced together their transient reporting on the DRV.

But at this time of arrival, after my predecessor had left for the ICC mess en route for the airport and home, between living-room and terrace I let the night grow around me, heard children's voices from the servants' quarters, sandalled footsteps in the street below, a ship's hooter in the Delta, smelled the sweet or acrid scents of Tonkin, saw the branches of palm and mango moving in the breeze, heard the clang of a gate, the hum of traffic on the boulevards.

In that stillness, a small, square Vietnamese, dressed in sarong topped by worn tweed coat of English cut, stepped resolutely from behind me out through the French windows. Bearing votive offerings high in either hand, he abruptly kicked aside my outstretched legs. Until revealed as the Residence gardener, his was a bizarre and alarming apparition, blind yet owning not only green fingers but the blind man's ability to move by tactile sense unharmed about the premises, however laden with pot-plants.

Thereafter, preceded by the flapping of his rubber sandals ('Ho Chi Minhs' allegedly manufactured from the wheels of shot-down U.S. aircraft), Monsieur Dong ingratiatingly entered the living room to bring coffee, seek instructions for the morning, and generally test the water. He was then just over 30, married and the father of two repellent children with permanent colds and coal-black teeth, all inhabiting, under the terrace, compartments approved by the DRV Government resembling loose boxes for Shetland ponies. These gave on to a spacious, if barren, compound over which washing lines were suspended. Half-a-dozen scrawny chickens scratched among the earth and thin grass. Small gratitude was shown when we eventually increased the family's living space by clearing out furniture, lent by the French Delegation, from an unused room adjoining the compound.

Dong protested his affection for the British and produced Christmas cards from various departed staff. With much wringing of hands and sycophantic body movements, he emphasized his own impartiality in political concerns, his disregard for state control and his refusal to follow the more distasteful orders of the authorities.

'But I must warn you, Monsieur,' he continued, sotto voce, 'none of that is true of the cook, Monsieur Nguyen, whom you will interview tomorrow. Monsieur Nguyen is a very bad man: be careful what you say before him. He is a police spy.'

I had assumed that all the servants, including Dong, who had served either in the pre-1954 Vietnamese army or as auxiliary with the French army, and doubtless had a debt to pay, were police spies. It was also reasonable, since there is no activity to which totalitarian régimes give greater attention than listening at keyholes, to suspect that the house was wired from top to bottom. Because Dong unquestionably would have known this, his whispered confession and accusation were comprehensible but hardly credible. He could, given his history, scarcely have escaped recruitment as a low-grade agent. It was a reflection less on himself, although he plainly lacked initiative, than on the infantile system of domestic spying that the only documents that he could possibly have passed to his masters were old envelopes, and the only oral information that imparted in conversation by Bloc diplomats and European fellow-travellers or Party members.

But he was an engaging fellow with his quick smile, good manners and willingness to help: rather a lonely one, devoted to a family of which, however distasteful in appearance and behavior, he was fond and whose frequent evacuation to 'the countryside' during bombardment caused him pain. Nor was it possible to condemn the prisoner in DRV hands that he — and many others persecuted or held in the North for origin, religion or youthful error — really was. He had to live, and if, as I surmised, feigned rage, eccentricity or simulated malady gave him material to report to the 'police' or to embroider at Lao Dong Party meetings, I saw no reason not to provide them. The dossier compiled would be satisfactorily inaccurate.

When, after my first morning in the office, I returned for luncheon to the house, Monsieur Nguyen presented himself. This cook, of whom I had been also warned, in culinary terms, by predecessors, had earlier followed the profession of sheet-metal worker. At no time was I able to ascertain the crime against the state which had brought about his punitive transfer to my kitchen. A gnome of wizened features illuminated by evil grin and periodic cackling laugh, his myopic eyes barely visible through bifocals whose steel frames were bound together with sticking plaster, Nguyen was rogue, existential man, scoundrel, wide-boy, damn-you-Jack-I'm-inboard, indifference paramount, a survivor.

His honesty, at least so far as I was concerned, was not in question. The weekly pencilled accounts checked with, or even undercut, the prices for pork, vegetables and fish easily established in central or sidewalk markets. When I once asked him why he never charged for the mangoes, papaya and bananas liberally provided, he grinned and jerked his arm upward and downward to demonstrate that, rather than waste money, he pulled fruit off other people's trees.

His stove, burning wood or charcoal and little bigger than a typewriter, stood on a small table in the tiny kitchen. Nguyen, in agitated attendance, his spectacles obscured by smoke and sweat, seemed unlikely ever to absorb the contents of the illustrated *Larousse* that, in response to Shepherd's severe judgment, I had bought for him in Saigon. His knowledge of the French language, only slightly more comprehensive than of English, was exiguous, but he enjoyed the coloured pictures and would spend idle hours riffling through the pages. Little improvement resulted.

In particular, I could never prevent him from carving, and then returning to the oven, long before needed at table, the roast leg or shoulder of lamb that he had prepared for weekend luncheon parties. The reputation in this regard of British Missions was hardly increased by my table, but Nguyen was, if not a proud, a stubborn man, and I refused the kindly offer of Anne de Quirielle, wife of the French Délégué-Général, to have him instructed in her own excellent kitchens.

Nguyen, at this first encounter, with elfish secrecy and in tones low enough to evade the hovering 'boy', his gaze darting in all directions but mine, counselled me to avoid antagonizing or otherwise providing material for police-spy Dong. 'Monsieur Dong is not to be trusted, he is not a person worthy of confidence: Monsieur Dong is a criminal, he works for the flics and his morals are bad. So are his wife's.'

To begin the mission in this atmosphere of domestic farce, with the parties, although their purpose, other than mutual hatred, remained impr netrable, perfectly aware that I was conscious to chicanery, was agreeaole, not unlike the role of a Nanny in a contentious nursery. Monsieur Nguyen's customarily insipid fish at lunch that day seemed a light price to pay for such rewards.

The Office of the Consulate-General, some two hundred yards round the corner on the Ly Thuong Kiet, was a low building almost entirely hidden in trees, situated directly opposite a factory the purpose of which I never determined, but which appeared to hold ancient vehicles and mechanical parts of every description. (Sounds of banging and the light of welders' torches emerged from therein from time to time; on the rare occasions that the gates were opened, the place resembled both repair shop and junk yard.) Behind the Consulate lay the Vice-Consul's balconied apartment overlooking a courtyard and his cook's loggiaed quarters.

The Vice-Consul, Geoffrey Livesey, then about 22, was at once the most gallant, level-headed and humorous of his generation, an invaluable companion. Only after I had left did he sacrifice accustomed prudence to the rash curiosity involved in too adjacent observations of a low-level air attack. He was fortunate that damage to his eardrums was temporary. His British Empire Medal was well earned.

At a desk just inside the front door of the office sat Monsieur Xuan, our elderly secretary and interpreter, better conversant with French than with English, but a functionary whose experienced advice it was sensible to consider, if not always to accept. He was in his late 50s by that time, his children and most of his family safely in the South or in the United States.

Xuan's stoicism, kindness and equability in those conditions of loneliness, under a régime that he certainly detested, commanded to betray his British employers, in continual fear of bombardment, immured in one small room, deprived of the open consolations of his Catholic religion, were then, and in retrospect, moving. (At the time his deliberate, lengthy thought processes and certain physical eccentricities, not then recognized as accompanying fatal disease, sometimes obstructed the patience which he deserved.)

Xuan was a good man who served the British well. Although he occasionally prevaricated or changed the subject if confronted with questions which should probably not have been asked, I never knew him to lie. Many of the less superficial truths about the nightmare Government of North Vietnam would not have been available unless deduced from Monsieur Xuan's subtle directions, from his silences, or from fac tual exposition regarded as secret only by Marxist-Leninist governments.

Behind his small office lay the main Chancery, a lofty room usually empty since Livesey preferred to work in the premises beyond, filled with desks bearing old copies of Hansard, Vacher and other reference books. The waiting room, carpeted, containing three or four armchairs and a table with English newspapers and magazines, was separated from the Chancery by a long counter. Beyond that again, in the north-west corner, was my own office and in the north-east the 'secure' area consisting of grilled strong-room and cypher office. The complex was dreary, and I passed as little time as I could there except during Livesey's absences in Saigon, my duties being rather to visit foreign embassies, Vietnamese offices and generally to circulate around town, than in Consular or Administrative work, of which there was, as already indicated, a noticeable shortage.

There were, however, occasions, apart from the daily minutiae of business, when attendance was either necessary or rewarding. One of our responsibilities, for example, subject to the approval of the Hong Kong Government, was the issue of visas for that Colony, and although Livesey dealt directly with most applicants, there were times when I should take a more interested role.

The Tri-Continental Commission, an international communist organization in which Cuba played a prominent part, had met recently in Hanoi. The First Secretary of the Cuban Embassy, a lady fair of face but of cosy proportions, sought — since North Korea had no diplomatic relations with the United Kingdom — visas for three North Korean participants in the Tri-Continental to transit Hong Kong en route to Pyongyang. (I do not remember, so long after the event, why the Koreans could not have returned home via Nanning and Peking, but imagine the period to have been that either of the Cultural Revolution or of growing Sino-Soviet dissension, or both, when travel by air or rail across China was as difficult for communists as for Westerners.) The applications, to our surprise, were approved by the Governor of Hong Kong, with the single proviso that the travellers should not hold military rank.

This condition was transmitted to the Cubans, who assured us that their charges were bona fide civilians. (The Cuban First Secretary, on a previous visit to the office, had left behind her a substantial bunch of keys which, discovered by Livesey 24 hours later, had not by then been reclaimed by her. We should have been unwise to assume that the keys had not been planted as a provocation. But the lady's relief on learning from my Mission of their discovery was considerable and served to eradicate that supposition. She behaved to us thereafter, indeed, with a sort of conspiratorial gratitude which suggested that she had not reported the loss to her superior.) Livesey instructed the Cuban Embassy that the travellers should report to the Consulate-General the following morning: I decided that I would take formal responsibility for the issue of the visas.

The North Korean trio, dressed at random and a more cheerful group than most of their grim compatriots, arrived at the front door with the plump First Secretary, to whom Livesey introduced me and with whom we exchanged pleasantries. I agreed later with my colleague that her attractions would have been less evident elsewhere than at Hanoi. The Koreans hung about in the background fidgeting, smiling winningly and behaving without the marks of military discipline.

But when, flanked by Livesey and Xuan, I barked out their three names in rapid succession in tones as near to the parade ground as I could affect, the impostors sprang to attention one after another, took a pace forward and saluted with martial precision. The Cuban rolled her eyes in despair; the unmasked Korean majors placated consequences with sheepish grins, snatched their passports, bare of Hong Kong visas, and, among coloratura Spanish imprecations, climbed back into their Soviet-built automobile. Crippled with laughter, Monsieur Xuan took discreet refuge under the stairs. Neither my first day in the Consulate-General nor subsequent attendance provided many such prizes.

VI

DEALING WITH THE VIETNAMESE

THE FIRST DUTY OF AN AMBASSADOR is to present himself to the local authorities at the most senior level available, to the monarch in Kingdoms or to the President in Republics. Consuls and Consuls-General operate at lower levels, in my case, since the Mayor would not receive me, the External Affairs Bureau of the Administrative Committee of the Hanoi Municipality.

This insignificant body was housed in a nondescript building in the middle of the city near the Petit Lac, a long stretch of ornamental water notable for the annual appearance, or otherwise, of a giant turtle, presaging a favourable year. Both the head of the Bureau, Monsieur Pham, and his assistant, Monsieur Dung, received me when I paid my formal call, one of considerably longer duration than the 15 minutes customary in capitals. The conversation was general, dwelling mainly on past postings. Both officials came to life when I recounted my role in the Liberation of 1945, of which my curriculum had rightly, since I was then in the Navy, not the Foreign Service, made no mention. I made plain at the outset my own view of the truth of this period. The reaction of both officials was not that of offence, but of keen historical interest.

Monsieur Dung, with whom I had many interviews during the months that followed, whether on administrative detail or in the presentation of the Secretary of State's Peace Initiatives, spoke excellent French and conducted himself with invariable correctness. Although one could well have dispensed with the oceans of black tea and the incessant boiled sweets preferred in this office, Dung would have made, and perhaps was, a first-class diplomat, factual, polite and imperturbable.

And if I never succeeded in extracting from him or his superior the least snippet of unpublished political information, still less speculation,

41

no more did my other diplomatic colleagues from their contacts in the Ministry of Foreign Affairs. Facts are released in totalitarian régimes for a purpose, not as part of a more or less cooperative relationship between equals, and the purpose is directed to class struggle. But Monsieur Dung, efficient within his limits, intelligent and conciliatory, made tolerable these encounters, with other interlocutors stiff, even menacing.

Meetings in the Bureau were not always free from reproach. During a visit by myself to Saigon in December, 1966, the USAF had mounted a raid against a factory to the south-west of Hanoi. This installation, as I myself observed on return from Saigon, had been put out of action, but in the course of the raid, damage was also said to have been inflicted in the centre of the city itself, on houses in a 'village' west of the Red River Bridge and in Russia Street, level with and 50 yards from the Bridge. Three or four terraced houses within 200 yards of the Consulate-General and some 30 yards south of Pho Hoama and east of the tramway had also been destroyed. The DRV authorities asserted that this damage had been caused by American bombs in a deliberate attack on populated civilian targets: their claim achieved wide media coverage in the West, including the United States, and aroused anti-war protest there.

I was not, unlike my other diplomatic colleagues, invited to join an official inspection tour of these sites, but visited them nonetheless on the morning after my return from Saigon. The downtown buildings, which then consisted of the back walls only and heaps of gray rubble, had certainly not been destroyed by an Act of God, but the inaccuracy, under North Vietnamese gunners, of Soviet surface-to-air missiles (SAMs) had already become plain enough to raise doubts in some minds, including my own, about the incident. These doubts concerned not the observed tendency of SAMs to miss their targets by large margins, but the frequency with which, due to inexpertise or faulty design, they misfired and fell to earth. They were of considerable weight. This thought, as I say, had also occurred to impartial but qualified observers in Hanoi, and is referred to in most works on the period.

Three days after my inspection, the aged messenger of the Post, Telephone and Telegraph (PTT), the department through which passed all my cables, inward and outward, in cypher or plain language, dismounted from his bicycle at the office in Ly Thuong Kiet.

The telegram that he delivered was Immediate, Plain Language, from the British Embassy at Washington; it conveyed the text of an article by Joe Alsop in that morning's *Washington Post*. Alsop had therein reported me by name and title as having declared that I could not confirm that the damage at Hanoi had been the result of American high explosive, that it might rather have been caused by unexpended North Vietnamese air defence missiles which, after partial misfire, had fallen back onto the city. Mr Alsop in 'quoting' me, had predictably emphasized the second of the two explanations.

This piece was carried worldwide and is referred to in *Homo Hominem*, Trombadori's book on Vietnam in which the author, after various complimentary remarks, goes on, nevertheless, to accuse me of having been corrupted by the enticements of 'American culture'. (I was glad, exactly ten years after the event, to deny to him, in Rome itself, this soft impeachment.) The only means at Hanoi by which I could, had I been so ill advised, have made a 'declaration' of this or any other kind, was through the local correspondent of the *Agence France Presse*. But, although I knew the current representative, I had not seen him for some days. Alsop's informant – or disinformant – remains to this day unknown to me. I realized, however, that he had rendered, at least personally, a major disservice, and I was grateful for the advance warning in the Washington Embassy's telegram.

I knew that the range of punitive measures against my Mission open to the DRV authorities included normal harassment (delays in official business, interference with basic services, etc.), with all of which we could live. But even though Alsop's article had put a small but reasonably effective spoke in the gathering momentum of North Vietnamese propaganda in the West, I doubted if my expulsion would be contemplated.

I had, fortunately, no time to ponder the spectrum of possible consequences, being summoned instantly to the External Affairs Bureau where, unusually, Pham, who began the interview, and Dung were both present. Since there then had been no other issues likely to be the subject of discussion, I had brought the full text of Washington's cable in my pocket, its plain language content and delivery to the Consulate-General from the PTT being obviously no secret to the Vietnamese authorities.

I was not mistaken about the cause of the summons. Pham at once referred, not to this cable or to other sources of information, but to the article itself which had, incidentally, also been carried by that time in the London Press and by the *South China Morning Post* in Hong Kong, if not elsewhere. (In both those cities, but not in Washington, the DRV had official representation, as they had in Paris, Delhi, Djakarta and, of course, in every communist capital.) He asked me if I were aware of the article. I said that I had read it.

'The facts are not just incorrect,' asserted Pham, 'they are lies, subversive of the integrity of the Democratic Republic of Vietnam. What explanation do you, as the source of this fabrication, have to give?'

His situation, whether or not he recognized it, was not a strong one, and this long-hop could only be followed by half-volleys which, nevertheless, it would be sensible not to hit over the pavilion. I therefore replied that I had not spoken in the terms referred to, asked rhetorically to which agency I could have addressed myself in Hanoi, and concluded this part of my response by emphasizing that, as Her Majesty's representative at Hanoi, I was not responsible and could not answer for the contents of the American or any other press. I took pains to repeat this point throughout the long interrogation that followed. Having made my position impregnable in this regard, I noted that Pham then changed direction.

'But what are your personal views on the brutal, cowardly American attack on these localities? You have seen the damage, have you not?' Pham shuffled through his papers: 'The North Vietnamese authorities provided facilities for all foreign representatives here to witness this atrocity on December 15.'

'I was not invited, Monsieur Pham.'

Pham seemed, for the first time, confused. He had plainly forgotten, which Dung had not, that the British Consul-General was not formally treated by the DRV as part of the Diplomatic Corps.

'But I agree that I have seen the damage,' I continued, 'on my own initiative. I am not a technician or otherwise qualified to comment on the results. I could not, in these circumstances, have a personal view other than that of deep regret for any loss of life.'

'But surely you have seen bomb damage before, in London during the anti-Fascist war? Does the destruction you have just witnessed not resemble that in your country also caused by enemy bombing?'

'London suffered devastation on a scale which I hope that Hanoi will never undergo. The damage here, distressing though it is, is in no way comparable. And I have not said to you that the incident on December 13 was not caused by bombing. Had it been, no doubt it was error, for my acquaintance with Americans assures me that it could be no part of their policy to make war on innocent civilians.'

'You have not said to *me* that our martyrs were not killed by imperialist high explosive,' said Pham, 'but what have you said to your Government?'

'As you know, communications with Governments are privileged. I am not at liberty, am expressly forbidden, to divulge them to third parties.' My interlocutors, after a few minutes' probing, were obliged to admit this reply as check, if not checkmate, and their questions became edged with desperation.

'But Mr Colvin, you were present during this unprovoked and sneaking American violation of our airspace. You heard the arrival warning, saw the bombers, heard the noise of their unprincipled attack.' Pham and Dung knew that I was among the few inhabitants of Hanoi who, lacking access to any air-raid shelter, had no choice but to endure the raid above ground. 'There can be no doubt in your mind that this destruction was the result of cruel and conscienceless aggression; the article's alternative is a disgraceful insult to our country.'

'But Monsieur Pham, I was not in Hanoi on December 13, but in Saigon, on a bag run for my mission.'

The two officials, who had conducted the interrogation equably and without threat, looked at each other in astonishment. I wished that they had not asked the question, for I had not sought for them the loss of face which ignorance of my absence had now brought about. I took measures, including a radical if ludicrous switch of subject to 'repairs to the residence', in an attempt to assure them that I had not noticed that the Municipal left hand had been rudely ignored by the Security right. Dung, in the remaining minutes, occupied himself by trying to persuade me to give a 'purely personal view, off the record', of the truth of the 13 December raid. He did so with charm. I felt very sorry for him and for Pham and wished, as much for their sake as mine, that I could help.

No perceptible harassment followed the incident. Harassment as a sporadic feature of life was, anyway, often difficult to distinguish from bureaucratic incompetence or general breakdown, taking such forms as delays in the issue of exit visas, the latter demanded by all Communist régimes and the equivalent on a much smaller scale of the Berlin Wall, or interrupted supply of power and light. The reasons for harassment could sometimes be clearly determined. The role played by Britain in support of her American ally was, as I have indicated, insubstantial, but Ministerial statements at home favourable to or even uncritical of U.S. objectives had occasional unfavourable consequences in Hanoi. And when the Wilson Administration chose to supply the Allies in the South with a team of trained tracker Alsatians, the local DRV reaction was not confined to predictable references in *Nan Dhan*, the main Hanoi daily, and Radio Hanoi, to the United Kingdom as 'the Running Dog of American neo-fascist imperialism'.

Apparent British Foreign Office indifference to abuse of this kind was tied either to the maxim that 'the dogs bark, but the caravan passes', or to the unlikelihood by specific protest of a softening of the long tradition of DRV invective, or to the effect on my own anomalous position, or to the hullabaloo likely to be made in London by the domestic left, or perhaps to post-Suez acceptance of reduced British status.

As to harassment, on a morning when I was to take the night flight to Saigon, Xuan told me that he believed that an exit visa might not be granted. He offered no reason, but repeated telephone calls, indeed, produced no visa up to two hours before the time that we should leave for the airport. I packed, had dinner with Livesey and waited out the twilight in the gloomy Residence, car ready under the porch. (As it was also possible that the Authorities might have known that the aircraft would not arrive and had, with customary secrecy, not chosen to inform us, we had been in touch with the International Control Commission, who had confirmed that the Stratoliner was en route.) We continued, Confidential Bags at hand, to wait, but with lowered spirits, for these journeys to Saigon, gruelling as they often were, gave access to friends in a happier and more open world.

One hour before our planned departure from the house, hope nearly gone, Xuan arrived on his bicycle with orders to report immediately to the Police Commissariat established during the French Colonial era next to the Law Courts, the Ministry of Justice and the Gaol, and maintained there without change. In this disordered office, supervised by a coloured photograph of Ho Chi Minh, a senior policeman told me that he had especially sought this opportunity to make my personal acquaintance, determine my state of health, inquire about my comfort, indicate to me infractions of State regulations of which I might be unaware, none of which had any connection with ourselves. He made himself pleasant, and I was interested to have this mysterious contact with the Vietnamese equivalent of the KGB; but greatly relieved when, in the nick of time, he handed Xuan my visa and other papers.

Apart from irritation at the cat-and-mouse game, one had on leaving the commissariat a certain sense, humiliating and familiar to political prisoners, not of contempt for the dilatory execution of a right, but of gratitude at a concession in a State where the individual had no rights and did not matter.

Other measures, as I have said, included arbitrary blackouts. At my first interview in the External Affairs Bureau, Dung had assured me that the Municipality would continue to provide, in spite of enemy action, all the utilities and other services available in Western capitals. Should this undertaking not be honoured, I should not, he said, hesitate to make appropriate representations.

We were well stocked with kerosene lamps and candles, so that the periodic absence of electric light was not a matter for serious complaint. Power for fans and refrigerators was different. After the first blackouts, I therefore sent a formal note to the Bureau reminding them of their assurance, drawing their attention to continued supply to all other foreign missions, for we firmly maintained our controversial status in all representations to the Vietnamese and, referring to an ancient but embarrassing dermatological weakness, warned them that repetition of the blackouts might involve my involuntary withdrawal on medical grounds. Communism, according to the Soviets, *is* electrification, and irrespective of the circumstances, the Vietnamese would not have welcomed the derogatory publicity that withdrawal might have directed to their programmes. It is, incidentally, extraordinary that these régimes in their external propaganda emphasize those aspects of their countries in which most Westerners, for good or ill, are least interested.

The note and oral protest appeared in some weeks to have no result whatever, and in the heat then afflicting the country, I began to suffer effects which would, unchecked, sooner or later have led to evacuation. I then adopted, unwillingly but *faute de mieux*, and although Xuan strongly counselled against such action, the course of dispatching the latter to the Bureau at whatever hour of the day or night the blackout took place.

To be dragged out of his bed at 3 o'clock in the morning and forced to undertake a lengthy bicycle ride was no fun for him, nor do I imagine that officials of the Municipality much enjoyed being awakened at that hour on such a pretext. But ten days after the last protest, when I tentatively remarked to Xuan that we had had no recent power interruption, he replied that the Consulate-General had at last, thanks to incessant representation, been transferred to the city's industrial grid, not a privilege granted to other Embassies, or so he said, and one which we should therefore not advertise.

Blackouts, as harassment, were still within the capacity of the Administration and were enforced from time to time, but we now possessed a relatively secure service. When, indeed, Dr Pel, the disagreeable Ambassador of Hungary, included the regular electrical supply that he received as among the potential benefits that might accrue to my Mission were I positively to advocate the North Vietnamese cause to my Government, his own air-conditioning died as he spoke. To prolong the interview, as he sat mopping his forehead, was a temptation I found difficult to resist.

As regards other Departments of State, although I was familiar through conversations at National Days and other receptions with members of the Council of Ministers, Politburo and Central Committee, there was, as has been said, no official contact between my Mission and DRV Ministries other than the Ministry of Foreign Trade. Nor was there enthusiasm on either side for an expansion even of trade, most of the DRV's small traffic with the Capitalist world being conducted through Hong Kong, and UK/DRV turnover standing at little more than £100,000 per annum.

Accompanied by Xuan, I did, however, pay occasional calls on the Trade Ministry, as much to converse with the wise Deputy Minister, educated in French schools and institutions, as to collect the barren statistics fabricated by his underlings.

Xuan, or I, or Livesey, also visited the National Bank, a vast, empty, domed mausoleum echoing only with the footsteps of underemployed tellers and cashiers, to exchange telegraphic and other sterling drafts on London into the local currency (dongs), emerging because of the absurdly adverse rate prevailing, without our shirts. Personal finances, on the other hand, since, apart from sums expended on food, celadon and blue-and-white china, the consumer economy was wholly absent at Hanoi, took a modestly upward turn.

The collector's instinct led me, during my first weeks in the DRV, into glancing, unrepeated contact with another aspect of the bureaucracy. I had formed the habit of visiting the downtown antiquary, Dong Thung, otherwise known as *Le Grand Voleur* or 'Great Thief', the mystery of whose activities was a reflection of the difficulty of understanding the régime.

Dong's original profession, in the days of French Indo-China, was that of wood merchant. Shortly before the Geneva Agreements, he astutely foresaw the migration south of rich North Vietnamese and their need for ready cash, to be realized in part by the sale of *objets d'art*. He accordingly established himself in, or transferred his existing premises to, an antique shop slightly to the west of the south shore of Le Petit Lac, and over the door he nailed his sign, DONG THUNG, DE GRANDE VALEUR. (Below the legend could be dimly discerned the words *Marchand de Bois*.) For over a decade of attempted extortion he had been known as *Le Grand Voleur*, a sobriquet, possibly because his French did not enable him to distinguish the two phrases, in which he took no shame.

Monsieur Dong was a small, tense, not to say hysterical figure in his 60s, dressed in hat and corduroy suit. He was principally engaged in supervizing the construction of a house for himself outside Hanoi and was usually in the shop at weekends only. When he was not there, his two unintelligent sons, who understood even less about the trade than himself, managed the business. His sales technique was one of consistent overpraise and overcharge, followed, when faced by expertise, which, fortunately for him, rarely occurred, by immediate and, one would have thought, humiliating collapse. (He was persuaded not only that I understood ceramics but that I would not expose his grosser forgeries to friends; the prices paid were those which, at his request, 'I would have asked if I were the vendor.') The opening of a certain Madame Ho's shop in the suburbs did not seem to affect his prices; indeed, although he closely interrogated his clients about their visits to that lady, he was curiously indifferent to the whole scale of his business.

The shop was one of the social rendezvous of the capital. It consisted of three communicating rooms. Ninety-five percent of the stock was 19th or 20th century rubbish, but, among the remainder, it was possible to find objects of value, good blue-and-white of the Ming and celadon of the Sung. Monochromes, because of the previous existence in North Vietnam of a copying factory, were more dangerous, but Dong produced also an occasional Ying Ching and a quantity of reasonable Ch'in and Swatow.

On arrival at Hanoi, I had assumed that if *Le Grand Voleur* were not working directly for the State, he must be under close official supervision. I discovered, or think that I discovered, that this was a false impression of an omnipresent state.

I had sought an export licence from the DRV 'Cultural Bureau' for my first purchases from Monsieur Dong, producing a signed receipt for the articles at prices which he had insisted on virtually decimating for the (tax) purpose. After habitual weeks of bureaucratic delay, I was summoned to that bureau and informed that, since two of the articles were national treasures (shallow bowls of 11th century Thanh Hoa celadon), they might not only not be exported, but would be confiscated. The responsibility for reclaiming the purchase price was to be mine.

I protested on the respectable but politically embarrassing theory that Annamite porcelain of that date did not exist either because Annam had then been part of China or because no ancient kilns had been found at Thanh Hoa or anywhere else in North Vietnam. My bowls were therefore Chinese (Sung) imports and so could not be described as national treasures. My interlocutor, who acknowledged the existence of the theory while rejecting it, would not accept this as a basis, and although we had an amiable, technical and non-chauvinist conversation, I left empty-handed. I subsequently explained the circumstances to the *Grand Voleur*, who was in no way distressed and refunded the sum that I had paid him.

On my next visit, however, I found him nervously clicking his knuckles and incomprehensible with fear. He had been, or so he said, berated by officials for his conduct in disposing of the articles, and was under the impression that his whole livelihood was at risk, that his shop was in imminent danger of closure, and that he might have to go to work in the padi.

Nothing of the sort happened, and he went back to the old stand, selling everything that came into his hands, Chinese or Annamite, without regard to antiquity. He told me that he had had no subsequent trouble from the authorities and anticipated none; he assured me that he would have a lot more Thanh Hoa during the next few days.

I believe that he declared an infinitesimal proportion of his income to the State for tax purposes and certainly not the vast sums he acquired from my spendthrift colleagues at Hanoi. I never saw anyone remotely like an official, or even informant, in his shop, and judging by his later attitude and the progress he made with his new house, he no longer had any fear of the authorities. If the latter allowed him to remain open for reasons of Foreign Exchange, they, because of his tax evasion, got pretty little out of it. Nevertheless, the need for a sales outlet for the 95 percent of junk that could be unloaded on ignorant foreigners, and perhaps even the provision of *something* at Hanoi for the Diplomatic Corps to do, may have been the main motives for continued non-interference with *Le Grand Voleur*. And after all, there were precious few officials in that mobilized country to spare for expert, if petty, oppression of that kind.

VII

COLLEAGUES

BEFORE I HAD BEGUN to make the formal calls on my diplomatic colleagues, Francois de Quirielle invited me to a farewell reception for members of his staff at the *Cercle Français*.

The French residence, behind a high brick wall, had once been that of their Commanders-in-Chief, including Generals de Lattre de Tassigny and Salan. It lay in its own park, with a hard tennis court, a small Club building (*Cercle Français*), staff accommodation, mess and offices. It was very large indeed and, set with great rain-trees, an hospitable oasis for those in less commodious and more isolated premises.

For this reception, tables and chairs had been placed under the trees outside the *Cercle*, the night sky lit with stars. Small electric bulbs were hung from branch to branch, and kerosene lamps illuminated the canapés, pâtés, cold and hot dishes displayed. My glass was filled with that excellent vin ordinaire supplied to French military and diplomats at nominal cost, last consumed in the French Sector of Occupied Vienna either as guest or in exchange for Haig, Johnnie Walker or Dewar.

The guests included, besides the staff of the Delegation and members of the Control Commission, the Egyptian and Indonesian chargés d'affaires, the Indian Consul-General, three or four ambassadors or senior officials from the Soviet Bloc embassies, but no members of the DRV administration.

Francois de Quirielle, the Delegate-General, was a distinguished diplomat with previous service in Europe and Africa and, subsequently, as Ambassador to Malaysia. His insights into the DRV administration, where his official contacts were, naturally, deeper than mine, his analyses and arguments, his unstinting cooperation with ourselves, were of permanent value to my mission. His kindness, although we seldom agreed politically, and that of his wife, Anne, handsome, warmhearted, ebullient, forthright, devoted to Francois but her own woman, gay, explosive and determined, can never be adequately requited. To meet under their wing those of their guests with whom I should deal bilaterally in the future was the first fruit of our later friendship. The French Mission, for reasons rather of history than present substance, still mattered at Hanoi, carrying a weight professionally nurtured by de Quirielle's sound conduct of Franco-Vietnamese relations. In these matters appearance frequently takes precedence, and with benefit, over reality.

The interest among a small community shown in the newcomer was a good deal more acute than I had expected. Francois de Quirielle, in particular, and Mr Dhawan, the Indian Consul-General, asked me detailed questions about British intentions which, I eventually realized, referred to some recent and specific event about which I knew nothing; these two and one of the Russians behaved toward me as if I were to be the special executant of a plan which was to have some major consequence for the resolution of the war.

The Soviet sceptically inquired about the channels that I proposed to use to the DRV for the U.K.'s new purposes. The Indian wondered whether the DRV would regard a cease-fire, without a unilateral halt in the American bombing campaign, as sufficient grounds for negotiation. The Egyptian, with whose government our relations were then uneasy, thought that a withdrawal of U.S. ground troops would also be mandatory. De Quirielle believed a cessation of bombing might be a necessary and sufficient condition, while the Indonesian thought that a halt in troop reinforcements would be essential. The resulting discussion which, in one form or another, would continue for as long as I remained at Hanoi, at least gave me time to try to reconstruct the events unknown to me which had led to such hopes in my person.

In fact, without consultation with the British Missions at Saigon or Hanoi, or prior warning to myself before leaving London a week ago, the British government had launched, on the day after my arrival at Hanoi, a 'Peace Initiative by Radio' which had been picked up in their own homes an hour earlier by those later attending the French reception. Lord George-Brown's virtues were so overwhelming that it would be foolish to reproach him for this and similar episodes, the domestic reasons for which, as noted above, were clear, although they had little chance of success. But that night one of them made his Department's emissary look more disorganized than necessary.

It was plain that the argument for a permanent bombing halt

expressed at that reception owed something to a general distaste for being — potentially, for Hanoi was not in my time often subjected to attacks as devastating as those undertaken elsewhere in North Vietnam — showered with high explosive. There was universal agreement, however, among my interlocutors that, in October, 1966, the U.S. bombing campaign as now conducted had not decisively affected the economy or the strategic capacity of the DRV. It might even have, under effective DRV leadership and by means of rousing slogans, stiffened the resistance of the inhabitants and would therefore lead neither to a North Vietnamese collapse nor to negotiations.

The facts were not in dispute. I subscribed to the view, and I still do, but I needed more time to understand that it was not at all the point. There are more ways than one of using the air arm, and the Americans had at the time chosen not only the wrong one, but one which ultimately guaranteed victory for the DRV. Nor was it for some weeks that I realized that the latter were uninterested in negotiations leading to any solution other than the unification of Vietnam and, eventually, of Vietnam, Laos and Cambodia, under the control of the Lao Dong Party (Vietnam Workers Party) at Hanoi.

I called next day on the doyen of the Diplomatic Corps, then the Soviet Ambassador, Mr Tshcherbakov, a career Foreign Service officer with previous experience in China who had, in 1966, already been at Hanoi for six or seven years. He later became Ambassador at Peking and faced problems of a more diplomatic and less administrative character.

Mr Tshcherbakov's Embassy, with the Chinese Mission the principal agents for supply of war material to the North Vietnamese army, maintained, apart from air transport and other logistic support, the range of services normally available as back-up to a Soviet presence overseas. These included, not only doctors, commissariat and repair shops, but air-raid shelters and even shallow-draught boats against a breach of dykes and consequent flooding of the city. I was therefore conscious that not only my position among the colleagues but, more important, facilities which might in the last resort include evacuation, depended on the good will of the Soviets, Co-Chairman with the United Kingdom, of the 1954 Geneva Agreements.

Driver Tien, complaining sotto voce, drove me to the massive bulk of this mission, doubtless once the palace of French Colonial Governor or other dignitary. I was escorted along corridors no more sub-fusc or impersonal than those of a British Government Department in London, up a staircase to a small anteroom looking through tall windows on to the driveway below. The room was furnished with comfortable armchairs and hung with Russian landscapes: a table in the corner bore glasses, vodka, vermouth, wine, aerated waters and various *zakushki* (snacks).

After a few minutes' conversation with my escort, an English-speaking referent, the Ambassador entered, accompanied by a First Secretary, somewhat resembling the late Peter Lorre, whom I had met the previous night at the *Cercle Français*. (The Ambassador himself did not attend functions at that grade.) Mr Tshcherbakov, although small, sandy, almost reddish haired, pale, a little remote and withdrawn, was an impressive figure and, when surrounded by Ambassadors of East European countries, carried a vice-regal air. It would, however, have been foolish to have expected him to show that dominance over his local clients demonstrated later in very different circumstances by the vast Mr Tshchetinin in Mongolia.

The Ambassador asked the conventional questions about previous posts, present living conditions and other topics aired on these occasions. When, glass of vermouth now in hand, he asked me to define my functions at Hanoi, I described the history of the British Mission and referred to our Co-Chairmanship established in 1954 at Geneva. The United Kingdom was, I continued, also a power with connections in Asia formed over many centuries and, as a trading nation, one with major commercial interests as well as residual military aid programmes. These factors and the current responsibility to resolve the war in Vietnam — and here I pointed to the Secretary of State's announcement the previous day — demanded a British presence at Hanoi. While agreeing with the Ambassador that present Consular functions were minimal, I said that they might not, in peacetime, remain so. In the meanwhile other tasks existed, and I hoped that, when expedient, I could count upon the cooperation of the Soviet Embassy.

Mr Tshcherbakov thanked me for my explanation and promised that he would ensure that I was regarded, so far as it was within his authority, as a diplomatic colleague. He was careful, presumably because he did not control the policies and prejudices of the Chinese, Albanian or North Korean representatives in the DRV, not to refer to me as 'a member of the Diplomatic Corps'; but by his example, if not his instructions, the treatment of my Mission by most of his Satellite colleagues was thereafter warm, friendly and, however it may have appeared in the narrow eyes of DRV officials, correct.

The Ambassador added that I should call upon him when I found it necessary, whether for discussion of Vietnamese and wider problems or with any material requests to which his Embassy could accede. I took advantage of this declaration on many occasions, either to clarify doubts in my own mind, or as instructed by my government. Mr Tshcherbakov was invariably polite, informative and direct. He had, it seemed to me, an understanding of the local scene and of the intentions of the Soviet government which was, if lofty and unencumbered by detail, a plain and simple one. This Ambassador was truthful and devoid of complicating guile. I wish, during the Wilson peace offensive of 1967, that it had fallen to my lot to negotiate with him direct on the hard and difficult intricacies of that bizarre imbroglio.

When I told a member of his staff that Tshcherbakov was an excellent ambassador, he sourly replied, 'All Excellencies are excellent'.

Soviet influence on Vietnamese policies was not a subject lightly addressed, and my first visit did not seem an appropriate moment to raise it. The Russians consistently claimed that the government of the DRV made its own decisions; that, no doubt, was technically correct. On this occasion Mr Tshcherbakov volunteered only that the Vietnamese, in his opinion, probably would negotiate if there were to be a halt in the bombing. But he expressly indicated that he could not speak for the host Government, seeming to suggest that his comment was only a reflection of DRV thinking, perhaps just an impression that he had gained from conversations with their leadership, certainly not an undertaking formally communicated by the Vietnamese to the U.S.S.R., still less dictated by Moscow.

The theme of a permanent U.S. bombing halt as a means to eventual peace in Indo-China was expressed by most ambassadors at Hanoi. My function, on these initial visits, was to listen, but the deliberate American decision to confine the ground war to the South made renunciation by the U.S. of their only other means of retaliation against the DRV improbable without reciprocal and verifiable concessions by the latter.

All these formal calls, each of which was returned in my own residence, were accompanied, at 11 a.m., by considerable quantities of food and drink, amounting frequently to a full meal of selected national dishes, whether tamales, gulyas, roast goose, sausages, cold-cuts, curry puffs or peppers, irrigated by curious East European wines, tea and an amazing range of vodka. The Cuban produced rum or banana liqueur, the Indian served beer, the Romanian and Bulgarian dry white wines, the Egyptian vodka, the Indonesian gin and tonic, the Chinese tea and

Mao Tai (rice vodka), the Czechs lager, the Hungarians tokay and Bull's Blood, the Mongols Scotch whisky. Owing to the absence of diplomatic relations, I had no opportunity to take Ginseng with the North Koreans nor whatever potable is favoured in Albania; the heat in the tiny Pathet Lao residence was so appalling that I have no recollection of anything consumed there.

Most ambassadors or their interpreters spoke French, in which we communicated. Neither the Mongol, however, nor his interpreter, who was a Vietnamese and Russian speaker, did so. Xuan, who was with me, therefore translated my remarks into Vietnamese for the interpreter, who then transposed them into Mongol for Mr Bataa, lounging powerfully on the sofa. Mr. Bataa, a Mongol of an agreeable and representative type, square, high cheekbones, stocky, his bowlegs acquired from a horse-borne childhood, later became Ambassador to Cuba. (I also saw him in the company of Mr Dambadajaa, Ambassador to Britain, in the corridors of the Presidium at Ulan Bator.) Although, as I subsequently learned in Mongolia, his country was then engaged in the supply to the DRV of cattle and ponies, nearly all of which died of heat, he did not appear to have views, at least none which he wished to express to me, on the course of the war.

Our conversation took the form of a short lesson, sought by me, in his own tongue, largely hallo, goodbye and thank you. At subsequent rare encounters Bataa maintained this genial approach, showing – after my return from a visit to London – apprehensive interest in the length of English mini-skirts. His National Day reception, at which his speech was not absolutely attuned to North Vietnamese requirements, was notable for the presence of a ravishing Mongol secretary in a pink sack dress. I can remember hoping, with no optimism, for an eventual posting to Ulan Bator.

The Cuban Ambassador, General Oliveira, on the other hand, was six-foot, seven inches tall. He wore battledress and a Castro cap; Hanoi was his first diplomatic appointment. He addressed me didactically, on my first visit, on the principles of Marxism-Leninism and the inevitability of the triumph of communism throughout the world.

I saw no reason to put up with this and politely pointed out to him that diplomatic relations, which Cuba and the U.K. enjoyed, were between states and should exclude ideological polemic or the export of political theory. Although this was not a welcome, or even comprehensible, idea to communists, particularly communists of fervid conviction and without experience of the larger world, it was one that Oliveira, after initial surprise, accepted. He offered me a cigar, which I refused, and then a cigarette made of cigar tobacco, which explosively disturbed my composure. This pleased Oliveira, and honours were even, after the consumption of a banana liqueur to become, indeed, heavily in his favour.

I have no idea what the Cubans actually did in Hanoi other than spit and throw stones at American prisoners exposed in carts, but Oliveira strongly advocated a Cuban paramilitary contribution in the south and was critical of North Vietnamese reluctance to accept this and other warlike proposals.

Irritation at Vietnamese refusal to permit direct participation by allies, tending in the latter's view to unnecessary inefficiency and lack of trained skill, was also expressed, *mutatis mutandis*, by other interlocutors, in particular by the Russians over Vietnamese management of SAMs and other weapons. I could understand their frustration at what amounted to misuse, even waste, of technical resources, but not their absence of political wisdom in proposing the introduction of foreign troops into a struggle which the DRV could satisfactorily represent as waged, on their side, by Vietnamese alone.

I liked the General and saw him thereafter as often as was decent; he was, speaking only Spanish and a few words of English, a lonely figure, nervous of diplomatic procedures and with a distaste for formal receptions. Uppmann and other cigars, the Cuban secret weapon and, although of reduced quality, still the best in the world, were within his gift. Oliveira himself, suffering from a digestive malady, neither drank nor smoked; this plainly made the tensions and etiquette of Hanoi's frightful diplomatic occasions, already for him lacking a comprehensible language, yet more intolerable.

Many of my colleagues were convinced that I was in some sort of direct touch with the American administration, if not with Dean Rusk himself. I had, in fact, no such contacts, my communications being only with the Foreign Office and with selected British embassies. But since they held this misapprehension, and many of them would have liked nothing better than to expound their views on the war to an American audience here unavailable to them, the approaches and revelations of one or other diplomat were, I feel sure, often seen by them as speeding along the air waves to Washington. I had, therefore, without claiming such access, *something*, however factitious, to offer. When, indeed, any communist ambassador or other contact had information or advice of substance which I could then incorporate in letters or telegrams home, if it could lead to better understanding of the situation in North Vietnam, I assume that it would have reached the U.S. administration by the appropriate route.

This comparative eagerness to seek my company obviously also meant that I had to analyse with minute care the contents of any conversation. Disinformation or even plain misinformation were as likely commodities for dispatch down such a supposed channel as information. There were a number of these canards: a rumour during heavy raids on the Paul Doumer Bridge that American POWs were being made to work on the bridge, transparent in purpose; others, including a story that Vice President Hubert Humphrey had landed at Hanoi airfield, obscure. Except for an early readiness, soon adjusted, to view the North as neither implacable nor opportunistic, I hope that I sorted the wheat from the chaff, not a boast that, whether intent on Nobel Peace Prize or in natural search of a quiet night's rest, could be plausibly maintained by some other non-communist missions.

Wholly different from any of these contacts was the Canadian element of the International Control Commission whose villa, shabby, comfortable and filled with prints of the Rockies, pine-clad lakes and prairies, stood opposite my own. Because the Canadian Department of External Affairs found it impossible at that time to persuade members of their service to head the Hanoi detachment, the latter was in the hands of a series of majors and lieutenant-colonels of the Canadian army, supported by a sergeant and three or four other ranks, all of whom rotated on a two or three-month basis. The war had by that time reached an intensity which precluded any movement by the ICC outside Hanoi, and the unit's duties were confined to self-maintenance and to such contacts with their Indian or Polish colleagues, and with the DRV authorities, as were necessary.

The villa, however, after a busy morning in the town or in the long evenings, provided a gathering point for many. Even when one of the atrocious movies provided by the Army Kinema Corporation had not arrived from Saigon, there were other distractions. Dr Deb from Calcutta would enlarge our evening hearts upon the sitar; the plump upper-class Alexandrian child bride of the Egyptian chargé d'affaires enlighten us on marriage in the Upper Delta; peripatetic Soviet secretaries discourse on the peasant wisdom of Georgian or Caucasus grandmothers; Mr Louhanapessy, Indonesian chargé d'affaires (Ambassador Sukrisno having defected to China after the failed PKI coup in Djakarta) inform us on Sulawesi and the islands; while Acadian

Corporal 'Boots' demonstrated on the dart board crafty aiming with his shaft.

Film nights were formal and unrelaxed occasions when the corps, including the French Delegate-General, Romanian, Czech, Russian and Egyptian diplomats with their wives, sat on stiff chairs before the silver screen. Some of the movies, stories of espionage in which the Black Hats were invariably Soviet, must have caused distress to the audience. The regular habitués sat respectfully sniggering at the back, drink in hand; since those days, going to the picture show has never been as much fun.

VIII

THE DAILY ROUND

DONG, NERVOUSLY BOBBING, would wake me at 7 or 7.30 with a cup of tea: the bedroom during the monsoon was dismal, its floor littered with the remnants of burnt-out mosquito coils, like skinless snakes, and the air heavy with their scent. Rust-coloured water trickled from the bathroom taps and showers. None of the curtains met. Outside, platoons of silent women, allegedly prostitutes under 'reeducation', soundless in conical straw hats and black pyjamas, brushed the street with long-handled brooms, the eerie spectacle of dawn.

Dong asked me on one occasion if I would like a kipper for breakfast. When either Livesey or I went to Saigon, we brought back a portable icebox measuring about 36 inches by 18 inches packed with items including crabs, bacon, quail, lamb, supplementing the extremely limited diet of Hanoi, but no kippers. 'Where did you obtain kippers, Monsieur Dong?'

'From the deep freeze, Monsieur.'

'How long have they been there?'

'Not they, it. Monsieur Ponsonby,' who had left North Vietnam some 18 months before, 'brought it.'

He produced, in its original wrapping, one of a pair of packaged kippers, the other long consumed. It was, if not a source of nostalgia, a change from North Vietnamese eggs, fresh enough but so small that one imagined local hens all to be bantams, stunted at that.

Monsieur Nguyen would then arrive, after preliminary circling with Dong, to discuss the day's menus, such as they were, plan our small weekend gatherings and, once weekly, present his scrawled expenses for reimbursement. The hot weather was beginning to end, replaced in October by the *crachin,* a thin, almost perpetual, drizzling rain, the product of the north-east monsoon with its intermittent winds, the tail of typhoons in the South China Sea.

In such conditions I put up my umbrella, turned left out of the gate opposite the lolling Vietnamese militia by the rear entrance of the Indian element of the ICC, turned right into the Ly Thong Kiet after a few hundred yards and thus to the office where Xuan, clad at this season in the tweeds of a long-departed British Vice-Consul, rose, bowing, to his feet.

'How is your tooth this morning, Mr. Consul-General?' He referred to a nagging pain from which I had suffered almost since arrival.

'No better. I think that I must arrange to see the Russians.'

'See them if you wish, Consul-General, but you would do better to follow my advice: Vietnamese dental services are excellent, preferable indeed.' This assertion seemed, on the visual evidence around me, in particular the teeth of Dong's children, improbable, and an exception to Xuan's level assessment of the capacities of the DRV. And, in those days, Soviet claims of material progress, including dentistry, had not been exposed to me as the myths that they are. More precisely perhaps, I still saw Russians as Europeans, with European notions of hygiene, anaesthesia and the needs of the individual.

'Yes, I know. But let us try first the Soviet Embassy. Please telephone the Ambassador's referent for me.'

I have always preferred, whether to avoid troubling others with my private affairs or through fastidiousness or because of a simple desire to control my own life, to make personal appointments personally, but this course was seldom practicable at Hanoi. The telephone in the residence rang frequently, but when I lifted the receiver the machine was invariably silent; when, on the other hand, I tried to call out, I was never able to achieve a connection.

I used the office machine rather more regularly, perhaps once a month, until one morning when Monsieur Xuan interrupted me with the news that two telephone technicians had arrived from the PTT in response to a request by myself that the set should be repaired. (I had, of course, made no request.) Two smiling Vietnamese, the male wearing a beige solar topee and a blue post office uniform, the female in overalls and peaked cap, entered the room and explained, when I denied asking for service, that *they* knew that the telephone was out of order, a hasty correction to their bland assertion.

I had, naturally, taken for granted that all the telephones were tapped either as open microphones when not in use or tapped when speech was in progress. No confidential conversations took place on the telephone or anywhere near it. I was, therefore, delighted rather than surprised when the male official seized the telephone, removed the base plate, extracted two presumably worn out devices which he asked me to hold, and replaced them with new objects from a broken spectacle case held by his giggling assistant. Although I knew little of these matters, I was able to recognize, from a short security course held before leaving London, both sets of devices as simple 'listening' apparatus. The whole episode was endearing and, in its naivete — unless it were some massive double-bluff — reassuring. But even to judge it 'reassuring' was to exaggerate: since we acted on the assumption of total technical surveillance, Livesey and I confined our confidential conversations to the open air or to writing, a process less inhibiting than one might suppose.

Xuan then, having spoken to the Soviet Embassy, announced that the Soviets had said that dentistry as such was not practiced in the U.S.S.R. There were doctors who dealt with ear, nose and throat complaints, and doctors whose speciality was reserved for all other maladies of the head. It was with one of the latter that he had, on my behalf, made an appointment that morning.

'I can't believe that the Russians have no dentists, Monsieur Xuan; you must have misunderstood.'

'Have you seen their teeth, Monsieur? Iron-mongers, perhaps; dentists, not.' Like an Oriental Jeeves, Xuan was remorseless, his advice ignored or not accepted: 'We must all hope that you come to no positive harm.'

The Soviet outpatient's department was a low, dark, humid bungalow, the waiting room lined with narrow wooden benches on which sat overweight Russian wives, their coiffures composed apparently of unidentified *matter* rather than hair and resembling spun-sugar beehives. Their bulky thighs, encased in tight, usually pink, crimplene skirts, spread at unappetizing right-angles below raised stomachs and heavy, shapeless breasts. Obesity is not unique to the U.S.S.R., reaching indeed its most grotesque proportions in the United States, but because of refusal to exercise, ignorance of diet, simple greed, male indifference and shortages of anything except sugar and other carbohydrates, more general in Russia than elsewhere.

The women talked freely, but as if to themselves, without looking at one another, unsmiling, in tones not precisely of complaint, but joyless, each seeming to recount her own catalogue of boring and minor events, probably ending in failure. Impatience, if not some unspecified contempt, seemed to fill their speech. They looked like charwomen playing the part of Memsahibs.

A doctor in soiled white coat seated me before a washbasin. After a cursory examination, he told me that I was suffering from a fairly rare illness, the cure for which was experimental and would involve ten years' treatment. I thought it best at this point to go home and reconsider the matter. Next morning I dispatched a telegram to the Embassy at Saigon in which I outlined the Soviet diagnosis and sought authority to pay a quick visit to the South for a second opinion and more conventional treatment. But although Saigon contained qualified European dentists, a subsequent telegram from the Foreign Office (to whom my own had been repeated) ordered me, on account of a new British intervention aimed at negotiations, to stay put at Hanoi.

When I returned to the outpatient's department some days later, speaking, in the absence of the referent, a mixture of Serbo-Croat and Bulgarian, the doctor injected me directly into the gum with a horse syringe containing, alternately, bitter aloes and some other compound, a process which continued three times a week without noticeable effect other than greatly increased pain.

I eventually began to fear that this treatment was a deliberate attempt wholly to incapacitate me and therefore sought the counsel of a visiting British doctor from St Stephen's Hospital in the Fulham Road, whom I had entertained to luncheon and whose received views on North Vietnamese intentions I had attempted to balance.

'A most interesting form of treatment,' he commented after some thought. 'Little seen these days.' He questioned me in greater detail. 'What you are undergoing is a well-known mediaeval practice, the object of which is to distract the patient's attention from the original pain by inflicting on him one different but yet more sharp.' I had no doubt that the anecdote would form an acceptable paragraph in *The Lancet*.

Xuan, as he made next day the inevitable appointment at a Vietnamese clinic, was gravely complacent.

This clinic, with its airy balconies, red-tiled roof and grass maidan, was not unlike the hospitals of British colonies, patients dispersed at random on the verandahs, leaning against pillars, sprawled on the grass. The difference lay in the complete absence of nursing staff and the presence everywhere of entire families, including children, equipped with pots, pans and other culinary devices, grouped around the related patient, surrogates for the nurses whom, even in the South, the Vietnamese psychology seemed unable to support.

The dentist, in a surgery equipped with modern Czech drills and other paraphernalia, was a handsome French woman in her 30s who had married a Vietnamese doctor, taken her husband's nationality and remained in the North. She was attentive, quiet and professional but wholly uncommunicative except on dental matters.

'You have two abscesses: two teeth should therefore be removed as soon as possible.' She stood back and gave instructions in Vietnamese to her assistant. 'There is no evidence to confirm the Soviet diagnosis.'

'When do you want to extract them?'

'There is little point in delay, Monsieur. I suggest that we go ahead now.'

'Do you propose a general or a local anaesthetic?'

'I regret that since anaesthetics are devoted entirely to the needs of the People's Army of Vietnam (PAVN) and to those civilians recently wounded by American imperialist air attacks on Haiphong and in the countryside, I shall have to operate without anaesthesia.'

'Yes, Madame. But I think I will defer this experience until later. I will make a further appointment with you for Friday at 11:30.'

On Friday, having instructed the domestic staff, I took a bottle of Haig Gold Label whisky from the reserves and, seated in the squalid gloom of the dining room, began gradually from a tumbler to reduce its level until, at 11 o'clock, about three-quarters — or such was my misty estimate — had been consumed. Arms on the shoulders of Dong and the blind gardener, I was then escorted, feet somewhat at the trail, to the Ford Escort, the driver's mouth agape. The pain of the subsequent proceedings must have been sensibly diminished by this measure. It did not seem so at the time, and the aftermath was even worse than recovery from the older type of general anaesthetic.

But the business was, after all, over. Asians, I think, if only because of the lack of an alternative, bear pain and suffering more equably than do Europeans. Furthermore, although the parallel is not exact and I doubt whether Britain was in such straitened medical circumstances even in 1940 or 1941, I am not completely confident that, say, a Swedish diplomat during the blitz on London or other period of reverses might not have been treated in similar mode to myself.

Although this episode rather overhung early days at Hanoi, it was permitted only intermittently to interfere with more usual occupations, visiting diplomatic colleagues, the administration of the consulate-gen eral and the continual investigation *à pied* of the conditions and the mood of the town and district.

The times were bad. A very large proportion of the state's resources was devoted solely to military purposes, whether to anti-aircraft defence, to the PAVN or to the support and maintenance of the National Liberation Front (NLF), that nominal coalition of all southern political forces, in fact controlled and directed in every respect, political, economic and military, by the Lao Dong Party under Le Duan and the PAVN General Staff under General Giap in Hanoi. While most, if not all, of the NLF's military equipment was supplied by the Soviet Union and her allies or by China, the manpower involved in its transportation down the Ho Chi Minh Trail, in the Cambodian sanctuaries and to a large degree in subsequent deployment in the South was northern and indigenous. And there were over 100,000 PAVN soldiers in the South. The consequent shortage of manpower for industrial purposes in the DRV, although accepted as an inevitable result of all-out war and partially compensated by imports, led not only to severe balance-of-payments deficits but to an almost negligible consumer economy. This and the evidence of bare shelves and counters was, again, less unacceptable to a people so unacquainted with the modern world, so disciplined, under so authoritarian a goad, but the effects on the population in terms of disease and sub-nutrition, of a similar neglect of agriculture, were more substantial.

In October, 1966, nine items were rationed, but other commodities were either scarce or, for many, prohibitively expensive. Pork was rationed, theoretically at 300 but actually at 150 grams of poorish quality a month. A good-quality escalope cost 1.20 dong* in local currency. Chickens, mainly scrawny, cost from 6 to 24 dong according to quality; some beef and buffalo were available, but this flesh was generally unpalatable to Vietnamese.

Rice, Vietnam's staple diet, was rationed at 13½ kilos per month for white-collar workers, 15-18 for light 'industrial' and 19-24 kg. for heavy 'industrial' and other heavy workers; children from one to 30 months received 4 kg. of rice flour, from 30 months to 5½ years 7 kg. of rice, from 5½-13 years between 7 and 12 kilos. The extent to which the ration was honoured varied, substitutes including baked bread, noodles, maize and manioc; rice cost .45 dong per kilo on the ration and .70 to 2 dong on the 'free' market.

Severe measures in December against the distillation of alcohol from

---

* 10 dongs were then approximately equal to £1.

rice were, however, not the consequence of a rice shortage but taken mainly in order to reduce the acreage of rice suitable for alcohol in favour of edible rice. (State distilleries used other ingredients such as manioc and sweet potatoes as a basis for alcohol.) A further reason for these measures, as under French Colonial rule, was the desire to concentrate distilling in state hands.

Other rationed items included soya paste at 450 grams a month, *nuoc mam* (the 'HP sauce' of Vietnam) at 1-2 litres a month per family, condensed milk at 4-8 tins for any new-born child whose mother could not breast-feed, 4 metres a year of cloth except for shrouds and bridal garments (5 metres), coal 200-300 kg. (14.35 dong) and firewood 15-30 kg. a year. Kerosene was rationed to ¼ litre a month per family; since there were total blackouts on three nights a week from November onward, as a result of the bombing on 19 April, 1966, of Vuong Bi power station, this shortage was serious and of major consequence to domestic life.

Items later placed on ration were sugar at 100 grams per month (500 grams for children and teachers) at 2.30 dong per kilo, washing soap at one bar per head for three months at .65 dong and one cake of toilet soap for children under one year of age; two boxes of matches were issued over a three-month period.

A sole or, rather, plaice, cost 1.35 dong and a piece of cheap-quality lake or river fish .35; owing to lack of regular communication with Haiphong, crab and other seafood were rarely available in Hanoi. Limes cost .35 dong each, tomatoes .30, papaya 1.35, aubergine 1.25, pamplemousse .30, eggs .35, three oranges .40, three bananas .40, one kg. of potatoes between 1.25 and 2 dong, one kg. of fat 3.50, one kg. of flour 3 dong.

In considering the prices and availability of these items, one remembered that salaries were very low: whereas my Vietnamese staff received 100 dong per month, a proportion of which nevertheless had to be deposited in the National Savings Bank, even a PAVN colonel received only 60 and a private soldier 2. For this reason, an arrangement whereby a bachelor might have two meals a day cooked for him at 28 dong a month, by a number of restaurants in Hanoi, to carry away in his metal two-tier tiffin carrier was not as cheap as it looked, although his rent might have been as low as 6-7 dong a month.

The '10 Month Rice Crop,' 40 percent collected by the end of November, was described in the press as — due to climatic difficulties and to lack of labour — only fairly good. In any case, although a unified

Vietnam might be self-sufficient in rice under a non-Socialist distribution system, North Vietnam alone, without supplies from the South, impossible under wartime conditions, was wholly unable to feed itself and thus remained dependent on Chinese imports.

Since July, 1966, there had been a noticeable reduction in the number of shops open in the middle of the city. Those principally affected were small craftsmen, basket and mattress-makers, copper and silver-smiths, mainly Chinese, to whom whole streets had been devoted; these, photographers, bookshops, electrical retailers, barbers, dress-makers, handicrafts — chiefly lacquer and mother-of-pearl — were either closed or open only for a few hours each day. Some of these restrictions were imposed by law; other closures were caused by frequent evacuation schemes involving up to 200,000 people at a time fleeing supposed imminent bombardment of Hanoi itself. (Closure of the bookshops, with their Soviet technical and propaganda publications, and of the dressmakers, stocking vulgar Soviet patterns, was no great loss.) There were also a number of stalls selling such items as Albanian cigarettes, zip fasteners, bulldog clips, combs, etc; itinerant cobblers repaired locks, fountain pens, even batteries, on the pavements, while the old women squatting on the sidewalks sold bananas and huge quantities of spinach grown to the south of the city.

Order, in these conditions, among the private sector of the civilian population, i.e. that proportion of the population not directly employed by the state, was largely controlled by Quarter Committees elected every three years in each of the four quarters of Hanoi. Applications to travel, without which the applicant would not even find a place on bus or train, or to buy consumer goods such as radios (ranging in price from 300 dong for transistors to between 140-220 for East European and Chinese sets) and bicycles had all to be routed through these committees. Their criteria for permission were stringent. A man would not receive authority to purchase a bicycle in order to visit his evacuated family outside Hanoi unless his home in Hanoi was also so far from his place of work as to provide the primary reason for the purchase. No one in the private sector speaking languages other than Vietnamese would be granted a permit to buy a radio. Persons in the private sector would experience difficulty in receiving permission to visit the only two private doctors practising in Hanoi. In the latter instance, although consultation fees and the price of medicine were payable from the patients' own resources, the fee was only one dong; unsophisticated medicines were available on the free market.

It was also the function of these committees to extract money from their flock, according to income, for National Savings.

People outside this sector, state employees and 'workers' received permits for their requirements through their own departments and organizations. Medical fees were paid by the *Service Sanitaire* attached to each such organization, which were in turn funded by levies of 25 percent deducted by the employer from each individual's salary.

But although the times were not the best, neither were they the worst. U.S. air attacks, as we moved into winter 1966, with its persistent spitting rain and low gray cloud, were reduced to a minimum, often confined to a single pilotless observation drogue or propaganda release aircraft. Pamphlets from the latter featured photographs captioned 'Born in the North, died in the South,' of dead soldiers of the People's Army of Vietnam. (Not all leaflets fell outside Hanoi or were immediately removed by the militia.) Such heavy bombers as did pierce the overcast, mainly in the periphery of the city, timed their missions so predictably that the onlooker was spared the element of surprise and thus the distasteful necessity of jumping, at militia command, into the cylindrical air-raid shelters, all much too shallow for Europeans, on the pavements.

The town roads were in reasonably good repair, although much patched with tar and gravel, but the secondary mud roads outside the centre were extremely dilapidated, especially those running to the highly cultivated Chinese vegetable gardens in the south. The trams, packed inside and encrusted with passengers outside, ran regularly, as did a few Russian and old French cars reserved for the administration. There moved also, on the tree-lined boulevards, a number of Chinese and Japanese motor scooters and small motor bicycles which eventually, for lack of spares, broke down beyond repair; and bicycles, in their thousands, like undecorative and dangerous flocks of butterflies.

'Morale,' so far as that elusive quality can ever be assessed in a totalitarian state, seemed from outward expression at least stable in 1966. The people, however obedient or brutalized, looked and sounded fairly cheerful, certainly neither rebellious nor at their last gasp. But continual government exhortation, threat, encouragement, the occasional display over the town of MiG aerobatics, ubiquitous political discussion groups on the pavements, the tension of public faces, acknowledged the problem which nearly twenty years of war, privation, hunger and suffering, without early expectation of peace, had produced.

IX

AROUND TOWN AND OUT OF IT

THE AUTHORITIES did not allow me to ride a bicycle in Hanoi. The reason given was 'security' or, sometimes, 'protection', not wholly implausible among the dense files of somnambulist cyclists. The real concern of the External Affairs Bureau was, however, not my safety, but my mobility and the opportunities this would have afforded. When confronted with a refusal on similar grounds, one of my successors, Baroness Park, proposed that the difficulty be overcome by permitting a tandem with a militiaman on the pillion.

To walk — for time was of no account and Hanoi not enormous — was the most agreeable and, in the end, the most expeditious means of locomotion. It was certainly the most practical. The alleys, the deserted pagodas stained with damp and buried in untended growth, the brown faces, wary or curious, sharp-turned eyes toward one and as quickly away, the shops and abandoned craft streets, the parks and the lake would scarcely have become familiar from the back seat of a vehicle. The children played in one's path or scurried into doorways; the life of Hanoi, on broken, neglected tarmac or in the dark recesses of the little houses on each hand, was instantly accessible. The old women in black pyjamas selling their vegetables from wide straw baskets, the fierce harangue to his squatting back-street audience of a political instructor, the bougainvillea hanging in swags over a crumbled wall, discontented youths with sleek, if duck's-arse, hair cuts, and jeans acquired by what strange channel, the fight to board the trams, the filth, vigour and some of the meaning of this secret town were at least visible to the pedestrian.

And in the excited crowd at Tet around the Petit Lac, although myself as conspicuous as the Eddystone Light, I waited as the minutes ticked by for the blurred, mysterious explosion, through the surface of the water, of that turtle whose appearance had for centuries prophesied victory to the Tonkinese.

My destinations did not much vary. They included the State Department, the 'bizarrely named edifice' referred to by James Cameron, open daily from 5 to 8 in the morning. The State Department was, in fact, the State Shop. It was always crammed with customers, sometimes fifty to a line, for the meagre stock of goods dispensed by one or, rarely, two young female assistants to each counter, but it made a wartime British Woolworth's or the Balkans in 1945 seem like Asprey's.

Here I used, without the master's genius, to play Kim's Game. The goods available in November, 1966, included footballs, enamelled basins and chamberpots in immense quantity, a guitar or two, Bulgarian' watches, Soviet and Chinese radios, hundreds of Chinese thermos flasks, two Czech bicycles and accessories, shelf upon shelf of torch batteries, one pair of Zeiss field-glasses, two crowded counters of foreign drugs (Caffein, Nivalin, Ematin, Philophran, Adrenalin, Progesterone), soap dishes, two or three showcases of local scent and soap, a few lipsticks, tin pots of face cream, one brand of tooth-paste, Soviet tinned and Chinese powdered milk, gumboots and poor-quality shoes, monocolour gabardine and other cloth, skimpy shirts and vests, faceflannels by the thousand, light-weight trousers. Clothes were sold at two prices, the lower by ten percent being for state employees.

Otherwise, apart from fairly good rubber sandals (not the famous 'Ho Chi Minhs') and what Lillywhite call 'yachting shoes', the stock consisted of ping-pong balls, repellent local lacquer and mother-of-pearl, vocational and polemical literature, shopping baskets, artificial flowers, bulldog clips, two self-coloured lady's bathing suits, three tennis rackets and a stimulating green bikini. A brave attempt had been made to lay out in window-dress this weird collection. Marked prices were the exception but, where shown, extraordinarily high.

An English traveller once defined a fully developed Socialist society as one where the lavatories at the airport did not function, and where hairpins were unavailable in the shops. The State Department had no hairpins.

The river bank near the house, with a little path running through high grass and not unlike the fen country, formed another of my regular 'constitutionals'. (In this barren stretch, young Vietnamese lovers, unlike their more controlled cousins in Peking, strolled hand in hand; but the girls, although racially akin to the ladies of Saigon, seemed of a different species. However much was owed by the erotic charm of the

Saigonnaises to maquillage and to the high-slit Ao Dai, it was hard to believe that even those adjuncts could advantageously embellish the simple forms and faces of the austere northerners, asexual, even plain.) Other strolls, apart from daily visits to diplomatic missions, led me to the dyke walls, to the lake ablaze with flamboyants, to the clang and squalor of the inner city, the great French palaces and the leafy grandeur of the suburban boulevards, their villas now streaked by rain and leprous with inattention.

Sometimes when the city became too claustrophobic, we took the car a little way outside the town to drive slowly past the neat viridian squares of sunken padi and other fields of irrigated agriculture. Here, surrounded by the stooped figures of the cultivators among their endless rows of rice and vegetables ranged in military precision, was the permanent Asia. Here one could breathe, reacquire perspective, slough off metropolitan tensions.

We were not, on the other hand, permitted to drive to Haiphong, a privilege granted to the French, or for picnics to the enchanting Baie d'Along with its vast, conical rocks protruding out of the sea among fleets of square-sailed junks. On return journeys from these excursions, the Vietnamese militia required the French to open and unpack not only the picnic baskets themselves but individual items, including plastic containers, even removing bottles from their straw.

Sometimes, as on journeys to Gia Lam airport, the car was essential. On one occasion in 1967, because the Paul Doumer Bridge had been put out of action by bombing, we had to cross the river by ferry. Earlier crossings had been shambolic: most travellers had arrived at the airport after the aircraft had taken off, and one unfortunate Pole did not get back to Hanoi until the following morning.

Before Livesey's next bag run to Saigon, we therefore sought a priority permit from the Hanoi Security Commissariat earlier described in the old French Sureté building located, soberingly if logically, adjacent to the Tribunal and Gaol. After waiting for 30 minutes in the concierge's lodge among other lightly clad supplicants, I was escorted to the waiting room where my interlocutor, a Tonkinese police sergeant slightly resembling Gene Kelly, helpfully informed me that 'the present difficulties were the result of American bombing'. He added that he thought it unlikely that we should ever again reach the airport until the bombing stopped; two Flying Englishmen forever to cross the river and forever forlornly to return. The portrait of Ho Chi Minh opposite seemed, at that moment, to represent *schadenfreude* rather than benevo lence. The functionary, however, promised to 'study the matter' with the Ministry of Transport. He replied to my thanks by expression of his simple duty and by reassuring strokes and pats.

We eventually received an 'introduction', itself a form of permit, for the ferry. Armed with this and with travel permits, identity cards and passports, we then wasted the afternoon, on the incorrect advice of the French, in trying to secure ferry tickets from an office on the steps of the Cultural and Historical Museum which did not, in fact, open until 5 o'clock. When the officials arrived, we discovered that our applications had succeeded and that we were to be second vehicle on the 5.30 ferry. After many expressions of esteem but, alas, no buck-and-wing from the sergeant, we departed for the vessel.

The ferry, oddly referred to as the 'tourist ferry', was not far from the museum, by a small piece of inland water where fishing was in progress. At this point we opened the ice bucket, broached the gin and tonic, offered some beer to the driver, who shared it with his mates, and contemplated the sylvan and unaccustomed scene.

The Red River, actually pink, lay before us. MiGs roared overhead, explosions took place in the south-east every five minutes with high columns of smoke, the ground was pitted with air-raid shelters, every bush concealed an anti-aircraft weapon, militiamen freely employed their loud-hailers, but while in no way resembling a day at Southend, a fresh breeze blew from the river, and we were, at least temporarily, on our way out of Hanoi.

The cars then boarded the ferry, and we joined them on foot after a short period in a sort of sheep pen. The journey upstream lasted about 25 minutes, during which we had opportunity to regard the landscape, passing ferries, picturesque barques with lateen sails and the Bridge.

The latter looked, as has been well observed, like a horizontal Eiffel Tower (it was financed by the Compagnie Eiffel) and was largely obscured from the river by scrub jungle, but we were able to note that one section of about 50 yards, or almost half a span, was completely missing. The remaining western section of this span was about five feet out of true, and three lorries and about 40 workmen were seen near the spot. Oxyacetylene torches were in operation on my return journey, but it was difficult to believe that the section could be replaced at high water. Rumour asserted, however, that the bridge would be in operation by National Day: and indeed it was.

We were a jovial, even euphoric, ship's company. Smiles were exchanged, a hero of the Democratic Republic exhibited his wounds, laughter was general. A young woman in black silk trousers and purple shirt passed her time in shyly giving us the eye and scratching her initials on the bonnet of the car with her fingernails. On arrival at the East Bank, H.M. Consul-General made his contribution to the evening's entertainment by removing his shoes and socks, unique apparel at Hanoi, and unnecessarily wading ashore before the ferry had settled.

The remainder of the journey was accomplished by car, initially over a dusty road lined by unused pagodas, rice fields, water, anti-aircraft guns and bombed houses, accompanied by shouts of 'Harosho' from strolling yokels. We also observed numerous troupes of relatively ravishing girl workers returning home with spades, hoes, mattocks, shovels, picks, yoked baskets, etc., who, despite their rags, here compared well with the disturbing but factitious charms of the prettier ICC air hostesses. The Customs at Gia Lam spent their usual quarter of an hour unpicking the seams of Geoffrey Livesey's underwear, but he was, after all, almost their only airborne client, and I had by then unpacked the bar again.

Take-off was not delayed, and apart from one short hold-up caused by bad traffic management, I reached the ferry in quick time on my return journey. Because the driver could not both drive and obtain the tickets, I was thus able to drive the car (illegally but unobserved) for the first time during my tour in the DRV, albeit for a few yards only. Unfortunately, owing to the sudden arrival of two high-level government vehicles, we were unable to get our car on to the first ferry; I went over by myself, leaving the driver to catch the next one. Seamanship was slovenly on arrival at the West bank where, back to reality, I was refused a lift by the sullen Vietnamese drivers of the ICC and walked the short distance home.

After this 'day in the country', I was obliged to agree that, considering shortages of manpower, the North Vietnamese had, at least in this particular instance, made good their claim to prescience and prior organization; there was nothing approaching chaos. I was also struck that many of them seemed positively, because of the active role they were enabled to play, to enjoy their difficulties. (Except for some of the Customs and Immigration officials at the airport, notoriously lacking in grace, we met with nothing but cheerful and friendly cooperation.) And finally, I thought, although there was nothing to be done about it, if *only* we could get out into the country more often.

To maintain consular pretensions, I also took the car to receptions, chiefly 'National Days' celebrating events as various as the October

Revolution in the U.S.S.R. or Mao's assumption of power in China. (One hour before the arrival of guests to our own Queen's birthday party, the balcony of the residence, weakened by climbing convolvulus and overladen with buffet tables, collapsed into the yard below. Since heavy rain began to fall as the first guest entered the porte-cochere, the catastrophe was more apparent than real.)

All these occasions, with the exception of the British reception, took place in the steamy heat of the International Club, a large building lacking ventilation of any kind in which only slow-moving overhead fans redistributed the humid air. They were gatherings of peculiar horror, taking the form of a 'cocktail' followed, as in all communist countries, by a dinner at which the only guests seated were the leadership and the heads of foreign missions; other Vietnamese and junior diplomats stood gawping in the background.

The table at which we took our place was round, with the Politburo, occasionally led by Ho Chi Minh himself, seated to the left of the host and the Diplomatic Corps to his right, both in order of seniority. As the most junior foreigner present, I was invariably placed immediately to the right of de Quirielle and, usually, directly opposite Ho Chi Minh.

Ho was then in the closing years of his life, frail but lively and alert. With his white hair, long, wispy beard and tiny frame in regulation blue suit, he resembled his photographs precisely: ambition and disregard for friend or foe had by that time metamorphosed into the lineaments of a twinkling Confucian sage; the treacheries and ruthless endurance of the past could scarcely have been guessed. Conversation with him was, for me, rare but genial, if superficial, concerning the culture of Vietnam, living conditions and, on one occasion, the changed architecture of London where he admitted to having worked at one period. (He was said to have been an employee in the kitchens of the old Carlton Hotel.)

I noticed at one reception that his patience was tried by the anecdotes of a Soviet astronaut named, I think, Titov. Ho's eyes, under the weight of boastful technicalities, closed, opened, intermittently flickered shut but, before he drifted off entirely, caught mine and saw me smiling. He laughed gently and shook himself.

'Who is that man,' inquired Titov, 'who is laughing at me?'

'He is not laughing at you,' the leader said. 'That is the British Consul-General. He is the only man who smiles in Hanoi, and he smiles all the time.'

All receptions took a similar bizarre form. After dinner and the spee ches — lengthy, more or less violently anti-American, illiberal and dog matic — the Politburo moved to the right in a crocodile and the heads of mission to the left, thus passing one another on the beam in line ahead while exchanging ritual handshakes. In this mode, but scarcely any other, it was possible for diplomats to claim that they had met Truong Chinh, General Giap and Phan vam Dong, the latter a figure of skeletal, almost spectral dignity.

One of these functions in Hanoi, on 27 August, 1967, when our Embassy at Peking had been attacked by the mob, was one at which the Chinese chargé d'affaires greeted me by spitting in my face. Restrained only by a wish not to involve my government in a public brawl, my first reaction, as the brother of a pugnacious sister and a product of British upper-class education, was to spit straight back. In the event, I turned my back on the Red Guard to receive, alas, the commendations of the Soviets and East Europeans. (Public fighting took place later that month between Chinese and Soviet citizens outside the Chinese embassy. The DRV militia had to be called upon to preserve order. Crossing China by train on return from leave, an East European diplomat was caught in the cross-fire of a tank battle near Wuhan. 'Communists were fighting communists,' he said to me in horror.)

The British, together with the Indians and Indonesians, were not invited that year to Chinese National Day. I decided to attend, instead, a function given by the Soviets and described by that Embassy as a 'Soirée Culturelle' which consisted, as it turned out, of the first of twenty-four parts of a film commemorating the life of Lenin. The Embassy was deserted on my arrival but filled rapidly with a large contingent of Russian diplomats, who greeted me with an enthusiasm I found difficult to interpret. It emerged, of course, that, unaware that I had not even been invited to the Chinese jamboree, the Soviets assumed that I had walked out of it in protest even earlier than they had themselves staged their own departure. Soviet congratulations for one who liked the *real* China were not easy to accept.

The only travels undertaken outside Vietnam, other than one flight to London for consultations in 1967, were those by the ICC aircraft to Saigon with the diplomatic bag. As the mission then possessed its own cyphers, the need for written correspondence was minimal and confined to routine matters such as the accounts and other administrative concerns. In theory, either Livesey or I took a bag every three months; in practice, because of the supposed need for my presence in Hanoi during British peace initiatives, they were more infrequent.

Their benefit lay in the opportunity for relaxation in the more agree able atmosphere of Saigon, still beautiful if marred by the incessant roar of jet engines from Than Son Nut, and for discussions with my own colleagues and friends in the Embassy and elsewhere. Life was narrow in Hanoi, and 'tunnel vision' needed periodic correction from minds not constricted by association with communists or repressed by the constant need for speech security. And how pleasant it was also to visit decent restaurants, to drive into the countryside — or that part of it not held by the NLF — to laugh and be frivolous, to hear English voices and to enjoy, for a little while, the special charm of my countrymen.

I was not encouraged, because of the fear that observed contacts would induce suspicions of 'espionage' in North Vietnamese minds, to associate with the American Embassy at Saigon, although I lunched once or twice with the American Ambassador, Ellsworth Bunker, and with Philip Habib, his senior counsellor. On one of these occasions, I tentatively raised with them the Hanoi rumour, which I had myself described as ridiculous, that Vice President Hubert Humphrey had landed at Hanoi airport for clandestine negotiations.

In reporting the conversation subsequently to the British Ambassador, I commented that I had sensed from glances exchanged between my two interlocutors that, after all, the allegation might have held at least some truth: both men had given me the uneasy impression of having been caught out in a secret which they would have preferred should remain for their eyes only.

'How little you know Washington,' Peter Wilkinson replied. 'If the visit took place, which I am sure it did not, then the message signalled each to each was rather: "One *more* thing the White House hasn't told us about." '

The return journey to Hanoi sometimes involved, because of the malfunctioning of the beacon and other flight arrangements, a stay of two or three days at Vientiane. This tiny capital on the Mekong appeared to contain little more than one main and unpaved street lined by few houses — other than that of the Prime Minister (then Prince Souvanna Phouma) — higher than one storey. The street was chiefly frequented by soldiers, hippies and shaven-haired bonzes in their yellow or russet robes; across it straddled a vast Arch of Victory erected in the '50s by a Lao General (Phoumi Nosavan) with United States funds intended for more substantial purposes, military or economic.

The Ambassador, Sir Fred Warner, took me on arrival to a reception given by the Lao Government in a modern hotel, where he presented me to a number of Lao Ministers. The insouciance of the latter was marked, the Minister of Defence showing pleasure rather than offence or surprise when the wife of the British military attaché affectionately blew streamers at his ear; the community was both small and intimate.

Staying with the Ambassador were Joe Alsop, the American columnist, Pamela Egremont and Kisty Hesketh. So absorbing was the conversation after dinner that it was only slowly remarked that in order to avoid the teeth of Fred Warner's pet otter, the company were all standing on the top of tables and chairs. Other animals collected by the Ambassador included a silver pheasant, two sloth hanging through the daylight hours upside-down, a deer and some civet cats; the otter was surely the only one of its species to express a violent detestation of water, running for its life at sight of the Embassy swimming pool.

To return to Hanoi from Saigon was always confusing. In Saigon were freedom, humour, grace, a struggling democracy − but gross corruption; in Hanoi, repression, penury, aggression, a police state − but a single cause which, however loathsome, produced spare, courageous human beings. Not that my communist colleagues would have been much interested in such matters, preferring to hear eye-witness accounts of the Vientiane 'White Rose', most lubricious of nightclubs.

X

CITY LIFE

BUT LIFE, OR WHAT LIFE WAS EVIDENT, among Hanoi's inhabitants in January and February of 1967 seemed less disagreeable than before.

Tet, or the Lunar New Year Festival, was celebrated in Hanoi from noon on 8 February to the beginning of working hours on 11 February. Defences in the city remained manned on 9 February in spite of the truce, and such government offices as maintained staff after evacuation to the country were manned by five functionaries each, working in shifts.

Extra Tet rations were issued. The town was hung with the national flag either singly or in clusters of four attached to shields; the traffic intersections were strung with coloured pennants and the streets with banners. I had not before seen the town so full of people, most of whom had come in from the countryside. Nearly everyone had made an effort to look presentable, and there were literally thousands of children, apparently well fed, happy, gay and extremely dirty, whose greatest moment came when the turtle showed its head and back above the surface of the Petit Lac. Thunder-flashes went off like Guy Fawkes Night, and the south end of the lake sounded like a juvenile Twickenham. In the middle of a yelling group of infants, I was little regarded. Earlier that morning, however, a Sikh major and the Indian doctor Deb were followed along the eastern shore of the lake by a crowd of children gazing respectfully at the Sikh's beard, spotted pugri and beard-net.

The Metropole Hotel, filled with peach-blossom branches and mandarin trees but otherwise as railway-station-modern as ever, seemed to be the only public restaurant open; and it was more than usually full with its own guests and with those of us who had dismissed our staffs for the holiday. The Vietnamese food was even worse than the European. In spite of the vile weather, most people had enjoyed this short break: the population had pinned their hopes on Trinh's offer of talks which they believed the Americans would find difficult to refuse.

At the end of March it seemed that there had been an even more substantial change in the atmosphere of the city over the past six weeks. Not only did the populace seem more cheerful and lighthearted, but the numbers of shops half-open had noticeably increased. This was not caused by an increase in the import of consumer goods (the shops were mainly barbers, tailors, small repair workshops, photographers, food shops) but by a feeling that Hanoi was, at least, not the very next target on the escalation schedule and that it was safe for evacuated shopkeepers to return more frequently and for longer periods.

The Tonkinese themselves, a more feckless, irresponsible and slapdash race than their dour reputation attested, wobbling down the tramlines on their pre-war Peugeot bicycles (£70 each at current prices against £35 for a new Czech or Chinese machine), seemed less tense, single-minded and xenophobic than of late. Now that the winter was over and they had removed the hideous sweaters, earmuffs and padded coats in which they encased themselves in November, they were certainly more attractive: the short, slitwaisted tunic coats worn by the girls over black silk trousers, the habitual pigtails and the occasional high heels offered small competition to their Saigon siblings, but at least the effort to appear presentable was maintained.

Neither did the men, in their off-duty moments, neglect their appearance, and if their double-breasted suits were more reminiscent of a Paris banlieu than W.1., that was to be expected; and it could not be said nor expected that factory, distributive trade, construction or other workers should be the glass of fashion in working hours. Their previous attitude toward oneself of suspicious wariness seemed now to be one of amazed curiosity; no more, perhaps, than the difference between being regarded as a potential enemy and as a creature from outer space, but welcome nonetheless. Greetings and smiles were almost invariably returned with warmth and the general politeness that was a secondary characteristic of this people. While the grimness inherent in their present difficulties remained, it was now less reflected in their behaviour.

I did not know how to interpret all this. Nothing, apart from the sentiment that Hanoi was not going to be subjected to mass air attack, had occurred recently to justify the relaxation. Food prices continued to rise, salaries did not, the war continued, consumer goods were scarce,

the town ran down from day to day, paint peeled from the houses, cas
ualties and damage in the provinces mounted, mechanical objects, from
locks to motor cars, collapsed with increasing regularity, families
remained often separated, the diet was a subsistence one, life was earn-
est, and there was not much light at the end of the tunnel.

The lifting of tension may have been due to a combination of factors. Since the North Vietnamese had really not known anything better
for a long time, if ever, and since material prosperity meant little as a
possible way of life for them and a consumer-goods economy was thus
not an alternative attraction, the 'siege', dangers and isolation under
which they lived had become a stimulating and even exciting way of
life. On, the other hand the bombing was still relatively light and the
Tonkinese may have believed that they were beginning to see a possible end, through negotiations or otherwise, to their tribulations, while
at least some Vietnamese were encouraged by sympathetic U.S. and
other foreign visitors to Hanoi, and the subsequent, favourable propaganda. An impression, in short, that spring had come, that the war
might not continue for ever and that, even if it did, they could take it.

None of this was to say that Hanoi had improved as a place of
residence. The essential services, light, power, water, telephones,
sometimes continued more or less to function, the wide, tree-lined
boulevards were swept and clean, the new antique shop had opened
in the suburbs, one or two small eating houses had reopened. Minister's houses, embassies and some ministries received a coat of paint,
but it was a drab and silent city, the silence broken only by the
infrequent army or state vehicle driving on its horn. The condition
of the French villas, each occupied by as many as seven families,
deteriorated weekly. The pavements were crowded by childlike male
and female yokels of the People's Army of North Vietnam and by
the village crones squatting on the pavement with their baskets of
spinach or onions. There were delays due to inefficiency, evacuation
and, perhaps, indifference on the part of the authorities.

Against this had, I suppose, to be set the astonishing beauty of lakes,
flowers, parks and gardens, French legacies which had been maintained
and, together with the zoo, provided an escape for those of the population who were not too busy to take advantage of them. (The zoo,
built around lakes, was quite beautiful: it contained an ancient elephant
and some monkeys, its birds numbered a peacock with arthritis of the
neck.)

Visitors to the countryside and to other towns of North Vietnam told me that my impressions of Hanoi were out of perspective. The city seemed to them, after the devastation of Viet Tri, Thai Nguyen, Nam Dinh and Than Hoa, 'swinging', the 'State Department' a combination of Harrods, 'the Grocer', Asprey's and Elizabeth Arden. Doubtless there was no absolute truth in that assessment; but compared to a half-destroyed hole in the wall in Than Hoa selling nothing but oil, cloth and salt, it was relatively true. And the fact that the air-raid shelters which disfigured the streets had not yet had seriously to prove their value, as opposed to certain provincial cities where they were almost permanently inhabited from dawn to dusk, was something for which to be thankful.

Now that the warm weather had returned, the open-air cafés on the Petit Lac in the middle of the city and on the southern lake had reopened, albeit with libations limited to Nescafé and fizzy drinks. Several theatres were open nightly with programmes of the Vietnamese variant of Chinese opera and of political revues. Cinemas regularly screened Vietnamese, East European and sometimes French movies. Other distractions included a mobile open-air brothel of five or six ladies in one of the parks, whose charges, except to Sikhs, seemed minimal. On this sort of subject I was never certain whether the apparently total isolation of North Vietnam from all outside influence, and the war atmosphere in which the younger generation had been raised, had exempted youth from the prevailing 'moral breakthrough', if that was the right expression, in Western capitals.

It was an important question, with obvious political implications for the leadership. It was certainly true that there was a surprising number of youths wearing King's Road haircuts and detached, if not resentful, expressions. In general, the absence of interference by the state with private behaviour, the relative decrease in political indoctrination and in the 'busybody' measures of a communist régime, while clearly due to the necessity not to goad the people too far under wartime conditions, must have had their effect in a diminution of singlemindedness, at least to some extent. And although most of the pagodas had been turned into Red Cross posts, one or two were still open and functioning, the Catholic Cathedral was packed for every Mass; so that in that respect also, and given that the state controlled the religious organizations themselves, those channels to another world had not been completely closed.

In the absence of catastrophe, such as a major bombardment of Hanoi or a failure by China to meet the short-fall in rice, this was the way that

I thought in March, 1967, it might remain. The people's troubles would, in fact, not really begin until the war ended, when the Lao Dong Party would have the occasion to start practising its political and organizational theories at full strength for the first time since land reform.

XI

NORTH VIETNAMESE INTENTIONS

UNLIKE THE SOUTH, North Vietnam possessed marked seasons. The winter, beginning in late October and lasting into February or March, was distinguished by temperatures as low as 48 degrees Fahrenheit and by the frequent drizzling rain, the *crachin*. Thereafter, although to speak of 'spring' would be misleading, the heat increased until reaching its maximum ferocity in May when it remained steady at about 100 degrees until October. Since there was no wind at night, the summer climate in Hanoi was perhaps the worst in Asia.

It was this seasonal difference, and in particular the relatively cold winter, that gave the Tonkinese, in relation to the more lethargic southerner, their cutting edge. This people had alternately accommodated with and resisted Chinese rule. They were as dominant in the peninsula as were the Javanese in the archipelago. They had beaten one Western power and were surviving against another. And yet, unified, indigenous control over the whole of Vietnam had extended only from 1786 to 1859.

The régime in Hanoi was a communist government of the most oppressive, blinkered and reactionary model which governed, by exhortation, through the fear that it could command. There was no section of the community which its actions had not damaged: its internal policies were supported only by its own cadres. Chinese occupation, dynastic wars, the terror accompanying land reform might explain its people's passivity under an ideology as hostile to their peasant interests as it was alien to their illogical minds, but I did not think that they explained the stamina with which the North Vietnamese fought the French and continued to fight the Americans. The missing factor was, I feared, still nationalism, now of a corrupt, wretched kind.

It was absurd to suggest in November, 1966, that had the West done

more to meet Ho Chi Minh since 1945, Vietnam would now be governed by a democratic régime led by a Ho converted to liberalism through
United States aid and shared anti-colonialism. Ho Chi Minh had sing-
lemindedly pursued the creation of a unified communist state since 1914
and had betrayed any of his collaborators who showed sign of dissent.
No Western concessions, however major, would have weakened his
ideology or deflected him from the attempt.

He was, however, with most of his compatriots, a nationalist and an
anti-colonialist. In forcefully opposing these concepts, the West could
only ensure, because the Lao Dong Party's cadre structure enabled it to
survive when all other parties were being decimated by the security
forces, that Vietnamese nationalism would become dominated by its
most doctrinaire component and that Ho's goal would thus be realized.
One could therefore only surmise that if the French could have learned
the lesson of India, there might have been a possibility that not Ho but
a genuinely nationalist régime would govern all Vietnam. For it was
nationalism, not its communist clothes, that provided the spark of
acquiescence in the DRV.

In spite of twenty years' war, the economy of Vietnam, at least in
late 1966, was not greatly worse than it had ever been. The damage to
communications was serious, but the labour involved in repairs helped
the unemployment problem. The damage on the Ho Chi Minh Trail
was also, no doubt, considerable, but on balance, the consolidation of
morale in every sector as a result of the lethargic technique of bombing
at that time had outweighed the material losses. The evacuation measures, air-raid precautions and dispersal of industry were indicators of a
determination to stay the course. The losses suffered by PAVN main
force units were heavy, but there was no great shortage of manpower,
and Vietnamese learned from their mistakes. There was no sign that the
DRV believed that the U.S. and South Vietnamese pacification campaign in the south would be successful. Food and certain other basic
commodities in Hanoi were tighter, but not decisively: the tenth-month
rice crop would not be disastrous. There was no visible evidence of failing will. External aid was being received, world opinion was favourable. Effective internal opposition did not exist.

It was the more difficult, therefore, to explain the conviction among
the Hanoi Diplomatic Corps in early 1967 that the DRV wished, sooner
rather than later, to negotiate, provided the United States were to stop
bombing the country and to halt further troop arrivals in the south.
(The previous pause in January, 1966, was described as inadequate since

1 'The British Residence, a square box-like structure, cream and brown with blue shutters'. (p.34)

2 The Petit Lac, home of the turtle 'whose appearance had for centuries prophesied victory to the Tonkinese'. (p. 68)

3 'The Office of the Consulate-General, round the corner on the Ly Thuong Kiet'. (p.38)

it had been accompanied by reconnaissance flights and troop arrivals.) The corps were also certain that Hanoi would, while holding to the principles of the Four Points, negotiate flexibly on all of them; reunification, so leaked an MFA official, would be a twenty-year problem: while the NLF must be seated at the conference table, the Front's rights after negotiation would be decided by the South Vietnamese people: United States withdrawal need be neither immediate nor unconditional. (Sources for this included the President himself.)

The undertaking to negotiate and the flexibility on detail were presented as a quid pro quo for a halt in the bombing. Military withdrawal would, it was argued, follow naturally in the course of negotiation, and furthermore, 'how could the Vietnamese trust the Americans after all their deceptions' by withdrawing militarily? (It would certainly have been harder for the Vietnamese to call up military action after a standdown than for the Americans.)

Unless these stories were simply what the Soviet Bloc would have liked the North Vietnamese to do or unless they were part of a campaign by the latter, through the Bloc, to improve their image further in the uncommitted world, why *should* the DRV negotiate and not fight?

Firstly, the damage might be more insupportable than we supposed. Secondly, Soviet Bloc diplomatic pressure and DRV military and economic dependence on the Bloc might be greater than we thought, as might be Chinese ability to match it. Thirdly (and on the other hand), the DRV might feel that Chinese pressure plus the bottlenecks in routing Bloc aid through China brought closer the day when she would be obliged to make an awful decision in favour of her neighbour. The Chinese knife might be at the Vietnamese throat, not the Chinese card up the Vietnamese sleeve. But fourthly, and as a result of all these factors, the DRV probably believed that their unaltered policy of reunification was now best achieved through political and subversive rather than through military means.

They would reason that skilfully conducted negotiation would lead to American departure from South Vietnam and to the collapse of present and future Saigon régimes without the monolithic structure of the Front and unsupported by American power. They could, in other words, afford to be flexible within their long-term programme: but since delay in negotiating might lead to a deterioration of their own position in the south, they might have no time to lose.

I have omitted from this analysis the theories that the U.S.S.R.

required an American presence in Vietnam because it freed her hand in Europe and provided opportunity for a Sino-American war *à outrance,* that the American presence was equally acceptable to China as living evidence of a paper tiger and as a real counter to the U.S.S.R. Both might have been true, but I doubt if the DRV would have allowed them to influence her actions.

So the voices prophesying peace might be authentic. But it would not be a peace of comfort to an Asian who, unlike General de Gaulle, did not believe that neutralism under a Greater (and communist) Vietnam, eventually to include Laos and Cambodia, was preferable to other solutions.

In trying to identify alternative courses of action for the DRV, one could not discount external influences on North Vietnamese power. The leadership of the DRV tried to retain both freedom of national action and its own (orthodox) interpretation of Marxism-Leninism.

Although immediately after 1954 it adopted Chinese measures such as land reform wholesale, it subsequently resisted Soviet and Chinese persuasion toward courses, such as negotiation on the one hand and the Cultural Revolution on the other, which in the North Vietnamese view would interfere with the objective of reunification. (When I once asked a Vietnamese cadre for his views on the Cultural Revolution, he replied that he preferred to read Shakespeare.) Nevertheless, the proximity, bulk, population and unpredictability of China were in 1966 and 1967 enough to ensure that that country could not be left out of account, and it might be that, while professing orthodox (Soviet) Marxism internally, the DRV felt themselves obliged to conform to Chinese revolutionary foreign policy, a policy which incidentally suited their present situation.

A 'pro-Chinese' faction in Hanoi was therefore not then one which sought control from or subservience to Peking, but one which considered that Chinese intentions and capacity to aid or interfere were paramount. (It would have also included those otherwise uncommitted North Vietnamese whose bellicosity matched China's own.) A 'pro-Russian' faction, by the same token, would have consisted of orthodox Marxists or followers of 'economism' and of those who deplored the loss of blood and treasure in favour of an advance into the 20th century: they were, so far as the leadership was concerned, in a minority.

The 'peace offensive' mounted by Hanoi in January, 1967, may have been prompted, inter alia, by the thought that China's internal difficulties might deprive her of the capacity both to offer consistent aid or effectively to oppose a negotiated settlement on DRV terms. It was frustrated not only by the American demand for reciprocity but by indications from Peking that the Cultural Revolution would not be allowed to affect China's support for Hanoi, and even that North Vietnamese peace negotiations *might* lead to some form of Chinese intervention.

It was, therefore, impossible for me to identify the Vietnamese 'pro-Chinese' faction so often referred to by the Russians with Western interlocutors as 'the main group opposing negotiations'. It was more than a faction; rather, a coherent and permanent reflection in North Vietnamese thinking of the facts of geopolitical life, which would only cease should Soviet aid become overwhelmingly preponderant. (Denunciation of China by such leaders as Nguyen Chi Tanh was no more than a riposte to Chinese criticism of Vietnamese set-piece military tactics in the south.)

In terms of power within the junta, the President, Ho Chi Minh, aside from his figurehead function, was probably the equivalent of a septuagenarian Chairman of the Board commuting twice a week from Sunningdale to sign papers. From my limited access, the Prime Minister, Pham Van Dong, appeared to be the primary decision-maker: Le Duan, the Party First Secretary, was deeply and personally committed to the southern war although *not,* in 1966–67, to a war on the extended time scale advocated by China: General Giap's military and possibly political reputation depended heavily on military victory; the Foreign Minister, Nguyen Duy Trinh, while at one time suspected of 'pro-Chinese' sentiments, did, however, seem to be at least the instrument for, if not the instigator of, any peace initiatives that the régime might from time to time feel inclined to put forward.

Truong Chinh, the sinister initiator of land reform and continuing revolution, could presumably be relied upon to maintain consistent intransigence. Unless Le Thanh Nghi, the Economics Minister, had more influence and was more inclined to peaceful reconstruction than I believed, I knew of no other leader likely to exercise a restraining influence on policy.

But the Chinese Ambassador (before his removal during the Cultural Revolution), Ch'u Chi Wen, an elderly and distinguished friend of the Maoist leadership and later Ambassador to Sofia and Mayor of Harbin and Mukden, told a French interlocutor in 1966 that, just as it was the duty of France to check United States hegemony in Europe, so did the Chinese see their duty as stopping Soviet hegemony in Asia.

The remark was presumably not unconnected with Mr

Tshcherbakov's remark, on the occasion of the Soviet National Day in November, 1966, that the Chinese 'had lost in Vietnam'; and it was certainly linked to private Soviet claims in 1967 that they and the DRV were together preventing the entry into Vietnam of Chinese military personnel in civilian clothes. China, as we have seen, bitterly opposed the new DRV tactic in the south, with its heavy casualties, of main-force action against United States and ARVN forces, in favour of pro-tracted war. But the ultimate intentions of neither China nor Russia were, at that time and in Hanoi, easily assessable. As for the Americans, perhaps two of Dr Kissinger's comments from *The White House Years* deserve the most attention. The first was that President Johnson 'took advice that he thought better informed than his more elemental instincts, finally cutting himself off from all constituencies as well as from his emotional roots' and the second that 'the U.S. in Vietnam was engaged in a bombing campaign powerful enough to mobilize world opinion against us, but too half-hearted and gradual to be decisive'.

XII

AMERICAN INTENTIONS

UNITED STATES INVOLVEMENT in Vietnam began with President Truman's decision in 1950 to fund the French military effort there. This decision was taken, if not as a consequence, at least in the light of the fall of Chiang Kai Shek, of the recognition of Ho Chi Minh's government by the U.S.S.R. and by Mao Tse-tung's new régime in China and of the possibility perceived in Washington of a major advance of communism throughout Asia. Desired French participation in common defence against the Soviet threat to Western Europe was a further reason why America should not antagonize that nation on its colonial periphery in Indo-China.

The aggressive Chinese role in the Korean War, as well as the evident influence of the U.S.S.R. over 'emergent' and other communist countries, was later seen as confirming the wisdom of the original decision. ('The loss', as President Truman and the National Security Council (NSC) said in 1952, 'of any of the countries of South-East Asia to overt or covert Chinese communist aggression would have led to critical psychological and economical consequences.') By 1954, the year of the Geneva Conference, American aid under President Eisenhower had reached the figure of $1 billion.

The only documents signed by any power at Geneva in 1954 were the cease-fire agreements. All others, including the Final Declaration and its statement on elections in 1956, were not only unsigned but tacitly recognized that the military demarcation line, as in Germany and Korea, was a political boundary. (In 1966 the East German Ambassador at Hanoi found himself in extremely hot Viet Minh water for suggesting to North Vietnamese interlocutors that a solution to the problem of Vietnam might suitably follow that of Germany. Mr Wolfgang Bergold was a very nice man. It may also be that his comments, which necessitated a subsequent absence from Hanoi for five months, were a reflection not only of his personal opinion but of Soviet policy at that time.)

Since, therefore, the unsigned Final Declaration at Geneva contained no collective obligation to free elections in Vietnam, the refusal of the Republic of South Vietnam (RVN) in 1956 to agree to pan-Vietnamese elections breached neither the agreement nor international law and certainly provided no justification for North Vietnam's subsequent military aggression against the Republic. At all events, the North had in 1954 anticipated Diem's eventual refusal. The DRV retrained thousands of Southern cadres from obligatory Viet Minh departures to the North, and left innumerable caches of arms behind, as well as arranging familiar links, including marriage, which permitted the later return to the South of further trained insurgents.

The apologists for the first use of force in 1959 by North Vietnam against the South have employed two arguments. One argument, tenable in neither law nor practice, attacked Diem's resolve not to subject his free country to the manipulated Elections which his country in fact had specifically abjured in 1954.

The second was that armed intervention by the DRV was a response to repression by Diem of anyone, not only communists, in the South who did not support his own régime. This theory, so warmly advocated by American and European intellectuals, has been since exploded not only by countless well-placed defectors but by the moving, if belated, abandonment of his cause by Jean Lacouture, its most prominent supporter.

Although Diem's harshness did create resistance in the South, he had by 1955, as we have seen, defeated the private armies (Cao Dai, Hoa Hao and Binh Xuyen), resettled the northern refugees, increased industrial and agricultural production and created a genuinely national régime. The DRV's decision in 1959 to go for infiltration and armed struggle was taken not in the South by the National Liberation Front (NLF), but in Hanoi by the Central Committee of the Lao Dong Party, the Communist Party of Vietnam. (The Lao Dong had already, between 1956 and 1959, embarked on a campaign of assassinations against effective southern local administrators but had not, until the 1959 decision, begun large-scale infiltration.)

By 1961, in spite of various proposals for greater U.S. manpower, the total number of U.S. military advisers in Vietnam was no more than 1,000 men; by 1962, it had risen to 11,000, chiefly in response to

ICC and State Department documentation of flagrant violations by the North Vietnamese of the Geneva Agreements. The effect on Vietnamese morale and ARVN mobility of these arrivals and the benefits of the Strategic Hamlet programme were initially promising. But on 1 November, 1963, Diem was overthrown and murdered. 'Whatever was already bad became worse — patronage, corruption, detention without trial or review.' The carousel of bickering generals began to turn.

In December, 1963, the Lao Dong Party commanded a major offensive strategy for the South. At the same time, Robert McNamara, then U.S. Secretary of Defence, reported to the new President, Lyndon B. Johnson, that the situation in Vietnam had greatly deteriorated. The first proposals were made, by General Maxwell Taylor and others, for bombing of key targets including lines of communication in the North, and the mining of DRV ports, as well as the training of an offensive guerrilla force in the South. But apart from the air strikes against torpedo-boat bases after the Tonkin Gulf incident on 8 August, 1964, the President then rejected any campaign of aerial bombardment until February, 1965, after the Presidential election of November, 1964, and before the arrival in 1965 of the initial wave of U.S. ground forces. By the end of 1964 the number of American military advisers in Vietnam had risen to 23,000.

Two American Marine battalions, the first U.S. *combat* troops, landed in Vietnam in March 1965, and by the end of that year their complement had reached 180,000. In December, 1965, General Westmoreland asked for 150,000 additional troops; in commenting on this request, Senator Mansfield suggested that a total of more than 700,000 men might eventually be needed. In 1967, after my arrival at Hanoi, General Westmoreland accepted a force ceiling of 525,000.

The land battle in the South — the enclave theory, 'search and destroy', main force actions, attrition, attacks on supplies, etc. — cannot be within the scope of this book. (The best critical account of that war is by Guenter Levy, *America in Vietnam*, New York, Oxford University Press.) It is, however, pertinent to note here that by the end of 1967 the enemy build-up in the South contained over 100,000 North Vietnamese infiltrators and, above all, that the overwhelming bulk of weapons and equipment held by these forces and by the Viet Cong had been supplied from the U.S.S.R. and China, via North Vietnam.

It was the contention of the Joint Chiefs of Staff and CinCPAC that this massive influx of supplies, whether of armour, artillery or missile, led directly to the huge U.S. expeditionary force in Vietnam with all its political consequences within America, and was a direct result of the failure by the President and his advisers properly to use air power.

The main argument of the Joint Chiefs of Staff (JCS) in Washington, of the Commander in Chief Pacific (CinCPAC — Admiral Ulysses S.G. Sharp), and of the United States Air Force was that mining of the North Vietnamese ports and interdiction in the north-eastern quadrant of Vietnam of war material reaching North Vietnam by rail or road from China would cut off *at source* the war-making capacity of the DRV.

Although 85 percent of supplies for Vietnam reached that country through Haiphong, most of the military equipment arrived by rail through China.

To neglect these targets was to ensure that incoming war equipment from Russia and China would be rapidly dispersed after arrival and dispatched to the south by a multitude of routes and trails all far more difficult and expensive to detect or strike than at the actual *points of entry* at Haiphong or on the borders of North Vietnam with China. The Joint Chiefs, in other words, sought a major, decisive application of air power aimed at strangling the military ability of the DRV *before* it could be used against, or even reach, South Vietnam.

Some of the President's civilian advisers preferred another course, the gradual escalation of aerial bombardment, initially away from the north-east quadrant and the Sino-Vietnamese border, designed to induce in the North Vietnamese a belief that worse was to follow, a system of deterrence or, rather, of graduated pressure. (Although this alternative programme (Rolling Thunder) had by June, 1965, been extended northwards as well as widened in scope to include land and amphibious vehicles, POL storage, bridges, airfields, marshalling yards, etc., it was at that time that the President found it necessary to dispatch U.S. combat forces to prevent the collapse of the Army of the Republic of Vietnam (ARVN).) The main raison d'être for a softer approach than that advocated by the Joint Chiefs was the obsessive fear, held by many civilian advisers, that the sustained bombing campaign near the frontiers proposed by the JCS risked massive Soviet or Chinese intervention.

It is depressing to realize that no such external intervention occurred in 1967 when the JCS programme had at last been largely accepted, or even in December, 1972 when, instead, Operations Linebacker I and II were directly responsible for the DRV's signature of the Paris Agreements, albeit on terms far worse for the U.S. and RVN than could have been obtained in the 1960s.

Expansion of Rolling Thunder in 1966 to include Hanoi and Haiphong and the rail and road lines of communication with China and the major ports was partial, irregular and continually interrupted by the perceived necessity to stand down aerial bombardment during 'peace initiatives'. (In a memorandum to President Johnson in March, 1967, John Roche wrote that Ho Chi Minh, 'like Lenin at the time of Brest Litovsk, would negotiate in cold blood for whatever goals he considers realistic, even if the bombs were coming down the chimneys') The campaign was, at least until early 1967, largely political. Because it had not struck the North Vietnamese import system at source, it had neither weakened the economy of North Vietnam nor much reduced the supply of arms to the PAVN and VC forces in South Vietnam.

Instead of bringing the DRV, in the favourite cliché of the time, 'to the conference table', the gradualist campaign, in the words of Admiral Moorer, former Chairman of Joint Chiefs, thus 'granted the enemy time to shore up his air defences, disperse his military targets and mobilize his labour force for logistical repair and movement. From a military point of view, graduation violated the principle of mass and surprise which air power has employed historically to attain its maximum effectiveness. Graduation forced air power into an expanded and inconclusive war of attrition.' And an equally serious disadvantage of graduation lay in the great increase in Vietnamese civilian casualties due to 'dispersal' of military targets — whether POL, anti-aircraft, SAM sites or mobile generators — in the middle of populated areas, or even next door to hospitals. Casualties among American pilots, at least until the advent of 'smart bombs', were correspondingly high and for the same reason. Both these considerations became decisive factors in domestic disillusion and dissent within the United States; the Secretary of Defence and the civilians in that department and in the White House must bear the blame.

But after the Tet stand-down in February, 1967, CinCPAC and the JCS, because of intensified North Vietnamese resupply to their forces in the south during that period, again recommended mining, strikes against ports, power, steel and cement plants and bombing of the north-eastern rail lines to China. Although the President again compromised, the 'buffer' zone near the Chinese border was struck over the next months, as were targets within the Hanoi and Haiphong sanctuaries; 85 percent of the targets recommended by the JCS and 52 out of the 57 targets isolated by the Stennis committee were, if only sporadically, attacked.

The campaign of bombing conducted against rail and other lines of communications in the north-east quadrant became continuous, day after day, round the clock, vital against the labour-intensive Vietnamese repair capability.

But the pros and cons of the bombing programme still continued to be debated in Washington. The participants remained, on the one hand, those who advocated strategic attacks on military and industrial targets which affected the capacity of the DRV to wage protracted war and, on the other, the 'gradualists', described in *Strategy for Defeat* by Admiral Sharp as either ignorant of the principles of warfare or 'frighted by false fire', paralyzed by the possibility of Soviet and Chinese intervention and by the activities of anti-war dissidents in the U.S. Anti-war dissidence was, of course, aroused precisely by North Vietnamese inspired propaganda made possible only by 'gradualism' itself and by its consequence, the southern build-up.

The gradualists in the office of the Secretary of Defense (OSD) Vietnam Task Group were led by Leslie Gelb and consisted mainly of civilians from that office. They were the authors of the Pentagon Papers, a document whose undeclared purpose seemed less to demonstrate the facts of North Vietnamese aggression or even of South Vietnamese disunity than of 'American culpability'. (In Admiral Sharp's view, most of them believed that the U.S. 'should have cleared out of South Vietnam early in the game and left the South Vietnamese to struggle by themselves'.) Their spokesmen — although far from taking the view described by Admiral Sharp — were Robert McNamara, John McNaughton at the Defense Department, William Bundy, Assistant Secretary of State, and his brother, McGeorge Bundy, President of the Ford Foundation. Walt Rostow, at the National Security Council in the White House, alone shared the perceptions of classical politico-military strategists and of the Joint Chiefs of Staff.

The Defense Department in May, 1967, wished to limit force increases, end the bombing in the north-eastern quadrant and concentrate air interdiction on the infiltration routes south of the 20th Parallel and in the panhandle between the 17th and the 20th Parallel. The JCS wholly disagreed with this course on the grounds that it would grant the DRV immunity on all other communication routes, increase enemy mobility, permit damage repair, increase both the concentration of North Vietnamese air defences and the release of men and equipment for infiltration and, by relieving pressure on Hanoi, strengthen North Vietnamese intransigence.

They once more recommended their own programme, the reduction by aerial action of external supplies to Vietnam, the destruction of DRV resources and the disruption of infiltration. At a conference in Saigon in June, 1967, and at the Stennis hearings (Preparedness Subcommittee of the Senate Armed Services Committee) in Washington in August, CinCPAC outlined the recommendation and additions to Rolling Thunder necessary to achieve these aims.

On the day that the hearings opened the President authorized strikes against targets within the Hanoi circle. In the China buffer zone and in the Haiphong circle. As a result of support by the committee for the JCS programme, further authorizations were given in September, 1967, for targets earlier rejected by Secretary McNamara. The latter resigned in early 1968.

Owing to cessations of bombing ordered in line with a 'new channel' for negotiations with Hanoi — a channel interestingly coincident with the increase in aerial bombardment — not all these authorizations were executed. When it became plain in October that no peace talks would be forthcoming, operations, including as targets the MiGs at Phuc Yen and objectives in Hanoi, were again mounted, but with little of their earlier consistency and perseverance, a reduction in which the weather played a major part.

But on 31 March, 1968, under pressure from Clark Clifford, the new Secretary of Defense, and from the Senior Informal Advisory Group, in particular Cyrus Vance and McGeorge Bundy, the President ordered that all bombing north of the 20th Parallel be discontinued. It is not necessary, in defence of the military strategists, to point again to the electrifying effect on DRV obstinacy of the bombing of Hanoi and the mining of Haiphong in 1972, nor even to the total destruction of the North Vietnamese economy that would have been achieved by 1968 had the United States chosen to bomb the dykes.

Discounting such draconian measures, the appeasers and the anti-war East Coast media had by April Fool's Day, 1968, succeeded in persuading a beleaguered President objectively to abandon not only the interests of South Vietnam and the United States but, à la longue, the soil in which could flourish liberty, justice and freedom of speech throughout the world. The ground continues to crumble beneath our feet.

XIII

BOMBING: THE BEGINNING

THE SUMMER OF 1967 BEGAN, or so it seemed, in March, with even less of Spring's transition than usual, moving from the drizzling chill of winter directly into temperatures of 100 degrees and corresponding humidity.

A comparable change from the relative absence of U.S. activity over the north-east quadrant in the fall and winter to aerial bombardment of some intensity began in April, although not yet within the ten-mile (prohibited) inner circle of Hanoi. Targets, most of them invisible to us, were struck all round the circumference of the city and included airfields, military complexes, industry, storage dumps and transportation. While the targets were invisible to Hanoi residents, the attackers and − at least in the early stages (for they later left the battle) − the defending MiG fighters could be plainly seen manoeuvring at high altitudes.

Although there were few combats in the classic sense of dogfights, the flash of anti-aircraft guns and, very occasionally, the twisting spiral of U.S. planes shot down in flames by surface-to-air missiles (SAMs) were within our observation. Smoke and fires from burning installations rose on the horizon: the crash of the northern anti-aircraft batteries alternated with the thunder of high explosive from projectiles striking objectives in the near distance.

All this, for the resident, was an unwelcome departure. Hitherto we had had to contend, as noted earlier, only with intermittent visits from reconnaissance aircraft and spasmodic raids from more lethal formations. Even the latter tended to occur in clusters over a period of a week or so and at predictable times, in particular at about 2.30 in the afternoon.

As I was accustomed to take a siesta every day after luncheon, I had been able to sleep peacefully through most of these raids, waking refreshed to a cup of Mr. Dong's tea, a later stroll through the streets, conversation at the tennis court in the grounds of the French delegation-general, visits to friends at the *Grand Voleur*, dinner and perhaps a movie with the Canadians.

Not much of that was easy after April. Even when attack was manifestly not against the city but against targets in the outskirts or even farther away, the DRV would insist on declaring an air raid on Hanoi itself. The sirens wailed up to thirty times a day: the din and that of the bombs and artillery often precluded sound sleep. No one was permitted out of doors during these incidents on pain of being incarcerated by the militia in one of the city's air-raid shelters, cylindrical concrete holes sunk some four feet deep in the pavements, uncomfortable for those of European height and bulk.

The unfortunate Mr Keller, Swiss Ambassador at Peking, who visited Hanoi four times between 1966 and 1967 and lunched at my house on each occasion, rather than face such immurement en route to his hotel was obliged by air-raids on every visit to spend the entire afternoon with me in the house. The Ambassador was a kind man, but the limitations of Vietnam as a subject for discussion must have tried his patience through these long hours. Nor did the work of calligraphic detection on the Chinese characters painted on the hall columns greatly tax his ingenuity. Although others have transcribed them as incitements to sexual desire, for the house was once a brothel, Mr Keller insisted that they advertised Horlick's Malted Milk. Indeed, the Hanoi agent for that product had once owned the house.

But at our final meeting, the Swiss Ambassador made me, after an immensely elaborate speech, a formal presentation, not as I had begun to hope, of a Longines watch, but a bar of Toblerone chocolate.

Another foreign colleague found the raids rather more tiresome. While playing tennis with his wife against another couple, he was induced by the sound of the air-raid sirens to quit the court at the double and in mid-serve, abandoning racket and wife in favour of the French cellar. Nervously emerging after the all clear, he leaped into his motorcar, bound for home, wife quite forgotten. Sirens again sounded. The timorous diplomatist jumped out of the vehicle while the latter was in motion, and into a cylindrical shelter, on top of which a militia-man then firmly placed the concrete lid; the colleague there remained in warm, green, stagnant water infested by mosquitoes and, he alleged, frogs, for over two hours. In the meanwhile, his car had proceeded unmanned down the boulevard, eventually to collide with the Hanoi railway station.

His Ambassador occupied himself by smuggling young Vietnamese prostitutes in the trunk of his car to and from their dwellings and his residence. (The consequences of this practice, also followed by the more dashing of the Russians, might have been severe in the event of discovery by the North Vietnamese authorities.) During one visit to his house, my successor was introduced by him to the latest of these girls, reclining voluptuously in his double bed; she seemed as insouciantly pleased with her sallow lover as he was delighted in her possession.

But during the height of the bombing, he sought, for reasons of self-preservation, his own government's approval temporarily to withdraw from Hanoi. For reasons of state unconnected with Vietnam, the request was not granted. The Ambassador had, however, assumed approval, sold the Embassy motorcars to his own profit and debunked to Hong Kong, leaving his deputy to proceed to diplomatic receptions on a bicycle, his pretty little wife on the pillion, an unusual form of loco-motion for Heads of Mission.

Anne de Quirielle was of sterner stuff. She made plain, when asked by a Western journalist for her reactions to the bombing of Hanoi, that she sought only a rifle and access to the roof of her husband's mission, from which vantage point she proposed to shoot at incoming U.S. air-craft. The Americans in Saigon took publication of this absurd state-ment uncommonly badly. But it was a sentiment shared, if not articulated, by several of those few in North Vietnam who wished the Americans no harm, indeed supported their cause; it should have been obvious that when one is being bombed, one seeks to ward off the bomber irrespective of the latter's purposes or flag. *Cet animal est très méchant: quand on l'attaque, il se défend.*

Others were less stalwart. In early May it seemed to me that the com-bination of summer heat, increasingly consistent bombardment and perhaps fear of further escalation of both phenomena was affecting the stamina of some Missions. I then determined, by indirect inquiry, that five of my colleagues had proposed to their governments, separately and without mutual consultation, that 'because of the current absence of political activity between the DRV and the U.S.A. and the consequent lack of a role for themselves', they should remove their Missions tem-porarily to other centres, Phnom Penh or Vientiane, or even place them *en disponibilité.*

One of these missions was West European, one East European, one Middle Eastern and two Asian. At least two of these represented communist countries, and all in various degrees opposed the policies of the United States and supported those of North Vietnam. None of them was likely to be asked to play any part whatever in U.S./DRV negotiations or in other 'political activity'; their proposals, all of which were refused, were in fact based on those more subjective and less stalwart considerations outlined above. To pretend, however, that I did not share them would be hypocritical; it was not hypocrisy so much as self-respect that prevented me from joining them.

I doubt if even the Soviets felt much devotion to their duties during those days of noise and sweat. Although Mr Gromyko had told a Western interlocutor in the fall of 1966 that U.S. escalation would involve not only Chinese but also direct Soviet intervention with troops, the threat had now been demonstrated as idle. The Russians had, it must have been clear to their Embassy, to grin and bear it like everyone else. One of their senior officials, converted from straight vodka to gin and tonic in the course of repeated visits to my house, found the prospect tolerable. (He later died of delirium tremens.) Another, with previous service in London, laid maddening emphasis on his acquaintance with Reggie Maudling, pronounced by him 'Moddling'. A Soviet military attaché, in the time he could spare from complaining about DRV mismanagement of SAMs or from chasing Tonkinese waitresses, recounted interminable dirty stories in an English which few, including Dr Deb, the Indian medical officer, could grasp.

Some idea of the effects of the bombing *outside* Hanoi had been given to me earlier by a traveller in North Vietnam. This reporter, although far from pro-American, was careful to distinguish his own *de visu* observations from the allegations of his North Vietnamese guides, this is an essential consideration in the highly charged ideologies of the time.

In this he agreeably differed from the distasteful performance, ultimately disastrous to U.S. policies, of Harrison Salisbury in December, 1966. Salisbury's first articles appeared in the *New York Times* as his own personal observations made during a visit to North Vietnam, the later pieces, however, heavily dependent on North Vietnamese propaganda and statistics. His description, for example, of Nam Dinh as a cotton-and-silk town with no military objectives, when the city in fact contained POL storage, a power plant and a railway yard, and was surrounded by anti-aircraft and surface-to-air missiles, ensured that Salisbury received no Pulitzer Prize. But the implication, drawn chiefly from

North Vietnamese falsehoods, that the United States was deliberately bombing civilian targets carried worldwide conviction. While only the first of many propaganda catastrophes of this kind, Salisbury's *New York Times* articles had a decisive effect throughout America in persuading Americans that their government was engaged in a brutal and inhumane campaign.

My traveller told me that there had been, as a result of the bombing, only one undamaged bridge between Hanoi and Than Hoa in the southeast of the DRV. All the others, including railway bridges, had been damaged or destroyed but subsequently repaired by teams on permanent standby using spare girders and adjustable parts stored in the vicinity. Pontoon bridges, hidden during the day, had also been observed.

Nevertheless, the journey of 170 kms, which took place in the spring of 1967 at night, by lorries in convoy under dimmed lights from the western exit from Than Hoa to 50 km. east of Hanoi, when lights were switched on and speed increased, took only 5½ hours. The convoy extinguished all lights under air attack; on one such occasion, which was no more than the dropping of a flare, the convoy had been badly bunched and was separated to secure distances by girl wardens apparently stationed in each area for the purpose.

Between Phu Ly, a town along the main route to the South which had been largely evacuated in 1966 and later almost totally destroyed, and Than Hoa, he saw electric light on two occasions only. The first had been in one of the less ruined streets of Than Hoa and the second in a badly damaged but just functioning power station near the Ham Rong bridge. He saw no piped water supply in any town or village of the area. The centre and the main streets of Than Hoa had been heavily damaged; shops open sold little more than oil, salt, cloth and, occasionally, cigarettes.

Brick buildings in the countryside, regarded by the North Vietnamese as automatic targets, were said to have been evacuated, hospitals, schools, etc., now being housed in bamboo houses. Education continued, and medical care under primitive conditions (mud floors, no piped water or light, insufficient doctors) was fairly devoted and as efficient as the circumstances permitted. Casualties, particularly those caused by bomb casings, were said to be widespread among the peasantry and not easy to cure. Doctors were mainly 'pharmacists', although there were a few good surgeons, frequently operating by pocket torches. In and around all towns or villages attacked, the traveller observed Vietnamese anti-aircraft guns of various calibres.

Bombing, other than along the railway line, where it appeared to be concentrated near halts, small stations and their attendant hamlets, had sometimes seemed in this area to lack the precision shown against targets such as bridges and oil tanks elsewhere in the country. Villages, ostensibly no more than agricultural cooperatives, had been 'wiped out' by 500-pound bombs, of which the craters were clearly visible; civilian casualties and damage to civilian housing in villages and towns seemed very high, again largely due to the presence of North Vietnamese AA defences sited in built-up areas on their perimeters.

On clear days air activity had been virtually continual from dawn to dusk. The constant series of alerts seriously inhibited schooling, repair work and cultivation; alert followed all-clear incessantly. Attacks against main road communications had frequently been successful and accurate in this region, but subsidiary roads had usually taken the traffic without excessive delays.

The diet of the 'Youth Volunteers', who had some responsibility for repair work, consisted of rice, vegetables, soya nuts and bananas. In spite of this adequate but limited subsistence, which was, of course, lower for non-cadres, and of the bombing and monotonous labour, the traveller had been impressed by the health, determination and high spirits of the population as a whole. 'After all, why not? They've never really known much else. And it is exciting and absorbing for them. Since they are unaware of what is certainly known to their leaders — the impossibility of military victory — they have also a goal which transcends self-defence.'

Petrol supplies were cached in drums (five feet round and ten feet long) at various points, virtually inaccessible to aircraft, along the roads. Industry, as generally recognized, was unknown in the area, although small workshops, mainly for spare parts, repairs, etc., existed. Mechanization of agriculture, apart from pumps, of which there were few, had scarcely begun. South of Than Hoa, because of damage to the roads, bicycles played a rather larger role in transportation than did lorries, each bicycle being modified to carry a load of 440 pounds; but a major cause of delay was the time needed to reassemble the pontoon bridges —regularly disassembled at dawn — at nightfall.

There had been considerable naval shelling of the coastline to the south of Than Hoa, and one village had allegedly received 1000 projectiles. The traveller had been forbidden to visit the beaches on the alleged grounds of 'defensive preparation against invasion'.

Salisbury, incidentally, called on me on arrival in Hanoi when he asked for my views on the situation in the Democratic Republic. (I do not complain that he included none of them in his articles.) When he revisited me toward the conclusion of his visit, he asked me plainly if I had 'a direct telegraphic link with Dean Rusk', then U.S. Secretary of State. I said that I had not, but added that if he had a message for the Secretary, I might at least be able to transmit it to my own government.

He then told me that after his reception that day by the Prime Minister, Pham Van Dong, he was confident that the DRV had made a decisive advance, in four points which they had not previously conceded, toward U.S./North Vietnamese negotiations. He asked me to telegraph them to my government for conveyance to the United States. I asked him in return first to outline the points. He did so: they were the notorious Four Points demanded by the North Vietnamese, in the person of Pham Van Dong himself, as long ago as April, 1965, unaltered and inexorable. I told him so. He said, in surprise, that 'he had never heard of them before'.

I do not understand people who will not do elementary homework before exposing their own solutions to complicated problems. Nor do I understand an institution, the Press, which will permit attacks on persons or governments on the basis of unverified information supplied by the subject's principal enemies. It seems to me that there is something wrong with a civilization in which the golden calf of 'circulation' can be exploited to promulgate, however unwittingly, untruth. If 'circulation' requires, or even permits, falsehood, then, without advocating censorship, must we not at least try either to establish a system of consultation and trust between the media and administration, or to ensure that the latter has proper channels of reply? If we do not do so, truth will not prevail, and all our decisions will then be as evil as are those of our enemies.

A profession which includes James Fenton, later on the staff of *The Times* who in 1984 said: 'I never thought of Saigon as My Story, but I did get a ride on a victorious tank' cannot always be regarded seriously or with respect, particularly as the tank was a PAVN unit!

Salisbury wrote to me some weeks later, cloddishly enclosing a list of questions on the DRV. I had by then seen the *New York Times* articles and did not reply.

XIV

BOMBING: THE CONTINUATION

ON THE MORNING OF 19 MAY, 1967, I visited my Vice-Consul, Geoffrey Livesey, in his quarters behind the Consulate. Below the apartment lay a green courtyard planted with small trees and scrub vegetation; his servant's rooms with their louvred doors were below the balcony running around two sides of the square.

Geoffrey gave me a drink. The overhead fan in the living room turned briskly, rendering a little more tolerable the damp, heavy midday heat. The thought of another four months of that cruel summer was depressing. But Livesey was not only young and adventurous, he was also uncomplaining, and I had no wish to intrude less stoical concerns on his self-sufficiency. The air-raid sirens sounded, and we walked out onto the balcony.

As we stood there seven or eight United States Thunderchief jet fighter-bombers, flying at scarcely more than roof-top height and no more, it seemed, than 100 yards away, shot across our vision at what appeared — so tight was the space in which the whole incident was framed between houses and sky — enormous speed. They had come on us suddenly out of nowhere, the hard, gray, sleek aircraft, in superb formation at 600 mph, disappearing for an instant behind the trees and buildings that lay between us and the thermal power plant less than one mile to the south, and then quickly climbing clear and away. As they had hurtled past, so close it seemed we could almost touch them or call to the pilots, we had seen the rockets fired from the pods under their wings.

Almost simultaneously, such lights as were on in the apartment went out, the fan stopped turning, and a column of dust, smoke and flame rose from the direction of the power station. (As the planes had penetrated the city's defences by coming in under the radar screen, the first anti-aircraft batteries opened up only when the raiders had not only departed but were probably twenty miles away.) As we were shortly to observe, the performance of this squadron disposed of every Communist or other illusion about the laxity of American bombing or the imprecision of U.S. bombing techniques.

The all-clear wailed: stillness descended. The apartment, without the touch of air from the revolving fan, was already crushingly hot.

'I wonder what the strong-room will feel like in mid-August? A bit warm, I should think.'

'Not very nice. I hope you've got your Right Guard, Geoffrey.'

Because no one would have benefited from accusations of our having acted as spotters or observers for the United States Air Force, we did not go out of our way to inspect the results of air raids. But on this occasion personal considerations demanded that we at least look at the target on the ground.

Anti-aircraft guns, surrounded by their agitated crews, were sited among the rain-trees in the park. There was an air of tense activity, almost hysteria; orders were bellowed in glottal tones. The men ran around their positions as if further attack were imminent. Fists were shaken at the sky; little groups of civilians whispered apprehensively together. The war was at last in the middle of Hanoi; the city, simmering in the heat, responded. The harsh determination on the faces of the gunners, the discipline and urgency gave an impression of devotion to country was frightening in its implacability.

It was also, because the air defences had no chance at all against similar raids, pathetic and oddly moving. Perhaps neutral diplomats in London during the blitz also caught the mood of the defenders and, if only subconsciously and during the height of the battle, identified with their guts and courage against the enemy. It was a strange, multiform and disturbing moment.

The power station, an oblong gray brick or concrete building, was about a hundred feet high with a ground plan of some 600 by 300 feet. It was topped by tall black chimneys and surrounded by terraced houses. The flames had died down by the time we approached it, but the dust still rose from fallen masonry. The building had been repeatedly struck by high explosive: the chimneys had collapsed, and the whole structure, gaping with holes caused by the rockets, seemed also to be listing drunkenly to one side. (We also viewed it from the other side, on our return home by the dyke road.) There was, in our opinion, no hope at all for it. The accuracy of the attack had also been such that, out of the complex of the fifty or so small private houses around the power plant, only three had been at all damaged and those from blast rather than direct hits.

Luncheon on our return to the residence included a rather disagreeable paté.

'What is this paté, Monsieur Nguyen?' I asked the cook in facetious inquiry. 'Is it dog?'

'Yes, Monsieur.'

'Black dog or white dog?'

'Black dog, Monsieur,' said Nguyen in shocked reply. 'I would never serve white dog to a man.'

'Why not, Monsieur Nguyen?'

'Black dog makes men strong.' He flexed his scrawny arm.

'What does white dog do?'

'It makes women weak.'

The culinary dogs were, indeed, especially bred in and sold from the quarter around the west end of the Paul Doumer Bridge, a practice which, I have been since informed, has endured into the Eighties. The particular incident seemed to fit in with everything else that had happened that day.

Power and light were still off that evening; the sirens had sounded almost incessantly throughout the day. Felix Greene, the British journalist and writer on Mao Tse-tung's China, then resident in California, dined with me by candlelight, and we listened to the thunder of bombing north of the city. Felix Greene told me that Cuban interlocutors from their Embassy at Hanoi had accused me of being an American spy. I replied that all I knew about Cuban activity in North Vietnam was their habit, to which I have earlier referred, of spitting and throwing stones at bound American pilots on carts or led as captives through the streets of the town. There seemed no reason, therefore, why their sly malignity should not include accusations of the sort that Greene described.

'Are you an American spy?' he asked.

'No.'

'I didn't think you were. You don't look like one.' The ridiculous exchange could only have been conducted between Englishmen.

Felix was staying in the Metropole, his room festooned with files, cameras and audio equipment; he told me later that the atmosphere under his mosquito net that night had been like a sauna. It was even worse in the little Residence, and I slept on a mattress on the balcony with a lighted coil nearby to deter the insects. The sound of bombing to the east was clearly audible. Before I went to sleep, I thought of Cozzens' words in *Guard of Honor*: 'Downheartedness was no man's part. A man must stand up and do the best he can with what there is.... if mind failed you, seeing no pattern; and heart failed you, seeing no point, the stout, stubborn will must yet be up and doing.'

And I thought too of that meditation of Marcus Aurelius which ran: 'Wherever a man takes up his post, either because he thinks it is the best place or because his officer has placed him there, there I think he should stay and face the dangers, taking nothing into account, neither death nor anything else, in comparison with dishonour.'

The North Vietnamese were probably thinking much the same things that night.

Next day the fans and solitary air conditioner in the residence remained silent; in the office, the temperature had mounted by late afternoon to 140 degrees, like the engine room of an old cruiser. Geoffrey and I sat shirtless or chatted with Monsieur Xuan. The latter professed to believe that power would somehow be restored within a short period. We had seen the power station and knew that he was finally wrong.

To the continued roll of bombing, I started to draft a comprehensive telegram to the Foreign Office on the past 24 hours' events. Having described the raid on the city, the condition of the power plant and its consequences, I concluded that there was no possibility known to me of restoring any electric services. Hanoi, my last paragraph would have read, must now be finished as a functioning industrial and economic city.

Geoffrey had started to work on the accounts, pausing from time to time to file his nails with an emery board. For all the apprehension he showed, he might have been sitting in Great George Street on an inactive afternoon. I handed him my finished telegram for encypherment and dispatch to the PTT.

At that moment the lights went on, the fans started to turn, and the rattle of the box air conditioner began. Across the street, the repair factory was once more brightly lit.

There was no more means then than there is even today of determining what had happened. The power station could have been less gravely damaged than we had supposed; mobile generators could have been brought into the area (for electric current was not restored to the entire city, only to our quarter and to a few governmental and other buildings); or another but more distant power station could have taken the load. The lesson, however, was of the astonishing preparedness and resourcefulness of the DRV. Only continual air attack of a kind that Rolling Thunder had not yet initiated would surmount those qualities.

But Rolling Thunder did, thereafter, or so it appeared to us, begin to do precisely that, although without again striking the power plant or other targets in central Hanoi. The objectives, attacked without respite for the next two weeks, remained on the periphery of the city. The noise of bombing and gunfire was almost continual, and the damage to Vietnamese equipment and weapons considerable. But by the time I left for London on consultations in early June, morale, health and the flow of war material to Hanoi had not decisively diminished.

In London I was received by the Prime Minister, Harold Wilson, in his room at the House of Commons. He showed chief interest in the conditions of life in Hanoi, in the 'feel' of the city; I was pleased that he really did smoke a pipe and sat with his feet resting in a desk drawer.

George Brown, then Secretary of State, allowed me an hour and a half of his time in the magnificent room in the Foreign Office once occupied by grandees like Lord Curzon. He was kinder to me, and certainly more relaxed, than I think the latter would have been, offering me an excellent sherry and rejecting all attempts by his private secretary to remind him of the Cabinet meeting in progress. ('I've got John here; I'm not going to waste my time there.') Mr Brown's main concern was for the possibilities for U.S./Vietnamese negotiations on which, from my knowledge of Hanoi, I could offer little hope and said so.

He listened carefully. His own views were balanced and extraordinarily well informed. It was impossible not to feel affection and respect for him. His departure in 1970 from the House of Commons deprived the United Kingdom of one of its most *human* men, and British life of one of its wisest political leaders; in discarding him as their candidate, the Belper Labour Party dealt a savage but, more important, a stupid blow to democracy. He was a good, lovable man.

'John, I don't see your telegrams until I'm in bed at night. I'm religious, you know. When I read them, I get down on my knees and pray for you.'

'That's a very ambiguous remark, Secretary of State.'

'You know damned well what I mean.'

After he had at last dismissed me and we were in the private office, I remarked to the Private Secretary, Murray MacLehose (later Governor of Hong Kong), that the depth and scope of the interview had been extremely impressive, particularly since the June, 1967 Arab-Israeli war was still raging.

'Yes,' said MacLehose, 'and bear in mind that you're about the only visitor in the last few days who hasn't come flying out of the door with the Secretary of State's boot behind his gallabiyeh.'

Rolling Thunder was not pursued during the early part of my ten-day absence but began again toward the end of my stay in England. Rumours in Saigon, when I passed through on my way back north, spoke of a projected American strategy to bomb the North Vietnamese dykes on a massive scale. Certainly millions of deaths had been caused under the French régime and untold agricultural and other damage by a natural flooding of the Red River; to breach the dykes artificially would bring the same result, putting even Hanoi under water to a depth of at least eleven feet. I do not believe that this option was ever seriously considered at the highest levels in Washington. Anyway, the policy was never executed, and the rumours may have been no more than deception, as a further means of pressure on the DRV authorities.

This did not deter the DRV from announcing almost every day on Hanoi radio (VNA) or in *Nanh Dan,* the Party daily, that the USAF was carrying out such attacks; although these statements were quite untrue, many of the Missions bought collapsible boats against the perceived likelihood of major flooding.

I was discouraged by my government from either buying a boat or commissioning the construction of an air-raid shelter under the Consulate. Both actions, it was thought, might have been seen by the North Vietnamese as an act of collusion by America's supposed ally at Hanoi with presumed aggressive planning by the United States against the DRV. The argument, it is worth recalling today, seemed sensible at the time.

In the fall of 1966 or the winter of 1966-67 a delegation from the Czechoslovak Government had arrived in Hanoi to advise the North Vietnamese on the modalities of carrying the propaganda war to the continental United States. The flow to Hanoi of grisly 'Western' journalists, television 'personalities', disaffected minority groups, 'tribunals', 'parliamentary' commissions, 'concerned' writers, 'independent' or 'international' jurists, doctors, trade unionists and other riff-raff, most of whose expenses were paid by the DRV Government, began and hardly ever stopped.

The tide of hatred for America, pulled by falsehoods of Marxist, neo-Marxist or Trotskyist professional manufacture, started thereafter to infiltrate the American media and eventually the 'intellectual' establishment. By the summer of 1967 it was clear, even to an isolated diplomatic mission at Hanoi, that the American effort to prevent a totalitarian régime from obliterating a free country was being resisted by the totalitarians as much – and with the connivance of their supposed opponents – in America as in Vietnam. (One publication described me as 'the lanky British Ambassador, a veteran of 22 years in Indo-China, who stalked the Hotel Metropole in white colonialist linen suit'.)

The picture presented of undersized and 'freedom-loving' northern democrats bravely struggling against a brutal aggressor was not one recognizable in either Saigon or Hanoi. In the South, aggression, atrocity and repression seemed, rather, the DRV's characteristics and in the North, regimentation and the absence of political liberty.

Neither the extermination by the People's Army of Vietnam of entire southern communities nor the massacres in the North during land reform distracted American intellectuals from the prospect of humiliating, if not butchering, their own country.

By late July, however, although no political movement was evident, there were signs in Hanoi of a growing sense of reality induced by the continued bombing.

Although 'neutralist' diplomats continued to report the allegedly private claims of DRV officials that a negotiated timetable for United States military withdrawal from the Republic of South Vietnam might extend up to three years, there now appeared to be unwilling acceptance that this would form no part of U.S. planning for the RVN until much greater political and military stability had been achieved in that country.

Some diplomats continued to assert their belief that a cessation of American bombing would, apart from talks, result in a drying-up of DRV infiltration to the south after an initial, say 15-day, increase. They would not confirm whether this was their view or that of their official contacts, nor would they substantiate their belief that a halt in U.S. troop increases would result in similar DRV concessions. Neither did they satisfactorily reply to my question whether the U.S. military could accept enemy reinforcement extending over 15 days on a scale comparable to that of the Tet truce. Otherwise, there was a fairly widely held belief that 'Hanoi was going to catch it again badly' before or after the Saigon elections, but that perhaps the next step in escalation was more likely to be the mining of the port of Haiphong.

A trained medical observer, who treated few North Vietnamese but kept his eyes open, told me at this time that he had seen early signs of malnutrition among between 60 and 90 per cent of children in Hanoi according to the nature of the symptom. These were lack of skin 'lustre', moisture at the outer corners of the eyes, scabies on the palm of the hands, fissured tongues, prominent ribs, swollen bellies and worms.

Neither I nor anyone else I knew had seen major evidence of such complaints except in very young babies, and my informant was quick to admit that he had been unable to examine the main indicators (liver and spleen) and that, for instance, swollen bellies were nothing like so gross as those in Africa or in parts of India. Lice were much worse, but that was another matter.

He asserted, nonetheless, that the present diet must result in serious ill health among children in two to three years, with permanent effect on their subsequent adult condition. (From scattered comment, I thought that all this might be more marked in the provinces, particularly near the Chinese frontier; it was thought anyway that there were now no more than 400,000 out of 1,200,000 permanent residents in Hanoi.) It was not his contention nor mine that these symptoms were visible in the army, among most cadres or among factory workers here; the food eaten by the latter was, as I had myself recently observed, adequate, although containing items visually repellent.

There was a noticeable increase in 'grimness', in other words, depression, compensated by a deliberate step-up in endurance which was probably to be attributed to the great heat of summer as much as to conditions of scarcity. (This did not apply to young women who remained neat, clean and cheerful, although − or because − there had been a definite increase in prostitution, perhaps due to the rising cost of living.) Bicycles were going slower, and there seemed to be a decrease in energy. Pebbles, even stones, had been thrown at Europeans, including myself, from unseen sources which had not, fortunately, happened to me before in generally well-mannered South-East Asia.

However silly it might have sounded, I recalled the remark of Anne de Quirielle, who arrived at my house one Sunday with a cut hand to which she applied Gordon's gin: 'I wonder if it might not be due to pro-Chinese Vietnamese who mistake us for Russians.' I did not myself think so; rather, 'it isn't the heat, it's the humidity,' or that children, or the xenophobia common to most countries in wartime, might be responsible.

I doubted if any of that meant more in immediate political terms than that the battle waged by brilliantly 'encouraging' Vietnamese domestic propaganda against the long, hot summer might have to be pursued with greater elan during the next few weeks. I thought that propaganda might win this time; but increasing efforts might have to be made in the near future. For the first time I was beginning to believe that, in spite of the history of that extraordinary people over the past 22 years, of their proven ability to withstand far worse suffering in other towns and villages of the DRV than they had had to withstand in Hanoi, of their tenacity, of the implacable aims of their leadership, they must have a physical limit sometime. I could not predict when it would be reached, perhaps not in 1967, nor what form it would take — presumably slow collapse — but unless the war were further internationalized, I thought that the limit might come.

As an incidental indication of the lack of seriousness with which the DRV's communist allies regarded the present juncture, heads of mission then absent included the Bulgarian, Cuban, Czech, Hungarian, Pathet Lao, Polish, Romanian and Soviet. (It was true, of course, that Le Thanh Nghi's annual economic mission was said to be about to leave Peking for some of those countries, but their absence was at least a sign that, as I said earlier, there was no immediate political initiative in view.) The Chinese Ambassador had still not returned to Hanoi after six months' 'sick leave'; the Indonesian Ambassador had still not been succeeded; the UAR had replaced neither their Ambassador nor their chargé *ad interim*. There was 'no one here' other than chargés, except ourselves, the French, the Indian, the DDR and the Albanian, and I was not sure about the latter, who kept the most narrow of profiles at the best of times.

Life, meanwhile, continued. In spite of the bombing, a crate of champagne and several of hock and claret reached me by the overland route via Nanning from Hong Kong. The Cathedral, guided by an Archbishop appointed not by the Vatican, but by the DRV régime, and boasting an inexhaustible supply of young male and female Tonkinese novices, held midnight masses at which both the church itself and the concourse outside were crowded with worshippers or, at least, with spectators.

Well-placed canards continued to assert that their Vietnamese captors were forcing American prisoners to carry out manual labour on the Paul Doumer Bridge or near any installation from which the Vietnamese sought to deter U.S. air attack. (The blast from the August raid on the bridge had lifted me bodily backwards from the Residence balcony and slammed me against the back wall of the living room.) A Vietnamese Customs Officer insisted on opening the icebox which I had brought up from a journey with the bag to Saigon; Livesey reported to me with pleasure that the only crab still alive therein had nipped the official's fingers to the bone.

Two more Peace Initiatives were received from London, via PTT bicycle, in the form of cypher telegrams of over 1000 groups each. By the time that we deciphered them, they had been announced on the wireless and were under customary attack by Nan Danh and VNA.

Mr Louhanapessy, the Indonesian chargé d'affaires, whose French was exiguous, told me of a district of Hanoi in which 'chickens' were available.

'A man near the Grand Lac took me by the sleeve and, muttering, *"Vous voulez une poule, voulez une poule?"* led me toward a dark alley which seemed to be full of girls. I shook him off, but I thought that my cook might be interested. One can't get much of that sort of thing here.'

One could not indeed. To ask Mr Louhanapessy, nevertheless, for the address would have been imprudent, still more to deliver a French language lesson or instruction on what he might have missed.

XV

VICTORY APPARENT

BUT BY SEPTEMBER, the time for *poules*, feathered or otherwise, had passed. The evidence of malnutrition was now clear, and among adults as well as children. Now food itself was not coming in from China, North Vietnam's main source of supply. American bombing of the entry points into Vietnam from that country, as well as Sino-Soviet differences, had had their substantive effects. In the streets, offices and factories, the population could barely get about their duties; even the Residence staff, better fed than the rest of their compatriots, dragged themselves around the house.

The hospitals were filled with cases of hunger edema as well as of wounds. (Bombing of the power lines to Hanoi at that time brought another danger, fortunately of short duration, that of failure of the electric water pumps; for three days there was no water supply throughout the district. Mass epidemic, in the already unsanitary conditions of the capital, could not have been far away.) The symptoms of disease noted in late July had begun to spread. The economy was at last breaking down. The country and its people were close to a collapse which, for the first time, no amount of excited exhortation could correct.

And every morning since I had first reached Hanoi, the streets of the quarter had been lined with war material brought in overnight from China across the Paul Doumer Bridge, amphibious vehicles, artillery, armoured fighting vehicles, Sergeant surface-to-air missiles on flatbeds, saucily parked even outside the British mission. By the time that I returned from London in June their numbers had a little decreased. By August and September there were none at all, and early-morning constitutionals in other districts and to the main railway station itself showed that the explanation did not lie in diversification elsewhere.

I had no authority to speak on the purposes of the war; they had been amply covered by observers as various as Professor P.J. Honey and Stokely Carmichael. Each step in the war, from the rearming of the *Infanterie Coloniale* in Saigon in the autumn of 1945 onwards, had had an apparent political inevitability which only hindsight showed to have been of its own time only, and not always even that. Nor could I discuss American military strategy or its results in the South. But if it were the American objective to destroy the FLN's infrastructure by military means in South Vietnam and by aerial interdiction of support facilities and lines of communication in the North then I could comment on the effects of the latter tactic on the DRV's ability to continue the war.

If the Viet Cong were really losing more men in the South than they could recruit locally or import from the DRV, then, failing Chinese intervention, the major war *was* over. The bombing was causing losses in men and *materiel* and serious delays, possibly unacceptable to a European power; conditions were mediaeval, industry suffered, to say the least, from dispersal, food was tight and agriculture undermanned, the distribution system was imperfect, electricity and power were variable, damage to lines of communication was enormous, no one *liked* being bombed or separated from their families, a high proportion of the manpower was devoted to repair. Supplies through China were certainly affected by the Cultural Revolution as well as, now, by around-the-clock bombing on arrival at the border. No matter how many non-return aid pacts were signed with the Bloc, the DRV knew that the Socialist countries preferred a negotiated solution.

I had once wondered whether the North Vietnamese were objectively cornered; their line of march (currently expressed as 'reunification') had, for centuries, been southwards, and I had doubted if they would give up. They had known that the Sino-Soviet Bloc *must* continue to support them and they did not therefore need to be too concerned about their own industrial capacity. Manpower shortages, at least in the north of the DRV, had been eased by Chinese labour with its own self-defence along the lines of communication; and again, since a political decision had been taken years ago to postpone industrialization in wartime, the 'wastage' of Mr McNamara's 'five million men' on repair work had not really been waste at all. The North Vietnamese majority had begun, as workers and citizens, from a nil base; their suffering and privation had not been, until recently, intolerable to them. Indeed, that majority, because of the purpose which it had been indoctrinated to assume and because of communal interdependence, even of pride, aroused by their difficulties, had probably been, until the summer of 1967, happier than it had ever been. Government and Party control had been pervasive, but it had not then, at least in Western terms, needed to be totally repressive.

Vast as was the damage, the country had until recently been 'run'. There had been just enough to eat. Movement had been possible. Trains had continued to arrive nightly on the east bank of the Red River where their freight had been either loaded straight into lorries for the south and south-east or, mostly, sent across the bridge or disembarked, re-embarked on pontoons, disembarked on the west bank and dispatched to the Hanoi railhead. But the trains were coming in no longer.

So that in the last few months I had come to believe that the country's endurance had reached its limit. If the appearance of the leaders at the recent National Day celebrations had been any indication, it might have been thought that they too might be coming to recognize this, in spite of the loss of political investment that negotiations might represent. But the tone and substance of some remarks by Pham Van Dong on 3 September, on the other hand, were harder and less flexible than ever.

And I had, until recently, to repeat my consistent impression that there was still almost nothing that the people could not be asked to do and almost no lengths to which they could not be persuaded to go, even if on their hands and knees. It was as difficult, I knew, to convey this mental climate as it was depressing to live in it. I had believed, until August, that the DRV régime would pursue the conflict even if they had, like Samson, to pull the pillars down on themselves and on all of us.

The Prime Minister's remarks might have reflected the DRV's position at that moment, that of an apparently cornered rat. But the corner might not have been as tight as all that. Even if it were, cornered North Vietnamese rats bit. I understood that this was well recognized by the South Vietnamese army, who tried to allow the North Vietnamese army an escape route while hitting them with 'gun-ships'. The U.S. Marines, on the contrary, tried to surround them and to fight it out on the ground.

I did not know what political conclusion should be drawn from that military analogy: not, presumably, a conciliatory one acceptable to the U.S. On the other hand, the total elimination of all the rats, through invasion and obliteration bombing, would also be neither practicable nor politically acceptable.

The Vietnamese had risen against their masters when moral and material circumstances had demanded in the past. If their circumstances had sharply deteriorated, if the role of 'victim' no longer seemed worth the sacrifice, if the equation of communism, nationalism and the charisma of Ho Chi Minh ceased to balance, then .... If the Americans continued to cut the railway lines from China and Haiphong to Hanoi and succeeded in putting the ports out of action, then, because it was now impossible to see how the DRV could both pursue the war in the south and keep the north running, the maintenance of morale − let alone enthusiasm − must become as impossible.

Until August General Giap's words to the 316th Division during the French war had probably been the key to the government's intransigence. 'The enemy will be caught in a dilemma; he has to drag out the war in order to win it and does not possess, on the other hand, the psychological and political means to fight a long-drawn-out war.' And peace itself might also have been uninviting to the régime, leading to payment for Bloc aid, charges of betrayal of the NLF, even their own overthrow and dependence on China.

But it was now the DRV's inability to fight such a war, failing Soviet air intervention and supply, that was plain. Giap's dictum was irrelevant. So, at last, were lorries and bicycles.

The DRV in late September, when I left that unhappy country for England, was no longer capable of maintaining itself as an economic unit nor of mounting aggressive war against its neighbour. 'The major war was over, in the sense that a game of chess conducted by Capablanca could actually be over in two minutes but might with a stubborn or less intelligent opponent drag on for hours without changing the final decision.'

It was at that moment of victory that Capablanca conceded the game.

4 The British Embassy, Ulan Bator: 'a fine semi-classical edifice with a large columned porch and balustered gallery'. (p. 131)

5 A Mongol gathering on the steppe.

6 H.E. with bird!

7 Joanna, aged 5, in winter attire.

XVI

VICTORY SPURNED

THE STRENGTH OF THE American bombing campaign of summer 1967 had rested not only on its weight but on its consistency, hour after hour, day after day. The strategy, as well as damaging or destroying — in ports, on railway lines and on storage areas — the capacity of the DRV to feed itself and to maintain invasion, had also, for the first time, allowed the North Vietnamese no time to repair war-making facilities. No sooner were they repaired than they were struck again. Tonkinese ingenuity had been defeated and, by the remorseless persistence of the campaign, their will eroded to near-extinction.

But although some spasmodic bombing in the north-east quadrant took place after September, it was on a greatly reduced scale and frequently interrupted by long periods of inactivity during 'peace initiatives', all illusory if not contrived, and anyway occasions when the campaign should have maintained, even increased, momentum. Above all, that factor — the persistence of the campaign — which had sapped North Vietnamese endurance, was discarded. And at the end of March, 1968, all bombing of North Vietnam north of the 20th Parallel was discontinued. Victory — by September, 1967, in American hands — was not so much thrown away as shunned with prim, averted eyes.

Even now, this renunciation is difficult to understand. Although the prompt use of air power against the north-east quadrant in 1965 would have brought earlier victory without the damage, misery and death to both sides caused by gradualism, the lifting of at least some constraints by Washington had brought the DRV to manifest defeat by 1967.

Some apologists have claimed that the equipment observed during the PAVN Tet offensive of February, 1968 demonstrated the failure of air power. But most of that equipment had been in South Vietnam or en route there before the summer air offensive in the North had even begun.

To attribute the surrender to a failure of will among the President's civilian advisers is to grant to those 'intellectuals' a will to victory which many of them did not claim, indeed rejected. A war directed by men who believed that it should not be waged at all was not one likely to be prosecuted with vigour nor one in which the military command, whom in their arrogance the 'intellectuals' anyway despised, would be permitted military decision. Nor would a war be enthusiastically pursued by men who thought that the North Vietnamese were not irredentist and aggressive Communists but put-upon Nationalist Social Democrats, or that America was not so much saving a nearly defenceless South Vietnam as 'intervening militarily in the affairs of another country when U.S. vital security interests were not directly involved', or even that South Vietnam, precisely because of her weakness, merited defeat and that her interests, anyway, lay in unity with her totalitarian neighbour.

Nor did the frightened 'intellectual' illusion that bombing would provoke Soviet and Chinese armed intervention help the effective conduct of the war. Nor could a war be won by men familiar with computers and academic theory but not with the battlefield or the ageless facts of South-East Asia. Nor, above all, could it be won by men ashamed of America.

The war, nevertheless, dragged on until the Peace Agreement of 1973. Thereafter, Watergate and consequent opposition to all Nixon's policies persuaded the U.S. Congress to withhold funds and equipment from the government and army of the Republic of South Vietnam. That country, thus carelessly abandoned by her American ally, now forms part of the renamed Socialist Republic of Vietnam, the conqueror also of Laos and Cambodia. Freedom is dead throughout the peninsula. Soviet navies and air forces move freely over the South China Sea.

But the 'treason of the intellectuals' ensured these consequences and ensured too that more than 50,000 Americans would not return home. The intellectuals, even confronted today by the Vietnamese invasion of Cambodia, the occupation of Laos and the mass exodus from Socialist Vietnam, still admit no culpability. Indeed, under the Carter régime, they sought and continued to obtain posts in the Government of those United States whose honour they degraded.

But despite them, the American effort in Vietnam, however ultimately unsuccessful in the peninsula, held the line long enough to permit the secure establishment of a democratic market economy outside Indo-China itself. The existence in liberty of the Association of South East Asian Nations (Malaysia, Indonesia, Singapore, the Philippines, Thailand) and the prosperity and independence of Japan, South Korea and Taiwan all spring from United States resistance to tyranny in Vietnam.

They are living monuments to the American dead in Indo-China and to all those men of the United States Armed Forces whose presence in Vietnam gave the rest of Asia the time to grow, unharassed and at peace. The war was not in vain. Were that not so, a man from a country which, for whatever good reason, played no martial part in 'America's war', would not have had the impertinence to write the story.

PART TWO

MONGOLIA

'Mongol nomadic society resists evolution into the higher, settled forms: it is so complete and independent that it is, in fact, incapable of evolution: it can only be replaced .... But the world is the less when a culture and a way of life disappear.'

Owen Lattimore.

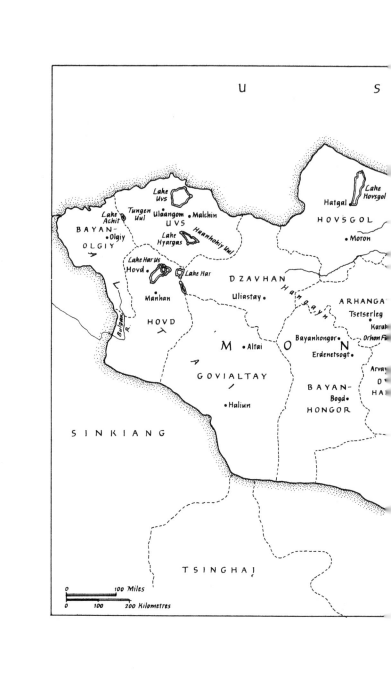

U S

Lake
Uvs

Lake
Hovsgol
Hatgal

HOVSGOL

Lake
Achit

Tungen
Uul
Ulaangom • Malchin

Moron

BAYAN-
OLGIY
• Olgiy

UVS

Lake
Hyargas

Haanhohiy Uul

Lake Har Us
Hovd
Lake Har

DZAVHAN

ARHANGA

Tsetserleg

Karal

Uliastay •

Manhan

Orhon Fa

HOVD

M

O

N

Bayanhongor •

Erdenetsogt •

Arva

• Altai

O

HA

GOVIALTAY

BAYAN-
Bogd•

HONGOR

• Haliun

SINKIANG

TSINGHAI

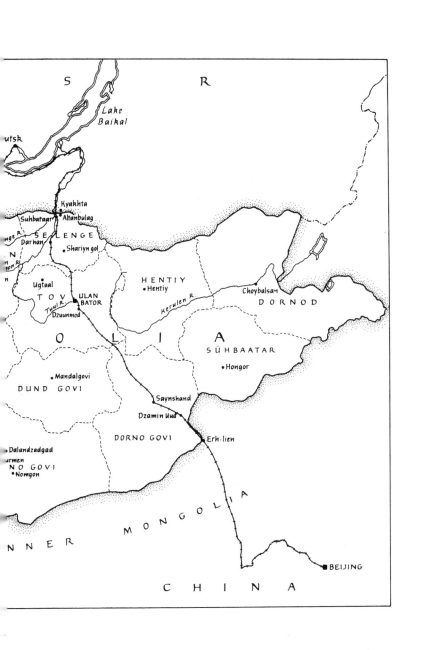

S   S   R

Lake
Baikal

utsk

Kyakhta
Suhbataar • Altanbulag
SE LENGE
nge R.
Darhan
N   • Shariyn gol
ton R.
n

Ugtaal   HENTIY
TOV   • Hentiy
Tuul R. ULAN   Choybalsan
BATOR   Kerulen R.   DORNOD
Dzuunmod

O   L   I   A

• Mandalgovi   SÜHBAATAR
DUND GOVI   • Hongor

Saynshand
Dzamin Uud
DORNO GOVI
• Dalandzadgad   Erh-lien
urmen
NO GOVI
• Nomgon

MONGOLIA

NNER

BEIJING

C   H   I   N   A

GLOSSARY

Aimag = province
Airag = distilled milk of horse, sheep, camel, cow and yak
Amban = senior Chinese official under the Empire
Argal = Central Asian sheep
Arkhi = Mongolian vodka
Artdel = small business enterprise
Bazmachi = Turkic rebels
Boodz = national dish of dumplings stuffed with mutton and
  onions
Buriat = Mongol tribe
Butachi = Criminal or other outcasts
Chantu = Muslims from Sinkiang
Deel = Mongolian national dress modelled on the Manchu
  robe
Dungan = Chinese Muslims
Ger = round, white tent
Gol = river
Hural = assembly
Hushoor = mutton pancake
Nuur = lake
Oirat = Mongol tribe
Olet = Mongol tribe
Saiga = small antelope of ungainly appearance
Somon = county
Stupa = architectural feature of Buddhist faith
Tarag = yoghurt
Tanka = Lamaist religious picture
Urum = clotted cream
Yurt = Russian word for ger (qv)

I

EN ROUTE FOR ULAN BATOR

FOUR YEARS LATER, in 1971, I landed at Moscow Airport en route for Ulan Bator, capital of the Mongolian People's Republic to which I had been accredited as Ambassador. I was accompanied by Moranna, my wife, with whom I had absconded on Armistice Day, 1967, two months after my return from Hanoi, our two children, plus all the paraphernalia of a young family — cots, perambulators and an elderly Nanny.

After our wedding at Chelsea Registry Office, the best man and bridesmaid had drunk champagne by the lake in St James's Park, without Young Lochinvar and his Ellen, who had hurried *ventre à terre* to Heathrow. To elope is to defy the world, to set it at naught, to discount family pressure, even the family itself. On return to England, however, our flight was not just condoned but instantly accepted by those feared hostile. We were home again, in my small flat in the King's Road.

Alexandra Mansions, although an agreeable bachelor establishment, possessed a fairly commodious drawing room, but only one bedroom. The future accommodation of a child, Joanna, to arrive in the world in 1968, as well as more immediate inconveniences of constricted space soon necessitated a move to larger quarters.

Armed with the property sections of various Sunday newspapers, we set out one winter morning for Hampshire. My wife had had a nightmare. I did not ever want to leave London. We were sullen house-hunters. Whether or not for that reason, we bought the first house inspected, a 17th and 19th century red brick parsonage on the Berkshire border. (One side of the road lay in that county, the other in Hampshire.) The village was nondescript, but the house engaging and large enough. The garden, on the other hand, looked, to my terrified eye, satisfactorily small. So it proved, but spacious enough to fulfil the urge to garden then belatedly discovered.

That garden and the house, although sources of sharp nostalgia, remained anchors to England for many years. The Old Parsonage, despite the conversion of a barn and other measures, retained its simple, English provincial charm, not a Country House but a house in the country. One *must* love the places one inhabits, but happiness in this rather ordinary Hampshire building was no illusion.

To live in the country and to work in the Foreign Office involved daily journeys by British Rail, at that time consisting of broken-backed conveyances, unkempt and subject to lengthy delays, although not then, in the Southern Region, mutilated by vandals. Basingstoke Station, too, lacked grace, with winds undiminished in ferocity from their origins in the White or Barents Seas, funnelling down its grubby platforms. Waterloo, at the other end, with its resentful Sixties porters, ubiquitous grime, broken windows and contraceptive vending machines, was little more seductive, the Underground Railway system even less.

The era was not one of civility nor elegance, those attributes being restricted to the clubs, or to the homes of our friends and family. The public times were bad indeed, not ameliorated by the appointment as Prime Minister of Edward Heath, a trimming, frightened, appeasing period without direction or courage, ending in surrender over principle: times without conviction. (It was said of Heath, as it was of William Pitt: 'Unfortunately he tried to find a middle path and he found one which united the worst of both extremes.') But our private time was reassuring, wrapped in home and friends and work, poor in money, rich in love and sanity.

After a dinner party at Greenwich, under Thornhill's great ceiling in the Painted Hall, it was, however, 'Abroad, and see new sights, your country's cause calls you away.' Geoffrey de Freitas had just led a delegation to Mongolia from the Inter-Parliamentary Union and had photographs: brown hills, Lamaist temples, round white tents, a camel-train, bow-legged stalwarts in huge fur hats. He observed that the current British Ambassador's posting was drawing to a close. I noted that my grade matched the post, and that the Serbo-Croat language, in which I was once fluent, might be 'converted', after short tuition, to Russian, an official language of the People's Republic.

My wife, although not seeking the fierce light which beats upon the wife of *any* Head of Mission, however small, was also persuaded that the opportunity should not be rejected. Nor was she deterred by the

Post Report's assertion that Ulan Bator was unsuitable for children. (It was a children's paradise.) Our preparations, linguistic and otherwise, thus went forward, marred only by an article in the *Daily Mail* which had unfortunate consequences, as will be seen later; our friends commiserated or congratulated; we acquired quantities of more or less useful information; Chambers of Commerce solicited support; companies canvassed views; in response to an advertisement in *The Lady* for a Nanny, one unqualified applicant declared her reason for seeking employment as a 'Sabbatical year from her husband'; we were summoned to Buckingham Palace to be received by Her Majesty, the ceremony known as 'Kissing hands'. 'Don't bite it,' I had been adjured. The Monarch was beautiful, kind and interested in our remote destination.

Nevertheless, waiting in the Parsonage garden for the cars to take us to London on the hot, cloudless, summer morning of our departure, the lawn clipped, huge scarlet roses around us, England was more inviting and Central Asia more intimidating than in earlier calculation. Both cars were late and, two hours later, racing across the tarmac at Heathrow, minutes before take-off, we resembled an Edwardian *Punch* cartoon of a journey to Clacton, not an ambassadorial envoi.

The Consul-General met us at Sheremyetevo, Moscow's main airport. His staff had under-estimated in terms of transport and workers the proportions of our monstrous baggage, but support was provided by representatives of the Malaysian and Singapore Missions, turbaned Sikh and jovial Hokkien; plainly the Commonwealth was alive and well in Moscow. That impression was confirmed on a later visit when confronted, in his morning coat and grave demeanour, by the British Ambassador's magnificent black butler, Grafton, of Caribbean origin, insouciantly present also at ambassadorial bridge tables elsewhere in the capital.

Immigration and Customs facilities were not facilitated by Nanny's insistence, unbeknown to ourselves, on completing her own entry and other forms without assistance. Since, in response to the printed questions thereon, she had declared herself in possession of firearms, wireless transmitters, dangerous drugs, silk-worms, and weapons of all kinds — and in a range greatly in excess of my error in 1967 at Hanoi — some delay, more confused than acrimonious, ensued. We soon left in ragged convoy for the house where we were to stay until departure for Mongolia, that of Joe Dobbs, the British Minister, and his wife, Marie, author of works on and, even, 'by' Jane Austen.

The children were put to bed, a destination also vainly sought by ourselves, in particular by my wife, who, in order to get her unwieldy caravan on the road, had not slept for over twenty-four hours. She did, nevertheless, succeed in dropping off intermittently at the Bolshoi on Denis Greenhill's genial shoulder throughout Swan Lake. (Anglo/ Soviet relations were customarily bad, and the Permanent Under-Secretary's visit was intended to negotiate an improvement. I do not remember if it did, and, in any case, after the expulsion in 1972 of 105 Soviet spies from the U.K., relations deteriorated yet further.) At dinner afterwards in the theatre, as well as caviar, vodka, red Mukuzani and white Tsinindal, we were offered an ambrosial fish from Lake Baikal called omul, whose consumption thereafter, because of conservation, forbidden, or at least restricted, for many years.

The worldliness and absence of polemic at this table, and at the other functions we attended, of Soviet officials working in the Ministry of Foreign Affairs at Moscow itself, were superior to the demeanour of their colleagues at Hanoi or, subsequently and with exceptions, at Ulan Bator and elsewhere. Despite the telling of boring, set-piece jokes, these diplomats' command of material, which included Mongolia, and their relatively liberal attitudes were a surprise. So was the rapidity with which the stumbling attempts of this neophyte in their language were fielded, unlike the gaping incomprehension of the peasantry who manned most Russian Missions abroad. Nevertheless, slyness and cunning, the principal characteristics of Soviet man, the wish to 'score' and 'put down', seemed never far away.

We enjoyed the furtive glances of Soviet officials at the portrait of King George V in the British Ambassador's dining room, with its haunting resemblance to the Tsar, his murdered cousin. (My wife, not hitherto part of an exiled community, was nevertheless daunted by the somewhat shoulder-to-shoulder unity of the British Club, however engaging its individual members.) We lunched in the country at an attractive inn from whose menu, rich as the Ritz or the Connaught, all dishes except one were 'off'. We visited the Kremlin, St Basil's Cathedral, the Armoury, monasteries, churches, the Tretiakoff gallery, the Galitzine palace, the Pushkin museum. We saw, in 18th and 19th century Moscow, but not in the new town, the classical European roots of the architecture of the capital of Russia, carried from Italy, France and the Austro-Hungarian Empire. We were, as always in British Embassies, warmly entertained by colleagues. I cast a good deal on Joe Dobbs's lawn with a new Hardy rod. We bought six dozen coathangers in GUM, that combination of Woolworth's and an oriental bazzar. We talked to, and learned from, David and Judy Bonavia, shortly before their expulsion by the Soviets and transfer to Peking.

But we had waited keenly for the play to begin and, four days after arrival, it was with relief that we returned to Sheremyetevo to take the TU-16 for Irkutsk, and onward to Ulan Bator. On reaching the Aeroflot service counter, however, with eagerly proferred tickets and passports, we were dismayed to see the Russian staff, as one man, silently leave their desks and scuttle through a door at the back. Subsequent remonstrations with senior administrative personnel did not compel their return, nor induce any response other than that the aircraft could not accept us and had, indeed, already taken off.

Even the Soviet workmen employed by the Embassy to manhandle the baggage, KGB cadres one and all, professed outrage: 'They turned you away, *with little children?*' We returned dejectedly to the Minister's house. Aeroflot's subsequent explanation, that the reservations had not been confirmed, was, as will later be seen, no more than excuse or, rather, cover for the more devious if infantile truth.

Our next journey to the airport, two or three days later, was enlivened by the sight of new Soviet automobiles, all of whose oil seals had burst in the June heat, abandoned every hundred yards or so along the route. We counted over ninety of these triumphs of Russian engineering.

This time no bureaucratic obstacles were placed in our way. We took off at last on the long flight to Siberia, landing in the early morning at Irkutsk, with its subsequently familiar crocodiles of shaven-headed Red Army recruits, at first taken for political prisoners. In the airport restaurant lightly boiled eggs were drunk, rather than eaten, in the Russian fashion, and other unsavoury dishes consumed before the short flight to Ulan Bator, our first jaunt in an aircraft of Mongol Air.

II

ARRIVAL

OUT OF THE CLEAR MIDDAY SKY our little turbo-prop came in
through the low green hills surrounding the airfield, touched down and
rolled to a halt by the control tower. The latter was housed in the 'International Airport', a building of impermanent appearance, not unlike a
rickety Tibetan temple. It contained, admittedly in parvo, the usual
facilities of an airport – restaurant, bar, lavatories, and ticket-counters
where Mongols alternately bickered and dozed. Although only one, or
at most two, international flights landed there on any given day, the
airport, like many other institutions in the Republic, was invariably
crammed with Mongols gossiping in their sibilant, almost surreptitious
language, staring, tramping up and down the stairs in felt or leather
boots, all quite indifferent to the business of aviation. The odours of
milk and mutton fat filled the air.

Ranged in ragged line by length of service en poste, my ambassadorial colleagues stood to greet me outside the tower. (I had not been
warned of this welcome and had devoted myself, before the call to duty,
to rescuing, at my wife's request, her wicker picnic basket from the
hold.) They were a spavined group and, varying in height as they did
from Mr Shchetinin, the enormous Soviet Ambassador, to the tiny
North Korean, the picture presented was, vertically as well as hor-
izontally, untidy if not grotesque. Nor was I adept in conveying my
pleasure at arrival, confusing the Chinese with the Vietnamese
Ambassador, greeting the former with froideur and the latter with
warmth.

This ceremony was later abandoned, initially in a one-time ukase
organized by the Soviet doyen to avoid welcoming a new Chinese
Ambassador, ultimately thereafter falling into complete disuse. Its
demise was a pity. As well as serving to bring us all together in inn-

ocent, regular, if rather unproductive conclave, it had marked almost the sole occasions when my Cuban and East European colleagues were obliged to venture outside their own premises into the open air. The fear, hatred and shame felt by these Marxist-Leninist worthies for the climate, as well as the culture, of their Mongolian ally was in notable contrast to their protestations of International Proletarianism. They felt that Mongolia was rather infra dig.

Thereafter, with Philip Shaw, Head of Chancery, who had received us from the aircraft, we drove across the steppe to Ulan Bator, a great river in the distance, hills on our right reaching down almost to the metalled road, but, on the left, dimly seen far away in the haze, blue skies above in the Land of Blue Skies. Cattle, horses and goats grazed on either side of the road. Behind wooden palisades, like the stockades of *Treasure Island,* could be seen the encampments of the Mongols, their round white tents (gers) unchanged for more than ten centuries. Children in various degrees of squalid undress played, shrieking, round the gers, their narrow eyes deep sunk above high cheekbones, nostrils dribbling. Wrecked vehicles littered the verges.

Ulan Bator ('Red Hero'), Urga in pre-Revolutionary times, contains few buildings other than the Opera, the Gandan Monastery, the Palaces of the former God-King (third in the Yellow Faith hierarchy after the Dalai and Panchen Lamas of Tibet), and a Taoist temple in the old Chinese quarter that are not inspired by modern Soviet industrial and domestic design. Were it not that some early architecture of the latter type had its roots in Europe, and that half the current population of the capital still lived in white gers which, however insalubrious within, were externally without fault, the city would have lacked all character.

Fortunately our Embassy, built in the 1930s, was a fine, semi-classical edifice with a large columned porch and balustered gallery. It had been occupied at one stage by the Cuban Embassy until the staff of that Mission decamped to Havana in the Sixties ('took French leave' said the Polish Ambassador, winking) in circumstances connected with shortage of foreign exchange. The British had then hastily concluded a lease, the rent for which the Mongols doubled almost every year, usually on the day before Christmas, correctly presuming that we would have paid *anything* not to return to the Ulan Bator Hotel, of Czech construction and Mongol management, the previous integument of the British Embassy, where the first Ambassador's wife had cooked on a primus stove balanced on the bath or the lavatory seat.

The house was raised above Peace Street, the main thoroughfare and

131

one of the few macadamed roads in the country. Trees planted outside it in the autumn had their roots embedded in blocks of ice which melted in the spring. It could be approached, supervised by militiamen in sentry boxes, either up steps from the road, thus producing an impression of dignity, if not grandeur, or through the little compound at the back, producing the reverse. Entrance by the latter route gave on to garages, the back of the house, a cottage and an undeveloped yard surrounded by wire mesh, eventually to become a tennis court; it was an unattractive, not to say depressing, prospect, but the one selected for us on our arrival.

There was no space for nurseries in the Residence. The children and Nanny were therefore settled into the cottage, ten yards from the back door of the Embassy. This building had been hitherto occupied by the Corps of Queen's Messengers, albeit only on the latter's fortnightly three-day visits. These retired Service officers, some forty in total, were not all best pleased, despite remorseless entertainment from ourselves, by the consequent rigours of accommodation in the hotel.

The building was assumed to be insecure for classified speech. (Furthermore, because of known Soviet exploitation of family dissension, the staff even conducted quarrels between husbands and wives in the compound, and sotto voce at that. There is no evidence that neglect of this procedure led to subsequent disaster, and there are no statistics to demonstrate whether, in outdoor temperatures as low as -40°C, the routine induced patience and self-control.) Philip Shaw and I, from the moment of my arrival, therefore began the first of many walks on the gravel. He had a tale to tell.

Some days before my arrival, when we were being refused passage at Moscow Airport, the embassy in Ulan Bator began to receive handwritten and telephoned messages, ostensibly from a senior Russian or Mongol official placing his services at our disposal as a potential informant. In all these messages, while seeking direct contact, the interlocutor had not specified an actual rendezvous until the day before we arrived at Ulan Bator, when he had announced to his unseen audience his intention to be outside the compound at 3 o'clock the following afternoon, to achieve an interview with 'someone who could help him and whom he could help'.

Shaw had, correctly, not responded to any of these missives. Nor did I propose to accede to the provocation. At the appointed time, however, kneeling on the floor of the drawing-room just below the level of the windows, I was able, without the use of periscope, to observe outside the gates a person of indeterminate race and with greying, marcelled hair, rather as one might imagine a trendy hairdresser in Croydon, talking gaily to a militiaman. (Without the latter's connivance, incidentally, no one was permitted to enter the Embassy grounds at all.) When it became clear after some thirty minutes that his appeal was not to be answered, the malefactor discounted his errand, making off down the path and into the town without apparent frustration or distress.

I did not see the creature again until some three years later when I was introduced to him at a reception which he attended in another capacity, that of a Socialist Bloc diplomat recently arrived in Mongolia. As he did not know that I had observed him in 1971, it was with no embarrassment that he greeted me in 1974. The encounter gave me secret pleasure. In his former or espionage capacity, he had doubtless been suborned for the role by the Russian Intelligence Services at Moscow, where he was then serving, and despatched by them to Ulan Bator for that single project. His task, of course, was so to interest the Embassy and, in particular, a new Ambassador presumed exhausted and off-balance from harassment in Moscow and a lengthy journey, that one or other would be driven to imprudent action, then to be exposed by Soviet propaganda with credit to all except the Mission and the U.K. Government. Perhaps chess is not always a successful guide to political action.

One seemed doomed to association with incompetent, hostile spies. Dong and Nguyen in Hanoi, however, had had a good deal more charm than the oafish Soviet marionettes in Mongolia. Similar incidents repeated themselves continually over the next few years, telephoned offers of defection, letters thrown through the windows, even attempts to enter the Embassy with 'defection' in view, all, since no aircraft other than those controlled by Aeroflot and Mongolair entered or left the country, rejected out of hand.

One, however, was both actual and more wounding. I had left the house one winter evening in order to visit Georges Perruche, my French colleague, in his quarters in the Ulan Bator Hotel. As I opened the garage doors to get out the car, I sensed that, although movement was neither seen nor heard, someone else was already in the garage.

Crouching in the darkness was a small, frightened Russian private soldier wearing stained overalls, who had climbed over the back wall into the compound. He was very young, very dirty, and chain-smoked nervously. He wanted to speak to the Ambassador. I declared my identity. Perhaps because of the casualness of my clothes in comparison with his mental picture of a Western Ambassador, or with the formality of his countrymen, he could not easily credit this information. His Russian accent was thick and difficult to understand. He seemed to be claiming that he wished to escape from the Soviet Army. He named his unit and location. It then occurred to me that if the house was vulnerable to electronic eavesdropping, so might be the garage. I moved him outside, forgetting until too late that the compound was illuminated and that I did not know where the switches were. The option of talking to him in the Embassy was closed. We were both trapped. (Since I could not command the services of an aircraft or any other means of transport, or rely on a friendly Security Service, we had, in fact, been trapped from the beginning.) I had no choice except to ask him to return by the way he had come. He started to obey but, suddenly, turned as if to go over the back wall. Would that he had. At the last moment he broke away and, in a sort of skittering run, made for the little front gate by the militia box. I heard the sound of his heavy boots outside as he doubled back away from the militiaman. There was shouting, a hue-and-cry, running feet. When I drove out minutes later, a small militia detachment had arrived under an officer. It was still there when I returned from the French Embassy, but I never knew if the Russian succeeded in getting away.

Georges Perruche had advised me that, although the incident was probably genuine, I would be wise to act as I would have done had it been another provocation or, at least, demonstrate to the authorities that our rôle had been passive. I accordingly telephoned the Soviet Military Attaché, an agreeable General who once told me that he 'loved' the Communist Party, and recounted the occurrence. He expressed interest only in whether the soldier had committed theft and whether he had been drunk. 'Was he drunk? Did he steal anything?' But when, the following day, after a call concerned with other matters that I had paid on the Soviet Ambassador, the Military Attaché formally thanked me for my part in preserving 'Socialist Legality' distaste and guilt were hard to suppress.

The Residence was on the top floor of the British Embassy with three other flats on the ground floor. The Chancery and wireless room were across the landing from the Residence. (The contiguity of office and home was perhaps a reason why we worked hard in Ulan Bator. Work and play were almost one, lacking the disincentive of mandatory commuting.) Our flat contained a large drawing-room and a dining-room, our bedroom and one smallish spare room in blue and white *toile de jouy,* off a central corridor. The furniture was supplied by the Department of the Environment, formerly the Ministry of Works, later the Public Services Administration, and was of rather second-rate design, in either rosewood or tubular steel. (This Department was in the habit of despatching to us crates of unwanted goods — forty pint teapots, sixty-five linen tea towels, four carpet sweepers without handles.) The pictures were slightly, but not much, better: the Ulan Bator Embassy did not rank high in Whitehall. The electrical, water and heating systems, all of which worked, had been installed by workmen temporarily imported from England.

Except our bedroom and the kitchen, which gave on to the compound, all these rooms looked across a valley filled with white gers to the Bogd Uul or Holy Mountains (one of the alleged birthplaces of Prester John), wooded hills stretching all the way to Dzuunmod, capital of Töv Province. (Wolves were said to infest these woods, deer certainly, shot in quantity by the King of Afghanistan and his entourage during a state visit, but not by us.) On the other side of the valley stood white buildings, named Xanadu by us, of extraordinary and romantic beauty at that distance, on closer inspection the 'palace' of the President of Mongolia, Sambuu and, later, of Jumjagyyn Tsedenbal and his Russian wife, like 'Lollia Paulina, hid with jewels'.

A hundred yards to the west was the Indian Embassy, led by a distinguished Ladakhi engineer from Leh, Sonam Norbe, who had qualified at Sheffield during the last war, later to become a Minister in the Jammu/Kashmir Government. Mr Norbe was married to an enchanting Tibetan, and they and their children, Deskett and Wongchuk (Pinto) — the latter eventually became Minister of Information in Srinagar — were our true friends. Buddhist, not Hindu, they were incomparably the nicest Indians we had met, then or later. We passed a good deal more time with them on picnics and other agreeable occasions than in trying professionally to unravel the tangle of Mongolian statistics.

Behind us was a Soviet-built agglomeration (microraion) of shopping centre and high-rise flats, windows broken, paint peeling or, at best, discoloured, foundations crumbling, rubbish on staircases and landings, bereft of maintenance within and without. Even vandalism might have been a more reassuring explanation for this moonscape than hopeless indifference to surroundings or, at all events, to modern surroundings, for the gers, on the other hand, were often models of order.

The Residence employed two maids. Delger, that rara avis, a Mongol beauty, was married, but her husband was in Moscow. In the meanwhile, a Polish lover enjoyed her favours. He was probably a lucky man. Unfortunately, absences from duty due to consorting with the Pole, and her lies to cover them, became intolerable and left no alternative to dismissal. That, we understood, also included tearful sessions of 'struggle' or, at least, self-criticism in the Ministry's Party Committee.

She was replaced by Daasha, a woman of character, integrity and humour, strong, honest, courageous, animated by decency and probably by religious faith. Her husband worked for the State Railways. She herself, if only from the evidence of employment in our house, was probably a Party member. But, like most Mongols, and like all Mongol women, she did not attempt politically to convert or proselytize. Doubtless she reported on our attitudes to her superiors at prescribed intervals, but her behaviour was that of a friend, and a watchful, generous friend. The later death of her young daughter broke our hearts as well as hers.

She and Tsirendidget, the number two maid, wore at dinner parties the blue, gold or red deel, Mongolian national dress modelled on the Manchu robe, fastened high at the neck with a toggle and falling to below the knee. Both became adept at serving at table, although Daasha tended to talk to the guests, chivvy slow eaters and perform dangerous feats of stacking. She was intrigued by England, but had comprehended very little, some of her comments seeming to refer to Dickensian London, some to another planet altogether. But, for her as for most of her compatriots, England was, other than an occasional French presence, the only window available to a world different from the collectivist universe of the Soviet Bloc.

The last member of our household was an enormous Russian tabby, who frequently refused to eat unless personally serenaded. The animal was also of uncertain temper, although my wife, when I commented on this, asked only, 'Wouldn't *you* be bad-tempered if you'd been castrated and everyone called you Lulu?' The operation was performed by an Hungarian doctor in the kitchen on telephoned instructions from the Medical Officer at the British Embassy in Moscow.

III

FIRST IMPRESSIONS

THREE DAYS AFTER OUR ARRIVAL I presented my credentials to President Sambuu at the Government Palace (incorporating the Praesidium, Central Committee etc., as well as the offices of the Prime Minister and President) on Sukh' Bator Square. The ceremony was faultless, preceded by my inspection, accompanied by the Chef de Protocol, of a company of magnificent Mongol troops in white uniforms, who roared a greeting. I did not then speak Mongol, but recited by heart the traditional reply. In my speech later, I compared our two nations — not easy between an island and a completely land-locked country — as 'peoples with a great past and a great future'. The reference to the two last Empires did not escape the Mongols, incessantly nagged by the Russians to abjure Genghis Khan. Toasts were then consumed, poured personally by the President, from a half-empty bottle.

The 'Palace' was monumental in scale. In front of it a smaller edifice contained the embalmed corpses of Sukh' Bator and Marshal Choibalsan, the Founders of the Republic, precisely as Red Square in Moscow contains that of Lenin. The leadership also stood on the roof to take the salute during parades. The Square itself was very large indeed. Improbably, and although its southern end looked upon mountains and not upon architecture, it carried faint suggestions of the Grand' Place at Brussels, even the Piazza San Marco. In its south-east corner, beyond hoardings bearing the likeness of Party leaders, lay the little ochre Opera House. Half a mile away, in front of the Academy of Sciences, stood the last statue of Stalin in the Communist bloc, tastefully airbrushed out in postcards of the site. In front of the Ulan Bator Hotel, Lenin gazed furiously toward China.

Next day the Foreign Minister entertained me to luncheon in a private room at the Ulan Bator Hotel. This took a form to which, in varying quality, we became accustomed in the years which followed, of mutton soup, cold mutton and the national dish (boodz) of suet dumplings richly stuffed with mutton, onions and mutton gravy. It was consumed by biting a small hole in the casing and, as it were, vacuuming out the contents. (It, and its sibling, hushoor, the mutton pancake, were extremely good, much better than the Chinese equivalents.) Three obligatory glasses of Mongolian grain vodka (arkhi) − so pure that over-indulgence, which later became habitual, never carried after-effects − were downed before proceeding to non-mandatory or voluntary libations.

Thereafter I took one of the Landrovers to the north-east of the city, for the first time over the rough steppe tracks through the hills to the bridge over the River Tuul, where we were subsequently to fish in the long summer days and, even, on occasion to pitch our tents. It was a day, like so many days in Mongolia, of unclouded happiness.

The Mongolian National Holiday, Naadam, is celebrated in mid-July. In 1971, for the first time in many years, a considerable military parade took place before the reviewing stands in Sukh' Bator Square containing the leadership and the Diplomatic Corps. The parade feat-ured a march-past, with troops, armour and artillery, then a fly-past by MIG 19s and 21s, followed by floats invoking industrial, agricul-tural and historical themes, excluding any exhibits that might have glorified the Mongol Empire of the 12th, 13th and 14th Centuries, ana-thema to Russia. (It was not, despite the Mongol Yuan dynasty embodied by Kublai Khan, anathema to China. 'The Mongol Empire,' observed my Chinese colleague, 'was a positive development, since it served the purpose of carrying Chinese culture to the West.') Except for civil manifestations, this parade was not repeated during my sojourn in Mongolia. On this occasion, unimpeded − I was lacking a Military Attaché − in photographing the equipment on view, which, I suppose, some department in London may have eventually found rewarding, I was encouraged by the example at least of my French and Jugoslav coll-eagues.

The Frenchman, Georges Perruche, had been a prisoner of war of the Germans. After the War, and after service in Paris and Saigon, he was posted to South Korea and captured in Seoul when the North Koreans invaded, remaining in captivity until 1953. Among his fellow prisoners at that time was George Blake, the British diplomat later convicted of espionage for the Soviets, who was then rescued from his English prison in an apparently daring coup and evacuated to the U.S.S.R. Georges, who had much admired Blake's courage and spirit in the appalling conditions of the North Korean camps, was reluctant to believe that the latter had turned his coat, preferring to think that the entire episode was a long-term operation on the part of British Intelligence. Nor was he convinced by arguments that Blake's 'bravery' in North Korea was exactly the result of his own knowledge that the Koreans and their Russian masters would not take terminal measures against him.

Because of these long periods of incarceration, Georges Perruche had made his appointment to and service in Ulan Bator conditional on non-residence there. He accordingly lived for nine months in Paris and on the Loire, visiting Mongolia only three times a year, accompanied by his wife Rachel and a small staff seconded from the French Embassy at Peking. When informed of this, it was alleged that Her Majesty the Queen, remembering the Mongolian reputation for horsemanship, remarked, 'I would love a job like that'. The sad fact was, however, that after the Shah's cousin had injured himself by falling off a Mongol pony, no foreigners were permitted even so much as to mount a horse, other than for photographic display.

Apart from one unseemly altercation over the distribution of vegetables and Tsing Tao beer carried by our couriers, Georges became a close friend, exemplary colleague and regular attendant at our table. When he left, eventually to become Ambassador to Afghanistan, I gave a small luncheon for him at which, in his farewell speech, he was good enough to praise our hospitality, my wife's cuisine, and 'the French wine habitually served'. With temerity, I interrupted him: 'But Georges, for the last three years, because good French wine doesn't travel, you have drunk nothing but Rioja.'

'Ah,' he replied, without checking his stride, 'I have always preferred *quantity* to quality.'

When I asked Rachel how he employed his time in Paris during that part of the year when he was not in Mongolia, she replied: '*Il lit Paul Valéry; il téléphonne*'. His death in 1982 has been the cause to us of lasting grief and sadness; he was a good, strong, civilized man.

Vladimir Milovanovic, the Jugoslav Ambassador, and his wife, had both been Partisans. We conducted political discussion in French, but that occupied less of our energies than hunting partridges in his Gazik (Jeep). The conduct of these expeditions would not have pleased British sportsmen. We shot the foolish birds on the ground, lowering the windscreen and blasting them with double-barrelled twelve-bore shotguns as they pecked at their exiguous nourishment. (One observer said that the Jeep, during these operations, looked like a mobile gun-turret.)

Milovanovic, indeed, once called out to me: 'Don't shoot. It's flying!' When I remonstrated with him, he replied: 'You think all this is deplorable. But neither of us is a first-class shot. If we shot them on the wing, we'd wound them, not kill them.'

Milovanovic was a Serb, and Serbs are determined, not to say obstinate, people. I was therefore unwise, in mid-winter, to counsel him against setting the Gazik up an almost vertical slope, the peak of which he believed to hold partridge. He immediately put the car in gear and by the time we reached the summit it had broken down irreparably. The Ambassador's only method of repair was to warm the carburettor with the flame of a petrol cigarette-lighter. The temperature was -35°C. It was getting dark. The nearest village, from which we were separated by a river, was ten kilometres away. But unless we were to dance together all night, or sleep in one another's arms, even fur-coats and hats and five woollen layers below the coats, would not prevent us, if we stayed by the car, from freezing to death before morning. We set off down the hill. The faster stretches of the river, despite the terrible cold, were still flowing. We moved downstream until we found the stream frozen over. We could not, however, gauge the thickness of the ice nor the weight it would bear. If it broke, we should die quite soon. We looked at each other and stepped out, laden with guns and game, hand — incomprehensibly — in hand, across the ten-yard section, and reached the other side.

'That wasn't too difficult,' said Milovanovic. As he spoke, the ice broke up behind us.

We walked up the valley, all vehicles resolutely ignoring our signals. In the village Post Office, lit by guttering candles, an aged crone refused to allow us to use the telephone until Milovanovic distracted her with a bottle of Jugoslav brandy. I was then able to get through to the British Embassy and a Landrover arrived an hour later. The experience gave a firm foundation for friendship.

The alleged possibility of a Soviet invasion of Western Europe through Jugoslav territory was contemplated during these years, though Tito and the authorities in Belgrade had made it publicly plain that any such move would be resisted to the death by the Jugoslav Army and people. Milovanovic, at that time, invited the Diplomatic Corps to a movie in the appalling Lenin 'Club'. The film demonstrated Jugoslav para-military resistance to an invasion in circumstances which, although a conclusion could be drawn, were not explicitly those of the last war, the enemy not explicitly German – a shadowy ambiguous war. The action was bloody, frightening and brutal.

Mr Shchetinin, the Soviet Ambassador, was seated on Milovanovic's right. He looked shaken. During the interval, he turned to him.

'Was this film made just after the war?'

'No.'

'When was it made?'

'Early this year,' said Milovanovic.

The Russian smiled grimly.

Mr Shchetinin, although afflicted with an odiously common wife, was large in both stature and presence. He had earlier been an unusually popular Soviet First Party Secretary in the Ukraine. Except during an icy period after the expulsion of the Russian spies from the U.K., he was kind to our Mission and accessible to myself. (Sir John Killick, my colleague at Moscow, was denied all access to the Soviet authorities after the expulsions, reduced to addressing them through the listening devices in the Embassy walls. All the Mongols did, for their part, was to demand my wife's driving licence and order me to bring my car in for 'inspection'. We rejected both requests, and nothing more was said or done. Nor did I fail, then or ever, to secure appointments with officials or Ministers). He seemed to like us, the first English family with whom he had had acquaintance, although categorizing official Anglo/Soviet relations as 'unreliable', outlining them in a parabolic gesture of his vast hand. His general mode of discussion was to shout, a method initially intimidating but greatly modified, if not reversed, when confronted by adequate decibels or even reasoned opposition. At all events, he was a great improvement on his predecessor, Vyacheslav Molotov, nor was he remotely matched by Mr Smirnov, his grey successor. But the major charge against the Russian colonists is the contempt that most of them displayed for Mongol culture, and the spiritual and psychological distortion this wrought on the Mongol ethos.

The East German Ambassador, on the other hand, a former Luftwaffe officer stationed in Brest after the conquest of France, was uniquely disagreeable, patronising, aggressive and insecure. After a particularly offensive conversation, however, when he presented me with a cigar recently given him by the Cuban Ambassador, I was able to point out that the container was empty. 'Is this the way that Comecon relations are conducted?' I enquired, to the pleasure of the Prussian's East European colleagues.

Naadam, meanwhile, beginning with the parade, continued with archery contests and with Mongol wrestling between fighters representing eagles, but somewhat resembling Sumo wrestlers in Japan. The bouts themselves were slow, almost dreamlike, the contestants seeming to concentrate their efforts on one another's underpants as much as on their bodies. Each fight, and twenty or thirty went on simultaneously in the Stadium, ended with its curious birdlike dance by the enormous victor. Elsewhere archery competitions took place, preceded by chanting: the competitors were elderly men, suggesting an analogy with bowls at Brighton or Bournemouth.

The Games concluded with a fifteen-mile race across the steppe by ponies ridden by child jockeys, at the finish as dazed and exhausted as their mounts. As each child finished, its father and mother, also on horseback, raced forward to seize the reins, take their charge and rub the horse down with a piece of wood. For a second, all mounted, all confident and each an individual, the great past of the Mongols was plain in view.

In the evening light, we drove home through the thick sweet scent of wormwood crushed beneath the wheels of the car.

IV

LIFE IN THE CAPITAL

THERE WAS FOR US a great deal of 'home life', especially family life, in Mongolia, and because of our relative isolation and the absence of 'things to do' that particular life was extremely concentrated. Matters diluted in the vast societies of the West became here of prime importance and their savour sharpened. Christmas and Easter with such ceremonies as we could arrange; the temples and palaces of old Urga (Ulan Bator); the extraordinary weather, moving from temperatures (during 300 days a year of blue sky) between +30° to -50°; dust storms 100ft at the base and 150ft high; hail punishing the skin and denting metal; cold so intense that it froze every part of a car in minutes; our children and their progress; food and drink; central Asian culture; travel; 'picnics' on Steppe and hillside.

The Gandan Monastery, gongs, bells and horns ferocious among the hum of Lamaist chant inspired my small son's power of mimicry, while in his Communist kindergarten he had to be restrained from offering 'Gentle Jesus, meek and mild/look upon a little child' as a contribution to political verse. Despite our apprehensions Lenin was never more than 'the man outside the hotel' to his sister, but her Russian was beautiful and she made a pretty snowflake on Parents' Day. Both loved the services, the food, the customs of the religious feasts, not least the presents. I suppose it was the shortage of consumer goods that enabled Joanna to stand contentedly for most of Christmas Day, in the middle of the drawing-room, wearing a new beret with all her hair tucked into it, a poncho *round her waist*, feeding a doll in a home-made cot from a doll's tea-set. It was certainly what caused the beatific trance in which David regarded his train and aeroplane. But children whose favourite birthday dish is spaghetti with tomato sauce garnished with green olives and pickles are not over-indulged.

Not one moment of that happiness could have been achieved without my wife. Already a good cook, she became a paragon, both at home and on the steppe over dung and wood fires. Necessity and privation were her goads, whether in the acquisition of mushrooms, rhubarb, clotted cream, bananas (from East European commissaries) or in the organization of such large functions as the Queen's Birthday Party. In any other country, all the Ambassador's wife has to do on such large occasions is to hire temporary maids, an extra cook and telephone the florist, as opposed to climbing a mountain to pick the flowers.

In no other country, indeed, were cook and Ambassadress synonymous, nor does it seem likely that either functionary elsewhere would, for example, have to grind up granulated as opposed to icing sugar on her family's birthday cakes. Nor, come to think of it, are there many countries so cold that the champagne bottles explode in the larder overnight before the Queen's birthday: wine in club shape is unusual. It is similarly improbable that Lady Cromer at Washington would have helped out her French opposite number by bringing bags of ice to the latter's reception.

Restaurants were not thick on the ground. We only went to one in Ulan Bator, shaped, of course, like a ger. It was not everyone's cup of salt-and-fat-enriched Tibetan tea, although, on my wife's birthday, she claimed that it was hers. One began with various cheeses, the best being sheep's cream: if that article had had a French name, it would be fashionable in Western Europe. Soup followed, then boodz, then wild wheat mixed with cheese, cream and sugar. (At Russian receptions, however, cream cakes, buns, caviar, blinis, salami and cheese were served. It was unfortunate that their pastry included large quantities of sugar.)

In our house ingenuity was such that, when the appropriate machine was unavailable, the best sausages in the world were made with the aid of a funnel and one chopstick. (I do not know what was served at National Women's Day receptions, where the Russian hostess would shout 'Eat up! Today you are free' and later advocate the collection of rubbish to and by her audience.)

At Christmas we made do with slightly undernourished turkeys from China, but enjoyed homemade Christmas puddings of immense age and consequent richness. Fir branches were dispersed behind the pictures; apples, tangerines, nuts and fircones, sprayed silver and gold, formed the centre-piece of the table. The British population in Mongolia lunched here, all eleven of us. On Boxing Day, the dining-room was dominated by a boar's head, the ears of which, earlier removed by our Mongol suppliers, were constructions of polyfilla. At New Year we had haggis, goose and black bun. Snap Dragon was played at midnight.

There was much to see in Ulan Bator: the opera, the Gandan and Maidar monasteries, Art Museum, the great Prayer Wheels, the Summer Palace with the royal coach, the 'Religious Museum', actually a series of Yellow Faith Lamaist temples with minatory or pornographic painting. In the minatory category, sinners were portrayed hanging upside down with their organs detached, besieged by hideous figures of masked menace. In the porno sections, the guide would inform the visitor: 'This God is copulating with his wife,' or 'Sexual intercourse is taking place,' or 'Fornication is performed.'

The Library of the Academy of Science contained most of the surviving Yellow Faith scrolls and documents in Mongol, Sanskrit and Tibetan. Some were breathtaking, the script of gold and brass on silver pages. Inks were mixed from ground pearls, turquoise, coral, silver and gold, forming, for example, moulded Buddha figures on the 'front pages'.

The circus was sometimes in town, notable for the repellent turns of its contortionists, plus less sinuous camels, foxes, wolves, badgers, horses and performing yak. A blazing row broke out at one performance between two Mongols in the 'Royal' box, where my family was also situated, alas broken up by the authorities. One part of the safety net broke during the trapeze act. No damage was done, but a large clamp fell within inches of a spectator. A pole thrown by an artist was missed by the attendant and landed in the audience. Finally, the safety net got completely out of hand and enveloped a quarter of the spectators. The Mongols enjoyed all this immensely and would probably have been disappointed had things gone smoothly. Most of them were doubled up with laughter.

But most of our entertainment was outside the capital, shooting, fishing, inspecting wild life, collecting fruit and vegetables. My family also rediscovered the Mongolian Bush Cricket or Gollio, about three inches long, of fairly horrid appearance, nevertheless of great interest to the National History Museum in the Cromwell Road where our specimens have been bred on, if not yet given our name.

It was in the country, whether on day trips or in our own tents, that we saw the real life of Mongolia, learned about its rural domestic economy, heard the indicators of dissidents for whom Mongol culture was still alive and, from the interior of gers, glimpsed the evidence of religious and traditional survival, my wife more frequently than myself.

Such interest was, of course, looked down upon by our Socialist colleagues, possibly as a pit from which they had only just emerged. We seemed to be viewed by them as unsophisticated, bucolic, possibly mad, their comportment on a 'diplomatic' hunting trip to Hentiy illustrating these attitudes.

We left on this jaunt in October, 1971, in bitter weather, my wife the only woman in the party. After driving eastward for several hours, with extensive stops as more and more East European diplomats got lost, we arrived at our camp. There the British contingent were supplied with rather a grand tent, in which we leisurely unpacked before a good lunch and large quantities to drink. No sooner, thereafter, had we started to fish than it began to snow. We returned to the tent and slept in six layers of wool and one or two of sable and musquash until dinner, when it was pitch dark and snowing even harder.

We dined around a huge bonfire, eating excellent spiced steak in a blizzard. The snow melted from our hot faces while piling up around our frozen backsides, a remarkable spectacle. The Russians cooked their fish inside a wood-lined box held over the fire on a tripod, the result delicious, not smoked, but 'smokey' char. A sing-song took place, the British contribution predictably coarse.

In the morning woodcock and antelope were engaged until the Landrover, much heavier than the little Russian jeeps, sank ineluctably into a bog. Six very strong Russians, two jeeps and any number of trees were required to prise it out. The moment had been an alarming one, soluble, it seemed at one point, only by a crane from Ulan Bator a hundred and fifty miles away.

Hundreds of duck and geese seen on the homeward journey in the middle of a lake flew obstinately out of range. The Rumanian Ambassador pettishly loosed off at a magpie. Other animals included wild cat and a Griffon vulture, still and gigantic.

Under such crisp, clear blue skies, the four of us passed the best part of our Mongolian years.

V

THE OPEN ROAD

AFTER COMPLETING MY CALLS ON COLLEAGUES and on
Mongol officials in the glorious summer of 1971, we lost no time in
getting out of the city and into the provinces. For our first tour we settled upon Ovor-Hangay Province (Aimag).

My wife and I left Ulan Bator in a propellor-driven Iluyshin 14 of
Mongolair on 23 August, landing on the grass strip at Hujirt, the somon
centre or county town, an hour later. The flight, apart from the lamen-
table condition of the aircraft in those far-off days — broken lavatory
doors, indeed an entry door which did not shut — was unremarkable,
although interesting in its glimpses of the expansion of both vegetable
and grain cultivation into the steppe. (It was my wife's conviction that
passengers were permitted to stand as in London buses and *enjoined* to
smoke during take-off and landing.) 'Agriculture', on an intensive and
systematic scale at least, was really only initiated in 1957.

We were met at Hujirt by Batsuur, the young official in charge of the
U.K. desk at the Ministry of Foreign Affairs, who had driven up, in
great discomfort, in one of the Embassy's Landrovers, with Tsevgee,
the Secretary of the Executive Committee of the Great People's Hural,
and by Avirmid, the Director of the Sanatorium at Hujirt, who drove
us to the hotel attached to the Sanatorium. Batsuur was a keen student
of nature, constantly trousering animal droppings. He also told us that,
since Mongols owed their keen eyesight to the far horizons, he never
did more than thirty minutes consecutive work in the Ministry.

Hujirt, consisting of the Clinic, a cooperative, and, separated there-
from, a straggling village, lies in pasture at about fifteen hundred
metres, and enclosed radio-active springs of alleged value in rheumatic,
neurological, venereal and gynaecological disorders. Mr Avirmid told
us that his establishment contained four hundred beds for remedial and

post-operative purposes. 'Stomach, bones and migraines' were his chief concerns. We were not invited to visit the dormitories, but enjoyed hot mineral baths, in compensation for the absence of plugs, functioning waste pipes, or warm water in the hotel. My Indian colleague later stayed too long in one of these baths and thereafter refused to travel outside Ulan Bator.

The Director invited us, with Messrs Batsuur, Tsevgee and the latter's pretty 'sister', to dine that evening in the decorated, luxurious ger in the grounds of the Sanatorium. In this untypical yurt, (described by our hosts as 'normal for the Feudals'), Mr Avirmid devoted himself increasingly to the consumption of spirits and to praise of the British, in particular of Sir Terence Garvey who had taught him to fish, and otherwise earned his respect when Ambassador to the Soviet Union and accredited to Mongolia. He claimed that Garvey had caught a 300 lb member of the Salmonidae family on heavy ironmongery. (Sir Terence subsequently denied the compliment.) The Director's toasts and monologues were unremittingly disapproved by his wife, a living example of the bossiness of Central Asian ladies. He was unable to accompany us the next day to various springs or to the Orhon Falls, so that the planned Anglo/Mongolian fishing competition did not take place. Mr Tsevgee told me later, 'as a secret', that the Director had been too drunk to get up. When, however, we gave his wife a presentation box of Wedgwood biscuits, she said that he had had a sore throat. We did not, for whatever reason, see this genial fellow again.

The country between Hujirt and the Falls provides thinnish pasture because of its volcanic nature and the black rocks which litter the steppe, with a preponderance of horses, yaks and marmot, the horse being the emblem of the aimag. It also contains a quantity of kereksurs, Turkic burial circles. Below the Falls, East German tourists were swimming in their underwear but, further downstream, grayling and char were abundantly accessible to spinners, if seldom to fly. In the evening Mr Tsevgee, in a speech which referred to the British as 'the best foreigners' he had ever met, excused himself from accompanying us to Kharkorin (Karakoram). He was clearly unwell, and we presented him with a bottle of Teacher's whisky, enjoining him to take it freely, with or without Mongolian honey, for his cough. This official was also the country's champion fox hunter, with a gun, not horse and hound.

Next day we drove through hilly pasture, in which we observed two large flocks of cranes, to Kharkorin, once the imperial city of Ogodei Khan, now a somon centre and state farm lying in a great plain encircled by mountains. The ancient capital, of which little remains, covered sixty-four square kilometres. The town now contains a small agricultural/industrial complex, yurts, shacks and central modern buildings, some columned and referred to as 'Palaces' (Sport, Culture etc.). Mongol ponies, with good silver work on their saddles, were tethered in front of the store. Bleating goats roamed the square. Mongol horsemen, in deels and trilby hats, went bow-legged about their business. Kharkorin managed to resemble both the Middle West and a backward village of the Austro-Hungarian Empire.

The Chairman of the state farm, a former Mongol Air Force pilot aged 53, told us that the farm had 75,000 acres down to wheat and barley and about 10,000 to fodder. The grain was badly studded with weeds. Large numbers of tractors and combine-harvesters were observed, as was solid storage for grain and fodder. The farm was irrigated by a system of canals, constructed by the Chinese, but then in poor repair. The population of the combined somon and state farm, administratively more or less co-equal, was said to be 8,000, of whom 1,500 were employed in agriculture, as opposed to animal husbandry. The herd — horses, sheep, cattle, goats and camels — numbered 80,000.

In the course of a tour of the state farm's power stations, flour mill, fodder factory and bone meal factory, I learned that the official statistics showed a total for Mongolia of thirty-two state farms, as opposed to nearly three hundred cooperative farms. Kharkorin, because of its site at ancient Karakoram, may be rather more a show place than most.

The flour mill, equipped with aggregates of Hungarian manufacture, was said to produce fifty tons of flour daily in two qualities at sharply varying prices from a work force of 230 in four shifts. Elsewhere we were told that fodder and bonemeal, exported to the U.K., were produced by other local factories. The coal-driven electricity generating station contained three small turbines manufactured by Hick Hargreaves & Co, Bolton, England, with other equipment provided by Hopkinson of Huddersfield, a rum sight in these surroundings.

Our progress was enlivened by the unexpected and, to our Mongol hosts, unwelcome appearance in the coal-fired generating station of a gregarious Pole. This veteran, wiping his hands on an oily rag, told me that he had served in England under General Anders. He retained warm memories of our country. The British equipment in the station had, he said, originally been supplied by UNRRA to Poland whence it had been transported to Mongolia. I should have liked to prolong the reminiscences of this travelled technician.

On the surrounding hills stands one of the four granite tortoises which allegedly bore the columns marking the Imperial guard posts. Below, enclosed by railings, rests a phallic sculpture then exploited by our hosts to illustrate the delinquency of the Lamas of Erden Tzu.

The lamasery of Erden Tzu (1586), now a museum, lies at the western edge of the state farm, behind low white walls crowned by 108 stupas and pierced by four gate-houses. The square contains six or seven Tibetan Buddhist temples richly painted, wide-eaved and with sloping tiled roofs, together with one major white and gold stupa. Massive granite statuary unearthed from the Imperial city itself lay about the uncut grass of the yard. The guest house was in course of over-vivid restoration and the temples themselves, now well maintained, were filled with incunabula of the 16th and 17th centuries, images, silk hangings, masks, as well as innumerable brass and even gold statuettes of the Lord Buddha and of the jovial lamas. Batsuur behaved with nervous spite towards these relics, as towards the frequent indications in Mongolia, including cairns and prayer flags, of the survival of either Buddhist or Shaman faith.

After a night in the guest house at Kharkorin, and, for a change, some brick-hard beef in honour of British guests, the return journey to Ulan Bator of over 230 miles, on steppe track much damaged by rain, took eleven hours. We observed en route a fairish acreage of light standing wheat and evidence of a reasonable hay harvest, the latter a main subject of the Sixteenth Congress and to which incessant Press reference was made. (We also noted, throughout Ovor-Hangay, and in Töv aimag, new wooden winter shelters for animals, another priority of the Fifth Year Plan.) But in the unsprung Landrover this was a battering journey and, for once, the long valleys and the endless mountain ranges were a prison, not a liberation, Ulan Bator, our own beds and flush lavatories an impossible dream.

★　★　★

Darhan, the industrial complex some 125 miles due north of Ulan Bator, is connected by rail to Ulan Bator, and by a metalled road which I used for my journey in early September. The first hundred kilometres from Ulan Bator consist simply of unlevelled steppe track over which tarmac had been spread, but the remainder, under the constant attention of Soviet troops with a large range of grading equipment, assisted by the Mongol Army, most of whose members slept soundly by the side of the road, was a very fair stretch of road. It was, however, little used for goods transport on this occasion, and my driver, Major Damdinsuren, preferred to use the steppe track.

The country, up to approximately sixty miles from Ulan Bator, was pasture. From there until Darhan lay vast state farms of unfenced hay and grain, wheat, millet and barley, most of which had been harvested by combine. (The Mongol Army, and the junior staff of all ministries, took part in this process.) Of animals, during the last seventy miles, only one large flock of sheep was seen.

Darhan city, lower than Ulan Bator, was in three equally hideous parts. The southernmost section, to the east of the road, contained the main industrial complex. North of that lay the site of the new residential area, and north again, 'old' Darhan with the Administration and two major factories, on a plan of Soviet design.

Mr Suren, Mayor of Darhan and Chairman of the Executive Committee of the Great People's Hural, said that it had been decided to build at this site in 1961 because of its position as a railhead, and because of the richness of local mineral and agricultural resources. Underground water, waste, telephone and telegraph communications were already installed for the population of 30,000, targetted at 80,000 for 1980.

As we had run out of whisky, I presented Suren with a 40 oz bottle of gin from which, pleading local custom, he obliged us to drink before pouring for himself. Gin, one was reminded, needs angostura or tonic to be palatable.

The mines at Shariyngol, forty miles distant, produced the coal to power the Darhan complex. Industry now consisted of a Soviet-built electricity generating plant and high power distributor/transformer, a Czech cement works, Polish brickworks, Bulgarian sheep skin factory, Soviet grain silo and fodder factory, food (milk, bread, juice, sweets) factory, building materials factory, and a Hungarian meat factory. All these concerns were large and the property of the state. Other, smaller concerns, such as motor repair shops, were responsible to Darhan city.

Mr Suren, in welcoming me to Darhan, attached to me a 'referent' and gave instructions that I was to be shown any installation I wished to visit. In the event, I inspected all factories with the exception of those for building materials and for meat. In general, no attempt was made (except in the cement factory, and, perhaps, the electricity generating plant), to conceal the presence of Soviet and East European advisors who, indeed, on two occasions formed part of the briefing team. With one exception, I was politely, even enthusiastically, received. There was no means of checking the reliability of the statistics given, but I could remark the humour and apparent goodwill towards the U.K. of most Mongol officials in the province. While, no doubt, these did not act without instructions, they made their duty a pleasure for the visitor, particularly at their rough and ready entertainments, for which both teeth and digestion needed a sharp edge.

No work, for whatever reason, was in progress when I toured the food factory. A new batch of bread tasted strong but good, and the lemonade transported me to a Hampshire village shop and its ½d sherbet in the nineteen-twenties. In the grain silo a smiling Soviet official accompanied the Mongol guide. In the cement factory, the Mongol manager, pointing to an embarrassed compatriot said to be 'in sole charge' of the controls, alleged that all Czech technicians had left; three of them immediately walked into the shop. We averted our eyes. At the Polish brick factory the finished product was being loaded into Soviet lorries, with Soviet drivers, but I observed here only one European technician, a manual worker in the shop preparatory to 'firing'. The leather factory, built with Bulgarian aid, was to have a capacity of 700,000 sheep skins per annum. Curing and tanning would be carried out in one shop, and manufacture in another. The shoe factory was to open in mid-September. In the meanwhile, the only shop I was shown contained two Bulgarians and some Mongol girls stitching wool with sewing machines on to the hems of sheepskin coats. The product, (coats, linings, gloves, slippers, hats), was rather inferior, although not disastrous.

The departure, post-perestroika, of the Soviets and East Europeans from these and other installations will have lifted a burden from Mongol hearts.

The chief engineer of the electricity generating station was uncommunicative and disobliging, the only official during our visit so to comport himself. Dressed in a ginger brown suit of superior quality and an open-necked Hawaiian shirt, he was a personage of Bengali appearance, for whose conduct my Mongol escorts apologized. I replied that it did not matter in the least; the engineer, no doubt, suffered from toothache or from a difficult wife.

The Ministry of Foreign Affairs, on this occasion, provided an interpreter, Mr Avgandamin, in his New Delhi silk suit the very model of chic, whose English did not bear the weight of technical information provided. Idle, *dépaysé*, charming, this young man was not untypical of the younger generation of Mongol officials, from this Ministry at least; the phrase 'honorary attaché' occurred continually when trying to establish a parallel.

★ ★ ★

What the Mongols mean by '*Gobi*' is flat land with little water or vegetation; they do not only mean a desert, although desert forms one fifth of the South Gobi. There are four Gobi provinces, of which I first selected for travel the Southern or Omnogovi aimag, arriving at Dalandzadgad on 21 October. Events in Ulan Bator had delayed our journey and frustrated travel by Landrover; snow storms in the north and dust storms in the south delayed us further. The flight, over a snow-covered land, was made in an AN-24 with two Soviet officers and a fine mob of romantically attired Mongols.

Dalandzadgad, encircled by the bare eastern extremities of the Altai, was a typical aimag capital of white stone buildings with green roofs, gers and brick blocks of Soviet construction It had, new and in the middle of the pale steppe, an impermanent air. Its population of 7,000 was served by a bakery, meat combine, printing press, fodder storage, power station, 80-bed hospital, and 'artdels', or small enterprises, producing boots, horn objects, etc. It also boasted a lavish 10-year school presented by the U.S.S.R., providing a microscope, rheostat, sewing machine and carpentry kit for *each* pupil, together with excellent classrooms, dormitories and gymnasium. Classes were said to include physics, biology, chemistry, wood and metal working, domestic science and the Russian and Mongol languages.

The Omnogovi aimag was divided into eighteen somons or counties − averaging 1,000 inhabitants each. It administered a herd of 900,000 head, including Bactrian (two-humped) camels, yak, sheep, goats and horses. (Seventy-five animals might be owned privately by each family.) The aimag contained open-cast coal consumed locally, salt, wolfram and gold not exploited, or so we were told, because of labour shortage. Dalandzadgad means 'Seventy Dry Rivers': the aimag was desperately short of water and is dependent on wells. At two stone artesian wells, water had been found at four to five feet, a uniquely high level for the province. Distance and contours were said to have ruled out the construction of a canal system from the rivers of Arkhangay aimag.

After a tour of the town and an address by the Chairman of the Executive Committee, we then left for Hurmen somon and cooperative, thirty miles to the south-west. The road lay over flat, gravelly steppe with the Nomgon Uul (Nomgon Mountains) far away on our left and the Gurvan Sayhan Uul to the right. Scrub, tundra, thorn, steppe — wild wheat and grasses provided vegetation, albeit dormant at this season. The horizons on this stretch resembled most nearly the Western District of Victoria, the Altai Mountains an imposing substitute for the Grampians. No landscape could have differed more from the folded green hills of north and central Mongolia.

Hurmen somon comprised 300 families, and 50,000 head, with a school, hospital and doctor, shop, Culture 'Club', library, store house for skins, veterinarian, the offices of Party Executive Committee and Council of Cooperatives. The few main buildings were single-storey, white stone with blue windows, but some hundred gers composed the somon centre which also ran to a 'hotel', where we spent a night of simple rigour, with outside trench-sanitation and a wash-basin in the dining-room.

We were received by the Party Secretary and the Chairman of the Executive Committee, and, together with Batsuur, entertained in our tiny bedroom to bowls of airag (kumiss or mare's milk), curds and other delicacies of camel's milk. Luncheon was similar to most meals of Mongol provenance, cold, elderly mutton and pickled carrot, fat mutton soup, and boodz, a diet in Hurmen exceeded in monotony by unpalatability.

Although these repasts were relieved by the excellence of Mongol vodka and the generosity and joviality of our hosts, their prospect sometimes cast a shadow over otherwise happy days in Mongolia.

Under a hot sun, we then drove south towards the Altai and the desert over good, open steppe track. (We saw no vehicles except a Blue Cross motor-bicycle and a Red Cross van in over three hundred kilometres.) Mountains hung in the sky over a mirage and the golden steppe revealed the great, red Bactrian, treading in file on either hand. These noble beasts, on thin but nutritious Gobi diet, were in sharp contrast to their dejected kin on the richer pastures to the north. The Gobi camel were, we were told, fatter, and their milk richer. They are sheared in spring and slaughtered in November, their meat is eaten, their hair exported, they consume 60-70 litres of water in five days, their cartilages make key rings and their milk, boiled, is used to cure the hepatitis which, unboiled, it probably causes.

We stopped to inspect wells, stone sheep shelters and, later, to ingest further camel milk products, sing songs and ride camels at a felt-ger occupied by four adults, five children and two (single) beds. At this point, amongst the Altai spurs, a red plant faintly similar to heather, a green 'cactus' permanently wet and the Gobi tree began to make their appearance. In the southern distance the plains resembled the seabed from which, in the Ice Age, they had been formed. Small herds of camel moved in this desolate region. Moving south-west against the setting sun, the jeep put up, and furiously chased, herds of black-tailed antelope and the rare wild ass, with its strange long neck and oblong head. We sighted no wild camel, their skinny legs and pyramidal humps seen by us only in the local museum.

At last, some eighty miles from Hurmen, on top of a dune, we looked down upon the sand and gravel waste of the desert itself, studded with the brittle, tortured Gobi tree, the bed of the aridised ocean running to the horizon and the frontiers of China. Our hosts, asserting the impossibility of wheeled travel in the desert, would go no further.

We returned next morning from Hurmen to Dalandzagdad after tea and bread, both with mutton fat, not good. The temperature was -10°C, the sky cloudless, but a fierce wind precluded search for arghal (*ovis ammon*) and ibex in the Gurvan Saykhan Uul. (We penetrated these mountains next day, however, sighting up to fifty head of ibex and six arghal at heights between 5,000 and 7,500 feet, as well as seeing the spoor of wolf. Wild strawberry and gooseberry plant, incense pine and herbal 'dog's mouth' were observed.) I think that we must, that evening, have become the first English to witness a Soviet movie in the Gobi about Soviet repression of the Kazakh revolt, imperialist in character. The wily Bazmachi were, however, deprecated and Russian suffering commiserated by the Mongol audience.

At a dinner on the evening of our departure, the Chairman of the Executive Committee told me that his principal concern was for the improvement, through wells, shelters and local cross-breeding, of the quality of the herd, in particular the goat and sheep clip. Labour, shortage of capital and the absence of a railway impeded the industrial development he most desired, that of coal (he claimed the largest supply in the country), semi-precious stones and other minerals. He hoped that the despatch to the countryside from the towns of 50,000 youths throughout Mongolia would help. Stable progress must, however, await the straightening of the population bulge. We bought a whole Gobi sheep and took it back to Ulan Bator in the aeroplane.

Travel for us, in this ancient, beautiful and slowly developing country, was absorbing, and little spoiled by the minor frustrations described. Causes for frustration, at that time, lay in the waste endemic in the system, in Mongolia's geo-political position, in policies dependent on forces outside her control and in her inability at that time to turn to the lively enterprise of the West.

VI

MONGOLIA IN HISTORY

AS TO MONGOLIA'S HISTORY, there is nothing to surpass Charles Bawden's magisterial *Modern History of Mongolia* and every reason to repeat the opening pages, here reprinted with his kind permission:

'The Mongols are one of the great peoples in the history of High Asia. Their name has been familiar over the whole of the old world for close on eight hundred years. Yet at the most generous estimate it would be anachronistic to speak of a Mongol state, in the modern sense of the word, as existing before the end of 1911. The imperial adventure under Genghis Khan and his successors left the Mongols exhausted and disunited politically, and in the seventeenth century they fell, piecemeal, under Manchu domination which continued for over two hundred years.

'Yet a feeling of belonging together, a sense of identity as the subjects and posterity of Genghis Khan, seems never to have deserted the Mongols, and this was one of two internal factors which helped to give them the vision and strength to recover their independence from the Manchus when the last imperial dynasty in China was swept away in 1911. The other factor was the spiritual unity conferred by the universal acceptance of the Buddhist faith in its Lamaist form, and by the reverence accorded to the Jebtsundamba Khutuktu, or Living Buddha of Urga, the head of the Lamaist hierarchy in Mongolia. Undoubtedly this continuing sense of community would have been nugatory had not the international interests of Russia demanded the survival, if possible, of an independent or autonomous Mongolia, to act as a buffer along part of the frontier with China. Mongolia's inability to assure her own independent existence was clearly demonstrated, for instance, in 1919, when an aggressive China took advantage of the temporary impotence of revolutionary Russia to re-annex Mongolia. Nevertheless, had the

157

Mongols not had the capacity for self-assertion, preserved under long years of subjection to an alien power, it would no doubt have proved impossible for the Russians to create and shore up for very long an artificial Mongol state.

'Mongolia's situation between two great world powers forces her to a greater degree of adaptation and acquiescence than might be the case if her geography were different. An indication of this is that her frontiers are arbitrarily drawn, especially on the south, and exclude more Mongols, especially within China, than they embrace. But it is of great historical interest that the Mongols were able to keep alive, first some sense of group solidarity and, later, their newly gained but precarious independence, until it became possible to stabilize their frontiers, to create from the rump of the nation a viable state, and to profit by the exaltation of nationalism in the middle of the twentieth century to achieve international recognition of this new Mongol state within frontiers agreed with their two neighbours. No other central Asian people has been able to do as much, and Mongolia's present status compares very favourably with that of Tibet, whose historical development over the past two centuries is in many ways analogous to her own.

'For over sixty years Mongolia has been developing as the second socialist country in the world. The main point at issue is the extent to which the Mongol revolution was a native growth and the extent to which it was a reflection of the interests of a foreign power, the U.S.S.R. It is impossible that at the outset the Mongol revolutionaries, whose purpose it was to enlist Russian support in expelling the Chinese and who enjoyed the confidence of the Living Buddha, can have envisaged the sort of control the Russians were to exert over their party only a few years later. This party included men of a wide range of opinion. As things turned out, the moderates were soon removed, but theoretical Bolshevism played only a negligible part in the first stirrings of the revolution in Mongolia. Nothing in Mongolia's history presaged the rapid movement towards communism which took place after 1921 and more especially after 1929. There was no Mongol revolutionary movement until after the October Revolution had taken place, and for the first eight years or so the most influential figures in Mongol affairs were Buriats of Soviet nationality. The Mongol revolution in general followed the pattern of events in Russia. In the form which it took it was determined more by events in the U.S.S.R. and by direct Soviet intervention than by Mongol needs, and though of course it dealt with Mongol problems, these were often tackled in a way imposed by Russia. This analysis will not be acceptable in all quarters, especially as it points up the extent to which Soviet actions abroad under Stalin belied the conviction of Marx and Engels that revolution and socialism should not be imposed from without. Understandably, the relaxation of Soviet monolithic control since the victory of Tito, the death of Stalin, and the emergence of communist China, has made an enormous difference to Mongolia's situation, and in recent years she has been able to give effective expression, both at home and abroad, to her independence ....

'Mongolia has ceased to be a secret land: she has emerged on to the international scene. She has now reached a plateau of relative stability. The storm and stress of the early revolution are behind her, and the problems of the future — economic growth, modes of agricultural and industrial development, educational consolidation and so on — are of a different order from those which exercised her during the first three or four decades after the revolution began. Those classes and individuals thought to be hostile to the revolution, in particular the lamas, have been eliminated, religion has been more or less extirpated, certainly as an institution if not as a residual attitude of mind. The economy is now differentiated, and no longer limited to a relatively primitive, extensive form of herding. Mongolia has now reached a stage where it is reasonable to take stock of the past and suggest the general lines the future will take. Given the continuance of the present determining factors, international peace, an effective administration, the continuity of financial and technical aid from abroad and the will to technical development, Mongolia will move in the direction forecast in the Party's fourth programmes concentrating on matters of economic and technical development in a Marxist framework, rather than on social change'.

In 1971, however, an article in the *Daily Express* referring to Mongolia as 'Russia's cowboy colony' caused offence.

Unlike the Soviet Republics, Mongolia possessed all the centralized attributes of an independent State, and natives, at least nominally, manned the offices of Government and of the economy. It was, of course, the case that her liberty of action was heavily conditioned by external aid and by political and geographical factors, but she was not alone in this dependence. 'Tributary' State was at this time a nearer definition of her place than Soviet colony, province or protectorate, a tribute paid in international support and in the loan to her suzerain of a military frontier 600 miles to the south.

Czarist policy sought to limit Russian involvement in Mongolia to the minimum necessary to secure Russian frontiers. Successive Soviet Governments, while vastly increasing Russian investment and presence, also supported the creation of a buffer state. At no time since the revolution have Russia's Far Eastern interests, or her potential opponents, permitted her to consider annexation.

The policy of the U.S.S.R. appeared to be rather, through technical and budgetary aid, the establishment of an economically viable Mongolia serving Soviet strategic objectives in Central Asia. Natural conditions, and the lethargy and frivolity of the inhabitants, did not make achievement easy. The results of the fourth Five-year Plan, and the Directives of the fifth demonstrated mismanagement and imbalances in economic strategy which the Soviets plainly intended no longer to tolerate. Measures of control and surveillance were therefore introduced in 1971, disagreeable for the Mongols and, worse, ineffective. The Soviets questioned the practicability of the objective itself. But since they could neither annex nor withdraw, they were caught in a trap of their own devising, not released by the dismissal of senior Politburo members, nor by the issue of unverifiable figures concerning overfulfilment of the plan.

The fifth Five-year Plan aimed at economic viability mainly through a switch in emphasis back from industry to agriculture, including compulsory direction to animal-husbandry of 50,000 school-leavers, increased labour productivity in industry and increases in electric power and in the exploitation of mineral resources, but not only was the herd, at 21.8 million, smaller in 1970 than it was in 1929, but a figure of no less than 200 million was once forecast for 1958. Some material progress, albeit accompanied by more discontent, has since been made, but self-sufficiency did not follow.

Mongolia, under communism, deprived of outlets other than through Comecon, and, most important, without the use of the China ports, could not stand on her own feet. The wealth of the country lies in its mining potential and in its livestock. No amount of Soviet aid in these areas (or in irrelevant industrial construction) would ever lead to the production increases that would be generated by the demand and skill of that free market which Mongolia's obligatory vassalage to the U.S.S.R. compelled her to reject.

No Mongol would have then seen matters in such categoric terms, although in 1971 there was some slight diversification of purchase, towards the U.K., Japan and Western Europe. (96.1 per cent of foreign trade was, however, conducted in 1970 with Comecon and all Socialist countries.) And progress towards the signature of an Anglo/Mongol trade agreement seemed a more liberal indication.

But in political and commercial terms the leadership in 1971 remained firmly bound by training, faith and even marriage to the Soviet alliance. While the re-emergence of China might have appeared to offer an additional option, it was not one that Mr. Tsedenbal and his colleagues were likely to accept, other than in minor trading matters. In the light of historic Sino/Mongol relations, this dogmatic attitude, while unfortunate, not least for Mongolia, was comprehensible. In the absence of a Sino/Soviet rapprochement, the very thought of which must have terrified Mongol leaders, it was also likely to endure, even after the gales of the 1980s which shook the Soviet world.

VII

COLLEAGUES AND FRIENDS

THE VALUE OF A BRITISH PRESENCE in Mongolia lies in the visible witness we afford of a different civilization. While one could not expect Mongols to regard it as 'better' (for them), it is self-evidently different, and superior. Secondly, while we remain a Power, if attenuated, with Asian concerns, it would be absurd to deprive ourselves of the opportunity of observing events, not only inside this enormous country, but at the Sino/Soviet cross-roads which it forms. Our trade in 1971 was small, if not minuscule, but might increase; the Cultural Agreement had led to exchanges of people and of material which opened windows for the Mongols on alternative scenes. We had a local ability through vigorous representation to stifle, at least temporarily, Soviet-inspired Press campaigns hostile to British policies elsewhere, an ability to which the Foreign Office's excellent relations with the Mongol Ambassador in London reciprocally, and greatly, contributed. It could not, in short, be helpful to ostracize or lock a people in.

I was conscious of bias. Mongol Ministers and officials, compared with the self-righteous bigots of the DRV, were genial and approachable; we travelled freely in wild and outlandish regions untrod by English foot, or very few, and long ago; every evening throughout the long summer we fished fast, deserted streams ten minutes from the Embassy, while, in the winter, disgraceful battues of partridges took place on the snow-covered steppe.

It was less agreeable for the rest of the staff and, indeed, for anyone without their own young children at the post. There were few normal urban distractions. Strong inner resources, or special interests, were required, but, given these, political, human and scenic interest, plus the unusual effort needed for self-administration, were enough to make service at Ulan Bator rewarding, if not exciting.

Disadvantages for the staff included the small size of the Mission, the empty life of the capital, the total absence of Mongol friends resulting from the authorities' paranoia at that time, induced by Soviet norms, and the relative absence even of congenial colleagues from other Embassies. In fact, some East European, Cuban and, even Soviet guests attended staff functions, but infrequently. And the distrust implicit in totalitarian regulations caused us, too, to respond sometimes with our own phobias. These were particularly sharp when the régime refused to permit Mongol children to attend a Christmas party in the Residence. But, if foreigners express outrage in Communist societies, that will be recorded in some way or other. Later that afternoon the prohibition was lifted.

Occasional Cubans, especially negroid, the Hungarians until a new Ambassador lost his nerve, an intelligent and cultivated Pole, the Rumanians until the Soviets arranged the removal of their First Secretary for 'too close' association with ourselves, were permitted access to our junior staff. But the French, Indians and Japanese provided the bulk of acquaintance.

The Japanese, after negotiation over war damage, re-established diplomatic relations half-way through our tour. Their first chargé d'affaires, never wholly sober, was a Mongol speaker. At one of Ulan Bator's frightful receptions, he addressed a Mongol Minister:

'You have an Inner Mongol accent,' said the latter. (Inner Mongolia is in China, not in the Mongolian People's Republic.)

'Yes, I was based there in 1943.'

'In what capacity?'

'A monk at a Yellow Faith Lamasery, cover for espionage on behalf of the Japanese forces against your country. I was caught just across the frontier by an Outer Mongol military patrol. The soldiers did not kill or seize me because, knowing your customs, I instantly removed the saddle from my horse, and lifted it in the gesture of surrender.'

'And then?' harshly enquired the Minister.

'The patrol let me go, thinking that I would die in the desert. They took the horse, naturally. But they did not know that, behind a sand dune, I had another horse.'

'What!' said the Minister. 'We've been looking for you for 30 years.'

Mr. Tsuge, the eventual Ambassador, had been for some years a prisoner of the Soviets captured in their drive through Manchuria. When, in 1973, I returned to the capital from leave in England and sought from him news of local events, he replied, 'News? What news? There is never news in Mongolia.'

He continued, however, that Ulan Bator's only dry cleaner had recently informed one of the Japanese attachés that the concern had fulfilled its plan; no more clothes would therefore be accepted until the following April. This seemed to me a goodish joke, the logical collectivist consequence. It later emerged, however, that far from fulfilling the plan, the shop had run out of (British) cleaning fluid and forgotten to order more. The anecdote thus neatly illustrated both Leninist lies and Leninist incompetence, although it also may have demonstrated lack of British commercial competence.

This Ambassador also saved our Government large sums through the loan to me of a member of his staff, a qualified masseur who applied acupressure and heat (shiatsu) to my back, causing pain but eliminating the original complaint. The brandy offered to this Third Secretary, however expensive, was incomparably less than the airfare to London and an osteopath there.

Visitors provided entertainment. A few days after arrival, and informally dressed, I opened the Embassy doors to an American couple who, announcing themselves as Ambassador and Mrs Chernov, demanded to see 'the Ambassador'. (Howard Chernov had been a senior U.S.I.S. official and U.S. Ambassador to the Osaka Exhibition, although currently owning radio stations in California.) Like the defector in the garage, he showed disbelief when I acknowledged the soft impeachment. I suppose Heads of Mission should wear coats and ties in working hours, not shirt sleeves, even in Mongolia.

Chernov hinted that he might have been charged with a preliminary role in negotiating diplomatic relations between his country and the M.P.R. (His visit, some years later, led to a U.S. wrestling team which conscientiously lost every bout.) Nothing, then or later, came of it, at least until the 1980's.

The Soviets have always dreaded the effects of an American presence on their own local prestige in Mongolia. The Americans, for their part, rejected as exorbitant Mongol costs that were − however exaggerated − locally normal, while insisting on all the panoply of marine guards, nurses, etc., which the Mongols did not then accept. Nor could the two sides then come to terms on the construction of an Embassy. In the meanwhile a body of U.S. diplomats equipped with up to two years' training in the Mongol language was dispersed unrewardingly around the globe.

The Chernovs joined our fishing expeditions. Howard Chernov elsewhere distinguished himself by, against orders, leaping out of his official car into the state broadcasting studios, which he inspected at the double from floor to floor, his escorts in hot pursuit.

Small numbers of American tourists visited Mongolia every summer. They were shown round the city, driven to a resort (Terelj) near Ulan Bator and flown to Hujirt, a fairly boring itinerary, as well as being obliged to eat the hotel's food while in the capital.

Their considerable dollar payments for the privilege were invariably held up in Moscow on transfer from New York, so that the Russians could make something on the turn before passing them on to Ulan Bator. The Mongols would then threaten not to grant exit visas to the tour groups until payment was received, at which point panic-stricken U.S. citizens would seek help from us. Although the solution was simple, a telephone call to the U.S. Embassy in Moscow resulting in instant release of funds, it was irritating, even frightening for the visitors. Nevertheless, we were thereby enabled to entertain annual groups to large informal dinners. Had we been shrewd enough to take their names and addresses we would, on our later posting to Washington, have been able to freeload the whole way across the United States.

The Mongol authorities sometimes caused pain to these and other tourists by arbitrary expropriation of exposed film at the airport. This procedure was stringently applied to a mixed party of young British Trotskyists who transited Mongolia by train on return from China to the U.K. during the Cultural Revolution. I happened to be at the railway station when this sallow and unwashed collection stopped there, unsteady and reeking of marijuana. I was subsequently instructed by the Foreign Office to recover the Trotskyists' property from the Mongolian Administration. Mr Luvsan-Rinchen, supervising Western affairs in the Ministry of Foreign Affairs, told me that the film was being developed in Hong Kong and not yet available. (If that were true, I had no idea how the Government had arranged it, lacking as they did any kind of representation or contact in the Colony.) In spite of fortnightly requests, the films were never returned. I observed finally to Luvsan-Rinchen, most civilized of Mongols:

'I suppose that the value of these photographs of China compensate you for the lack of a Mongolian Intelligence network in that country?'

He smiled thinly and did not demur.

Among other English visitors, apart from our family and friends, was John Gibbons, Mongolist pupil of Professor Owen Lattimore at

Leeds University, who ordinarily lived on a house-boat in the U.K., in which he and his wife brought up a young family. In Mongolia, John resided in the University itself without complaint in restricted circumstances on a diet which was evidently insufficient.

'If Communism worked,' John once said, 'life here would be intolerable. But, thank God, it never does.'

John King and others taught English at the University. Caroline Humphrey of the Scott Polar Research Institute at Cambridge, with much experience of Yakutia and of the Buryat Mongols of the U.S.S.R., continued her Mongol studies in Ulan Bator. Jim Pringle, Reuter's Bureau Chief at Peking with prior service at Havana and, later, at Bangkok and Beirut, visited us to re-establish the reputation of British journalism, a task which, in more than one regard, he successfully completed.

We became, furthermore, for the British Embassy at Peking, Simla to their Delhi, visits beginning with one from the late Sir John Addis, the most knowledgeable expert on Chinese ceramics of his generation, who was able to see in Mongolia, for the first time, the cradle of the Yuan dynasty.

Eric Staples, retired naval officer, now Chaplain to the Embassies at Moscow, Helsinki, and, eventually, Ulan Bator, was Vicar of the English Church at Helsinki where he resided. Once a year, and sometimes more frequently, in spite of notable ill-health, he took the Trans-Siberian at his own expense to visit and conduct services with us, even before becoming our official chaplain. The ice on the floor of his compartment in the train at Moscow was, on one occasion, still solid when he arrived at Ulan Bator. Eric's entry in Crockford's Clerical Directory was the second longest in the book. The entry in the Diplomatic Service White List for the British Embassy in Mongolia was the shortest; we were the smallest diplomatic mission in the Service. After I had addressed the Protocol Department in the Foreign Office on the subject, however, Ulan Bator drew level with Tegucigalpa by the addition of one Chaplain, while Eric defeated the nearest rival in his professions index by a head. 'Chaplain to Her Britannic Majesty's Embassy at Ulan Bator, People's Republic of Mongolia' was, at least in terms of printed space, unbeatable.

All through our life in Mongolia we looked forward to the arrivals of Owen Lattimore, Mongolist, most electric of writers, teacher, friend and the greatest traveller in Central Asia of this century. Owen, brought up on the China Coast, after education in England worked into Manchuria, Peking, Mongolia and Chinese Turkestan (Sinkiang) until 1938, later writing books whose contents are as dazzling as their titles: *The Desert Road to Turkestan, High Tartary, Turkestan Reunion, Mongol Journey* etc. etc. From 1934 to 1941, he lived in America as editor of *Pacific Affairs,* although acting from 1941-42 as President Roosevelt's representative and political adviser to Chiang Kai-Shek. He was later arraigned by Senators McCarthy and McCarran as the 'chief Soviet agent in Asia', and, although cleared of McCarthy's charges, was not formally vindicated by the United States Government until 1977. From 1963 to 1970 followed 'the happy years in England', until his wife Eleanour died tragically as their aircraft landed in New York. During that time, and since, he taught at Leeds University, where he remained Emeritus Professor, and voyaged regularly to Mongolia, a full Foreign Member of the Academy of Sciences.

One day, while he was having tea with us, we heard him referred to on Peking radio as 'an international spy'.

'Owen, do international spies get a lot of money?' my wife enquired.

'Well, they ought to get *more*, oughtn't they?'

With his agreement, I started to write his Life, both in Mongolia and on our return to England, when he spent frequent weekends at the Old Parsonage. One day, when I had amassed some sixteen hours of tape recordings, he said that he had now decided to undertake an Autobiography. I did not try to remonstrate or dissuade him. I must, however, have shown disappointment.

'Don't worry,' he said soothingly, 'my book will create a demand which yours can later fill.'

Other visitors included foreign Ambassadors at Moscow and Peking accredited to but not resident in Mongolia. With these or, rather, with Ambassadors from N.A.T.O., the E.E.C. and other allied nations, we made it a point not simply to discuss local events but to show them my despatches, thus ensuring that our views, at a time when 'acceptance' of inevitable Communist triumph was all too widespread, had a wider distribution than Whitehall alone. Most Heads of Mission, unfortunately, made the journey out of curiosity or obligation rather than interest. One's information, therefore, tended to go in one ear and out of the other, the Shah's envoy, for example, remaining in Ulan Bator for less than a day, returning to Moscow in disgust.

The Turkish Ambassador, however, General Turkmen, later to become Foreign Minister, was a different matter and, with his Private Sec retary, accompanied us on country pursuits. I told him that I was afraid that my daughter might, in her little Mongol/Soviet Communist Kindergarten, become too dependent on the myth of Lenin. She had already begun to bawl songs about the protection afforded by the Soviet Army to 'little children everywhere'. (It emerged eventually, we have seen, that Lenin was for her no more than 'the man in front of the Ulan Bator Hotel'.)

Ambassador Turkmen was at pains to calm our fears. He pointed to a portrait of the Monarch. 'My children are at a Soviet school in Moscow. But just as, when they return home in the evening, we talk to them at length about Ataturk, so, no doubt, do you discuss the Queen. The two sides do more than balance out: the home side wins.'

The King and Queen of Afghanistan made a State visit to Mongolia accompanied by Ministers and a large retinue. One Minister told me that the country's revenues were greatly augmented by foreign hippies: 'We arrest such people, selected on the basis of their parents' known wealth, for possession of drugs. We then hold them in our uncomfortable prisons, and cause their fathers and mothers, in America or elsewhere, to be informed. So far, we have not yet had one instance of failure to secure large quantities of foreign currency in exchange for the release of these children. They are, after all, no better than criminals, and criminals dangerous to their own countries.'

I asked the Afghan Chief de Protocol, an elegant if anachronist figure in sponge-bag trousers and short black coat, uncustomary wear in the People's Republic, whether he had ever been to England: 'Not many times since I left Eton,' he responded. Most of these attractive people were murdered in the coup d'etat marking the overthrow of King Zahir Shah.

VIII

THE WESTERN PROVINCES

IN THE SUMMER AND AUTUMN of 1972 we travelled to four of the five Western Provinces. These areas, linked under both the Jungarian and Manchu Empires, form a historical, if no longer an economic or political unit.

Hovd, the capital of Hovd aimag, a centre of the Jungarian Khanate until 1758, and thereafter, until 1911, the seat of a Chinese Manchu Amban, was an oasis city, in semi-desert and bare mountain, in the west of Mongolia. Nothing remained of the Yellow Sect monasteries, nor of the Fortress, nor of the Amban's palace, their sites occupied by a children's garden, an empty swimming pool and a stadium, shabby and mosquito-ridden, with modern grandstands in Moghul style. Yet it was a pretty town, shaded by poplars from the hot sun, low white walls replacing the dilapidated plank fencing common elsewhere. Horsemen wheeled elegantly about the streets. The white tents were here varied by the clay huts of Chantu and Dungan and even Soviet architecture seemed lighter and less depressing. But the gaze of wily Habdal, Chairman of the Aimag and a Kazakh professional administrator with previous service in Bayan-Olgiy and Uvs aimags, was as indirect in avoiding discussion of Mongolian history here as in denying incidents on the Sino/Mongolian border, 'with the exception of strayed cattle', over the past two years.

In this Province Manhan somon incorporated a cooperative farm reached across a barren plateau in the fierce prevailing drought. I cannot recall a drive, even in Mongolia, of such boredom and discomfort, enlivened only by the Kazakh driver's resemblance to Elvis Presley, by the Kereksurs (Turkic burial circles, of which Mongols usually profess ignorance) and by the Black and Black Water Lakes in the eastern distance. Here Mr Baasai, the elderly and dishevelled Farm Deputy Chairman, earlier mistaken with his staff by Avgandamdin, my Ministry companion, for wandering Mongol drunks, stumbled through his duties with worried attention, concerned that, owing to the drought, no animal of the cooperative was less than thirty miles from the centre itself. The inhabitants of this somon were exclusively Dzakhachin, a Mongol (Oirat) race, perhaps 15,000 strong, with their own dialect, not always comprehended by the Khalkh Avgandamdin.

Habdal told me subsequently that he intended next year to submit plans for irrigation by canal from the rivers feeding the two main Hovd lakes, a draconian innovation for the conservative, pastoral Mongol. He also appeared receptive to suggestions for fodder crops of the type found south of the Karakorums, but nothing would come of that.

Hovd aimag seemed a thin place, in rainfall, topography and the character of its peoples, an area without qualities. But this was not always so, for the region produced in the 18th century the last great Oirat leader (Western (Jungarian) Mongol), Amursana, who in treacherous grandeur surpassed even the Achinese and Ayush in the 20th. Both are celebrated by public statues in spite of earlier Soviet disapprobation of the former. To meet, in this *galère* a jet-set Austrian hunter related to my daughter's godmother was disconcerting.

Hovd covers 30,000 square miles, of which little is wooded, but is well supplied with lakes. The Altai Mountains run through the province, their highest point at about 13,000 feet. We were told, with what accuracy I do not know, that the aimag produced coal, meat, skins, wild pigmeat, fish, mica, wool, furs (mainly wolf and marmot) and that the total herd of livestock was 1.6 million. The population was said to be around 60,000 including Mingat, Olet, Kazakh, Dzakhachin, Urianghai, Khalkh, Chantu, Torgut, Durbet, Bait, Hoton, and Dungan minorities and 'some Chinese who had chosen to stay with us'. There was, nevertheless, a serious labour shortage, attributed oddly to the large proportion of young people in the population.

There was little ploughed land. Cucumber, tomatoes and apples were grown in the south-west on the Bulgan River. Three kinds of melon were grown by the Chantu, and very good we found them, including Huluu Amtat Gua and Tarvas. Medicinal herbs providing oils, vitamins, fodder and the ingredients for certain alcohols are also found. One rare white flower, the Burkhan Tsetseg, sometimes known as the God-Flower, (literally, the Buddha flower) grew two feet tall in the high Altai. I was surprised to be told by Habdal that the Hovd fish spawned in June and July, and that fishing would be poor until mid-

August or September. The Soviet Military Attaché had earlier informed me that there had been no limits to his catch in June on the Black Water Lake (Har Us Nuur), but I certainly caught nothing there.

We were shown, among other enterprises, a free-range egg farm producing 118,000 eggs per annum, one of which was drunk raw in our presence by the Manager, possibly of Chantu or Dungan origin. The hens looked over-used by their roosters, although this may not be rare on chicken farms anywhere.

The Hovd museum contained, inter alia, a vast 7th century iron cooking pot with a 12th century Mongol inscription, and a perfect Tzu Chou vase. The theatre was closed, half the company being on tour and half on holiday.

★　★　★

Kazakhs formed a large proportion of the population of Bayan-Olgiy aimag and did not care who knew it. (There were few Khalkh, and the remainder were said to consist of Urianghai (Monchok or Altai) and Tuvans.) These descendants of the Naiman Middle Horde were a charmless people, bullying, impolite, between whom and the Khalkh there was no affection; their only noticeable virtue seemed an absence of financial greed, almost unknown elsewhere. The Kazakh Deputy Chairman, Nasilen, hidden behind black spectacles, wore badges bearing either Lenin's profile or views of Moscow. Speeches were rather propagandist and pro-Soviet, a phenomenon rare elsewhere. Official contacts with Alma-Ata are frequent and I believe that Kazakh attitudes here were conditioned as much by Soviet as by Mongol policy. Although one authority asserted that the MPR encouraged the Kazakh to look to the U.S.S.R., and although both Governments have used the Kazakh to foment unrest in Sinkiang, Avgandamdin's shocked reaction to Kazakh behaviour seemed more socially significant.

Olgiy, the aimag capital, stands on the Khobdo River, at a height of some 10,000 feet in the Mongolian Altai. Dwarfed by its magnificent surroundings, the pink Opera House alone saved the town from the dreariness of modern construction. (Khamza, the Kazakh Party Secretary, told me, however, that the French Ambassador had referred to Olgiy as having 'accomplished more in fifty years than had Paris in a thousand'.) The Kazakh female white wimple and bib were still to be seen, the splendid male headdress, however, reduced to a round embroidered skull-cap of many colours.

At the Tsengel somon, reached through precipitous mountain ranges, their peaks still snow-capped in the evening sun, vast draughts of airag were consumed and brick-hard curds surreptitiously trousered. Even greater difficulty was experienced with the appalling Kazakh national dish, half-boiled legs of mutton reposing in a tin wash-basin, surmounted by a sheep's head, the teeth jauntily protruding. It is the privilege, and duty, of the honoured guest to slice, and eat, from this memento mori, the gristly lips, cheeks and, dear God, the ear. My wife and I met the delicacy head-on on three occasions: neither vodka nor the testers, carpets, hangings and chests of the Kazak gers were adequate distraction, while our hosts rudely conversed with one another in their own language. (It must be noted that the women, at least in this region, are often ignorant of Mongol.)

But the fish in the Khobdo River, the latter crossed by pontoon ferry also carrying motorbicycles and Bactrian baggage camels, were plentiful and full of fight, more so, indeed than the fisherman, under orders to take a cup of vodka after each catch. And two female eagles tethered on the fiery plain, trained to stoop in winter on fox and wolf, had a weight on the arm evidence at least of Kazakh muscle. (The Kazakhs claim sole use of these birds, although we know from Douglas Carruthers that the Kirei (Kirghiz) were employing the method in 1911.)

This province in the extreme north-west corner of Mongolia, bordering the U.S.S.R. and China, contains the beginning of the Mongolian Altai with a high point at Mount Friendship, described in Tsengel somon as somewhat less than the 15,000 feet claimed in the capital. The province has twelve counties including eleven collective farms, a state farm and a fodder farm. All somons were alleged to have 8-year schools and kindergartens; one in six of the population were receiving education. Instruction was in the Kazakh language as well as in Mongol. Specialist schools existed in the Kazakh language only. Newspapers were printed in Kazakh in addition to the Mongol language press. Tsengel somon was said, on different occasions, to have either thirty miles of common border with both China and the U.S.S.R. or to have a border which stopped ten miles short of the Chinese border. I did not know if that meant that there was dead ground on the Mongolian side of the Chinese border, or that another somon intervened. The former seemed more likely.

Leopard, ibex, bear, wolf, deer and arghal abound. Tiger, mentioned as existing in Hovd, were not referred to and even their existence as a species was denied on our visit later to the Gobi-Altai. A mineral water is found in the somon. Although the County Chairman, a domineering, red faced, hook-nosed, pork-butcher of a man, assured me that lorries could get out to Olgiy from November to April, I think that, in this mountainous country, Tsengel may well be isolated from time to time during that season; the temperature can then fall to -50°C.

★ ★ ★

Uvs aimag was approached with reverence, in immortal memory of Carruthers, over the Yamaat (Goat) plateau and through the towering canyons of the Turgen and Hahiraa ranges. Behind and before us lay the blue lakes of Achit, Uvs and Hyargas. In the aircraft the Kazakhs vomited freely.

The province, in beauty, and in goodwill, gaiety and kindness is close to paradise, and the capital, Ulaangom, ringed by large ger settlements, with its tree-lined streets, a sleepy hollow of some charm. When I said to the somon Chairman that we did not usually drink more than three glasses of vodka for breakfast in England, he correctly commented, 'You are not in England now'.

An experimental research station had been in operation for about six years at the western edge of Ulaangom, producing red, black and two kinds of yellow currant, currant wine and 'cognac', five strains of barley, vegetables, apples and 'wild' strawberries. The station was fly-infested, bred presumably from the irrigation canals. Two glasshouses contained young plants under 'whirling-sprays'. The apple trees were trained almost to the ground and they, and most of the fruit trees, were covered in winter. Some of the apples were pathetically small. We were enchanted to find that the sign on the gate of this establishment, announcing its function, was in very fair English for the occasion.

Eastwards for ninety miles stretches a broad, green plateau bounded to the north by the salt Uvs Lake and sand hills and to the south-east by the Haanhohiy mountains, allegedly onomatopoeic for 'falling rivers'. In the reeds by Uvs Lake were found gull, tern, stork, crane, duck, goose and heron, while coveys of partridge and sand-grouse rose from the plain. The officials of the East Gobi somon provided lunch, a guest ger and fishing at Lake Bayan and, in Bait custom, accompanied us halfway to our destination of Malchin.

Malchin somon and cooperative farm is also Bait, lying in the foothills of Haanhohiy at the site of a monastery mapped by the Russian geographer Potanin. (The monastery, its winged roof replaced, is now a storehouse). Vodka and rice pudding for breakfast were followed by a tour of the somon, by a superb demonstration of cutting out, roping

173

(with the western leather lasso) and breaking of young horses from a herd numbering six hundred and fifty. This practice, brutally compressed into three days, would not suit English conditions.

Quantities of liquid, milk or grain, non-distilled to triple-distilled, were absorbed in the Brigade leader's ger, gregariously crowded and periodically invaded by calves. Luncheon was committed in a guest ger, the stalwart chairman, Batam, a one-armed veteran of the battle of Khalkhan River against the Japanese, belching unrestrainedly. Singing, drinking and wrestling, with the members of the cooperative, their wives and children, continued almost until dusk, myself contributing Old Macdougall and Roll me Over, and being forcibly lifted head high by the local wrestling champion. So far as he was able, Batam sang us the Homi, entirely vocal but somewhat resembling the sound of a Jew's harp, an extraordinary effect among Mongol singers. We parted with embraces and emotion. It was a good day, under blue skies and flat-bottomed Mongolian clouds.

Uvs aimag contains agreeably few Kazakhs, the population being Durbet, together with Hotons, Bait and seven other minorities. The humour, good manners and insouciance encountered here were refreshing, while Dashdonner, the Deputy Chairman and a Khalkh from Selenge aimag, had a shrewd and reserved wit. It is worth recording that the Ulaangom museum contains the helmet and chain mail of Amursana. Legend relates that he left them with a herdsman in exchange for a horse, when fleeing towards Russia from the Manchu. And some of the most savage Lamaist armed risings against the Communist State, as savagely repressed, occurred in this aimag in 1930 and 1932.

★   ★   ★

We arrived in Govialtay aimag by mistake, re-routed there in midair in an unheated Ilyushin 14 (its clock set for Moscow time), the weather prohibiting descent in Dzavhan. The journey thus took us through the Hangayn Mountains at 19,000 feet, not a cosy height in a copy of the Dakota. The authorities had five minutes notice of our presence in their aimag. At one point we had flown for some miles through a canyon heavy with snow and ice, so close to the mountains that they seemed to be within reach. My wife, as was her practice, went instantly to sleep. On arrival, I congratulated my son Mark, visiting from Australia, on his sang froid.

'You don't know, father. I read the same page thirty times.'

This vast south-western province has a border over 300 miles long with Chinese Sinkiang. Although, as in Bayan-Olgiy and, to a lesser extent, Hovd, there was strong evidence of Soviet 'cultural' influence, in particular Russian language training, there was no sign of a Soviet military presence or of other than commercial activity. Whereas we were debarred from the two aimags on the eastern frontiers where the main Soviet military presence is alleged, we were at least allowed into the western provinces. But as we were not given access to their frontier areas, I would not draw any firm conclusions. Certainly the wastes on either side of the Sinkiang/Gobi border seem little suited to military activity.

The aimag is divided between desert or semi-desert and the Altai mountains, red and purple in the afternoon sun. The Shargyn Gobi, en route for Haliun somon, a vast plateau of sand, clay and shale, supported in this rainless season only meagre scrub and pasture. The landscape is typical of the aimag, the southern third of which is, indeed, an uninhabited waste frequented only by antelope, wild camel and wild ass. In the dark surrounding bulk of the Altai roam lynx, snow leopard, arghal, wolf, saiga, bear and ibex, upon which tourists inflict light flesh wounds in season.

The chairman (Mr Bazar) of Haliun somon was a zoologist who, apart from the gallant but unpromising task of growing fruit and vegetables, had devoted himself to the cross-breeding of wild and domestic camels, sheep with arghal, goat with ibex, and horses with wild ass. Some results seemed impressive, and perhaps central to the problem of subsistence in this windswept, barren region. No sightings, according to the Province Chairman, had been made in 1972 of the Tah or Przevalski, the ancestor of all horses. It seemed possible that this semi-zebra striped animal, found only in the Tahriin Shar range, or zoos elsewhere, might have finally succumbed to natural extinction or the bullets of Chinese frontier guards.

The aimag contains, besides unexploited iron and copper ore, large quantities of open-cast coal, but the economy was based on animal husbandry and the capital, Altai (once Yosonbulag), contained no industry whatever. Altai was, indeed, no more than a couple of streets with a hotel facing the wrong way, Party and Government offices, some houses, and a museum, all surrounded by large fenced ger encampments. The roads, or tracks, led, as everywhere in Mongolia, straight on to the steppe. It was surprising that this lost tract of land should contain so many Turkic and Chinese artefacts. Although caravans may have passed through under the Manchu, only a few troops and junior officials can have resided in this appanage of the Western Region.

The First Secretary of the aimag's Party Committee, Mr Hurlee, seemed to pride himself on the barley, potatoes, cabbages, apples, water-melons and onions which he said were being grown in his unrewarding territory. Certainly we saw some of these in Haliun somon, but the only hope for this province lay in an improved livestock, dependent in turn on more wells, shelters and labour.

Haliun somon and cooperative farm is to the south of Altai. Founded in 1959 on territory which had hitherto carried only a few gers, it was a compact village with accommodation in the VIP room little short of comfortable, always excepting the outside sanitation. Mr Bazar showed us, besides his herds, including the amazing sight of a thousand camels roaming round a single ger, cabbage, garlic, onion and potatoes, thousands of apple trees standing in four hectares, and some ill-tended currant and gooseberry bushes. He claimed that his potatoes yielded twenty tons per hectare and that he harvested 500 lbs per acre of fodder crops.

Round the fences of an enclosure attached to the somon raced a herd of saiga, eternally attempting escape, indifferently observed by a flock of geese, a wild ass foal and a brown antelope. On the mountains Mr Bazar showed us the magnificent result of an ibex-goat cross. The local goat are black with spatulate horn, but the cross was a pure white miniature ibex giving nine lbs of wool per shearing. The local sheep much resemble a small arghal, but we did not see any progeny of their cross-breeding programme. In a further enclosure we saw a Mongol chestnut pony with a wild ass dam. Mr Bazar told us that they were 'becoming intimate'.

On the way to see a projected reservoir, we observed two large combines cutting a fodder crop for which a hand scythe would be considered adequate in Scotland. This reservoir was to be fed by a nearby stream and by snow-water. It was cut out of sandy soil, but unlined with stone. When I asked Mr Hurlee whether the water would not run away into the sand he said that he thought it might, but that they were 'going to try'. The canal to the valley below was, on the other hand, well if crudely stone-lined. They were, it must be admitted, unusually conscious of irrigation at this somon, and had not done badly.

The party and administrative buildings here were crammed to an unusual degree with Soviet literature and posters. Haliun had the customary 'club', 8-year school, hospital, bath-house, hostels, kindergarten etc. In Govialtay as a whole, half the somons were connected by aircraft and all by 'road'. The nearest settlement to the Sinkiang border was the somon of Altai in the south-west (there are two Altais in the aimag), ten miles from the frontier. This comment, coupled with that at Tsengel in Bayan-Olgiy, led me back to an earlier thought about 'dead ground' on the Sino/Mongol frontier.

In these provinces we again received welcomes whose apparent warmth much mitigated the discomfort and even squalor of their conditions. Traditional Mongol hospitality, although bureaucratically yoked to the Pan-Marxist bandwagon, in a country whose beauty is scarcely corruptible and whose people maintain robust humour, continued to make travel an agreeable duty.

We have been, in a few provinces, the only British in living memory ever to have been seen by the inhabitants and, in nearly all, the only British diplomats. These visitations, from outer space as it were, excited well-mannered curiosity, but no goggling. We tried to react similarly and also, within dignified limits, to abandon our reserve to our hosts' often strenuous requirements. It seemed to us that this response, in contrast to the hectoring, alcoholic and domineering behaviour of Soviet guests, offered an image, to which Mongols were reasonably attracted, of a different and more civilised people, energetic, moderate, unassuming, ready to listen and of decent appearance.

★   ★   ★

In Mongolia as a whole, however, 1972 brought no economic or political advance. Stalin is alleged to have prophesied a Mongolian population of 30 million, and a herd of 200 million by 1958. In 1972 the population of 1¼ million was about equal to Birmingham's but in a territory half the size of India, while there were fewer livestock even than in 1929. People left, or did not greatly breed, in this harsh territory and the slight rise in the birth rate under Socialist incentives was more than matched by animal losses under Socialist centralism.

Not only the Scots left a barren land for Empire. But Genghis Khan in the 13th Century could rely only on the Mongols, and perhaps only on his own line. His Empire faded in dynastic squabbles, over-extended communications, decadence, the awakening of the Catholic Europe and the Ming. A sort of One World faded with it. The Mongols went to sleep, or bickered; Shamanism and, later, the Yellow Faith, lulled; there was no other Genghis, nor demand for one. The Manchu, in the 17th Century, found little more to conquer than tribes who fought each other as treacherously as the invader.

When, in 1911, the Mongols rediscovered enough unity to expel, or slaughter, the Chinese colonists remaining at the fall of the Manchu Empire, the dilemma had not yet been resolved. Mongolia, although economically unrewarding, was for others strategically vital. Bolshevik policy, under Chinese and White Russian armed pressure, moved from the gingerly detachment of the Tsarist Far East Department, to intervention. Mongolia became, in 1921, 'The First Satellite', led initially, as the old institutions collapsed, by a class of criminals and illegitimate outcasts, butachi. In the past 50 years Mongolia had developed as a Soviet military base, in exchange for a hope of economic viability which the Soviets, of all people, were least competent to ensure. Settlement, in 1972, was visibly less successful than the limited nomadism which, without adequate preparation, collectivism claimed to supplant. Industry was spotty, labour-intensive and irrelevant, while the exploitation of mineral resources, arguably the last hope for Mongolia, had hardly begun. Soviet control now included Russian officials who sat without apology in most Mongolian institutions, including now, the Ministry of Foreign Affairs.

The MPR was an inefficiently, if lavishly, subsidized buffer State, but it was the Mongol's own State, and not a part of the U.S.S.R. Mongols are Asians, and their insouciance, even the practice itself of Communism, were no more than sly acknowledgements of the strategic value placed on them by their two neighbours. Since the Soviet Union provided four-fifths of the Investment Budget for the current Five-year Plan, the Mongols at least selected the most lucrative paymaster. And continued exhortations against religion, idleness, drink, irresponsibility and other 'survivals of the past' indicated that the paymaster had little modified the Mongol character.

In the service of the U.S.S.R., as well as providing real estate to meet an illusory Chinese military challenge, Mongolian Ministers in 1972 received from and paid visits to most countries of the Socialist world in the interests of solidarity and of the image of Mongolia as an independent, newly-developed State under Socialism. This latter concept was so absurd to us that we might have been at risk in underrating it elsewhere. The Chinese, on the other hand, while pursuing trade and other negotiations, treated the MPR as a Soviet puppet and, in October of that year, rudely rebuffed a probably disingenuous Mongol approach towards revived accord. Ideological relations were, if anything, worse than in 1971. The new factor in Mongolia's external affairs was the establishment of diplomatic relations with Japan, already resulting in a stream of Japanese commercial and other visitors. While the scope for trade and aid must not be exaggerated, an expansion of contacts with Japan could only ease matters for the Mongols, not least, in the very long term, politically. Much had changed since the Battle of Khalkhin Gol.

Anglo/Mongolian relations chugged along. We were there, according to the British Press, to provide a window on Central Asia, which we did. And we had, again, successfully knouted impertinent criticism of Her Majesty's Government's policies, particularly on Ulster. We were also still there to give to the Mongols an alternative window to that northward-looking thing with which they had landed themselves. However marginal and frustrating was the enterprise, it was a wise venture. Trade had grown, student and other exchanges prospered and would be renegotiated upwards in April. We continued to be seen and grudgingly admired. (We had recently aroused local pleasure by dressing the children in the Mongol deel). Another cause for grudging popularity were film shows about Hong Kong and whisky distilling, at which we served Tsingtao and San Miguel, much appreciated by our guests.

IX

OFFICIALS AND OTHERS

MONGOLIAN OFFICIALS IN THE CAPITAL, although reserved, were kind, scrupulous in meeting our requirements, and amenable, if gingerly so. Appointments were almost invariably granted within twenty-four hours.

We suffered an early incident in which post office employees opened and inspected a non-confidential bag containing newspapers etc. It seemed an honest mistake and apologies were professed in response to our protest. On one occasion a Queen's Messenger, who had been warned not to do so, was taken into custody for photographing too archaic a spectacle in the Sunday Market, but his release was rapidly secured. A militiaman removed film from my wife's camera when she was caught photographing the Venetian campanile of Dzamin Und railway station, hanging half out of the carriage window to do so. Had we been in possession of our identity cards, no action would have been taken. The Head of Protocol once publicly upbraided me for shooting pigeon in an area which I had not sought permission to visit. We were, on certain beats of the Tuul and Kerulen Rivers, arbitrarily told to fish elsewhere. We always obeyed, returning when the mounted game-warden had disappeared over the nearest hill.

In the interview with the *Daily Mail* referred to earlier, my wife had been damagingly misquoted as alleging that, since nothing suitable was available on the local market, she supposed that all comestibles would have to be imported. She said nothing of the kind. In fact, we imported only wines, spirits, tobacco, sometimes butter, olives and a few other delicatessen. This process needed care. Wine bottles burst en route in winter and butter liquefied in the summer, as my successor discovered. At a reception shortly after arrival, I was personally abused for this slight by a Minister more heavily in his cups than usual. At a luncheon we subsequently gave for him, however, we demonstrated that every item on the table, other than wines but including the enormous joint of roast mutton and even the vegetables, had been locally acquired. Mongols, as nomads, boil in gigantic cooking pots, not roast their mutton. But that did not reduce the quantities consumed on this and other occasions. No one who has eaten Mongol, especially Gobi, mutton will ever again find *lamb* exciting. 'You have done very well,' he said as he gave his jovial benison.

Our Nanny, Mrs Taylor, a determined walker and explorer, once had not returned by nightfall from an expedition into the Bogd Uul. These hills were wild and, as has been remarked, reputed to contain wolf. Murder was also rumoured to have taken place there and, since the area was a 'security zone', the police were said to shoot first and ask questions later. I was sufficiently concerned to report the matter to them. Richard Lewington, then Head of Chancery, and I thus visited the Central Reporting Station, a building dimly lit and resembling the cockpit of an 18th Century man-o-war, containing, as no doubt in Saville Row police station on a Saturday night, drunks, down-and-outs and prostitutes, one dishevelled but smilingly seductive and primed for sport. The officer in charge sat at his desk under a 'No Smoking' sign puffing away at a cigarette and glancing at us through narrowed eyes. We faced difficulties. The captain had, firstly, to be instructed in the role or function of a diplomat and, then, in the presence in Mongolia not just of a British Embassy, but of the British as a nation, leave alone people.

'But are you not Russians?'

'No.'

'Not even a little bit Russian?'

Our next step, myself in Mongol accompanied by Richard in Russian was to explain to the officer the concept of a 'Nanny' which he, by no means unnaturally, persisted in confusing with 'wife' and 'mother'. It seems unlikely that he ever grasped the concept, but a careful record was made of such snatches as he was able to understand. But to find *any* member of the staff, irrespective of title, at midnight in the mountains was all that we required. Nanny had, in fact, returned to the Embassy in our absence, so that any search party despatched went on a wild goose chase; I doubt, indeed, whether any was despatched. When the captain observed that I was looking at the 'No Smoking' sign, he searched in an embarrassed manner for an ashtray, but, finding none, dropped the cigarette into a cylindrical tin and gently dribbled on the glowing tip.

Contacts with officials were frequent and few days passed without calls on one or other Ministry, the Academy of Sciences, the University, Party offices, etc. These were, apart from the provision of large mugs of black tea, universally agreeable, even when I was there to protest regularly about mendacious coverage of Ulster and other British domestic events in the local press, all carried from Soviet media.

In the presence of Batmunkh, now the Prime Minister, but then Rector of Ulan Bator University, Shirendev, later dismissed as President of the Academy of Sciences, once asked me how my Mongol studies proceeded.

'Progressing. It is a difficult language for us. The constructions are the reverse of the English language, sort of back-to-front.'

'Yes, well. English is also back-to-front, so far as we're concerned.'

At a reception for President Husak of Czechoslovak I was presented to the latter by President Tsedenbal. As all the Heads of Mission had waited, standing, for over ninety minutes for this privilege, I had chosen to reply pettishly in Mongol, rather than Russian, to Husak's greeting.

'Who's this?' said the Czech.

'That's the British Ambassador,' replied Tsedenbal, somewhat the worse for wear. 'He only speaks Mongol.'

'Can't you find anyone in Mongolia to teach him Russian?' the President crossly but revealingly enquired.

These receptions were, as in all Communist countries, an ordeal — interminable speeches, toasts, unpalatable zakuski, glass after glass of vodka — exceeded only by the tedium of Praesidium meetings, at one of which even Ambassador Gunnar Jarring took forty winks. They did, at least, afford opportunities to discuss with colleagues such few subjects as were of interest, but the rigid segregation of men from women was unnecessary, causing the gatherings to resemble Australian social life in the 1940s.

We arrived at a Reception, held by the Chinese Ambassador, Mr Shu Wen I, in his ornate Embassy, at a time when Anglo/Soviet and, thus, Anglo/Satellite relations were at their lowest ebb. As we entered the Hall, the walls were thickly lined with glowering Russians, East Europeans and their wives, bulging untidily out of crimplene dresses, most of them successfully projecting disapproval and dislike. It would have been an unpleasant, even alarming, moment were it not that, far away down the room, we saw the Chinese, in a group, gently applauding our arrival. Chinese relations with their hosts and with the latter's associates were very bad indeed during those days, nearly every formal occasion until at least 1975 including comments by Mongol leaders taken by the Chinese as ideological or national insults with consequent walk-out by the celestials.

Mr Shu Wen I and his staff became our friends, with the Jugoslavs, Rumanians, Japanese, French and, although in no united forum, the Indians, forming at least, however unorganized, a 'shadow opposition', without which we should have been isolated. With them, and with the others mentioned, we were able to pool at least some knowledge and opinion of the extraordinary country to which we were accredited. The British contribution, since we travelled and the others — apart from the French who were rarely present — did not, was considerably the largest in these exchanges. The Chinese, who had a persecuted 'colony' with restaurant and vegetable stalls in Ulan Bator, and whose citizens were also dotted about in the provinces, were forbidden to travel. The others preferred not to.

Russians and some East Europeans, because all other forms of complaint were condemned as ideological or, at best political, complained endlessly about their health, in particular about high blood-pressure allegedly caused by electric storms. According to one Soviet informant, five Russian colonels had died in the Gobi in the first three months of 1972 from cardiac complaint resulting from storms and rapid atmospheric changes. (My interlocutor informed me that he himself took 'oxygen pills' against the contingency.) It was entirely probable, but the real causes were drink, lack of exercise and too much food, not the climate of Mongolia, outré though that was. The men drank and slept. The women stuffed themselves with jam and chocolate, crying 'Vitameen, vitameen!'

Russian technicians tended to gather in the 'dance-hall' of the Ulan Bator Hotel, furnished, other than with tables and chairs, almost entirely by the sort of coat-racks that still stand in pubs, and once stood in the halls of working-class homes. This establishment and its juke-box provided the High-Life of the capital. Because the shortage of women was extreme and the hunger of the technicians unappeasable, two other male members of my staff accompanied us when my wife and I visited it.

The other Embassy wives had expressed no inclination to attend. They were probably right, but the Russian artisans, all of whom were over-lubricated, not to say flushed with wine and music, were obliged to take no for an answer, if only because that answer was given by three men and not one 'unprotected' woman.

These pursuits, however, provincial, were of the city. Most of our days, and those of Joanna and David, were spent in the green hills and valleys, beside the rivers of Mongolia, every weekend in the summer — for myself almost every evening — and on those same hills in autumn and winter, now brown or dusted with snow. (In that continental climate with, anyway, only ten inches of precipitation per annum, snow did not lie for long, except on the mountain peaks.) The winter temperatures around the capital would then fall to as low as -30°C and the windscreens of the Landrovers would freeze to a 6″ patch of visibility. Our picnics on those occasions were short, with the motors kept running. But at least we saw the harsh beauty of the country, the terror for herdsmen in the approaching storm, the far peaks snow-crowned across the valleys.

For the children it was a happy time, both in the extended family of the Embassy and in the Mongol/Soviet nursery school, hung with portraits, not of Jesus Christ as in kindergartens in the West, but of Lenin. Children are not taught to read or write in the U.S.S.R. or M.P.R. until much older than in the U.K. Instruction such as there was, for they seemed to pass their time shouting, playing and sleeping, was oral and visual. Ours were, as 'capitalist' children and children of a capitalist Ambassador, treated like a prince and princess. It was, thereafter, in the rigours of British private and public schools, a difficult act to follow.

X

JOURNEYS TO CHINA

MY WIFE AND I visited Peking every six months, one journey being that made in November, 1972. No civil aircraft had flown between Peking and Ulan Bator for years, communication now being provided by one 'fast' and one slow train weekly, the former the Trans-Mongolian Express from Moscow and the latter going no further north than Ulan Bator. The Trans-Mongolian contained coupés panelled in mahogany and hung with blue Chinese silk, each coupé with its own shower and basin. The journey from Ulan Bator took 30 hours. The slow train was comfortable enough, but more basic and needed 47 hours. Both trains were Chinese-run, but the Chinese restaurant was not coupled until the frontier, while the Mongol restaurant was extremely bad and usually shut.

The windows in November were obscured by ice; in summer, they could not be opened. This was oppressive, as was, on the slow train, the constant bouncing movement and the absence of proper service. The conditions for second class passengers were fetid and rough: wooden bunks three deep, in a long open carriage, on which lay, cocooned, Mongol and Chinese peasants in huge sheepskin coats, babies howling or at the breast.

For most of the first day, on the southward journey, the train crossed the Mongolian steppe, snow-covered now, through the mountains and foothills, dropping down to the Gobi in the evening. All the length of the route evident marks were visible of the Soviet military presence: hangars, factories, huts, barracks, radar, runways reared out of the desert and fell back, with no attempt at concealment. Frozen Russian soldiers laid telegraph poles, handled huge concrete construction blocks, observed complacently by the idle Mongol. Buzzards perched on the overhead wires. Most gers were in for the winter, but the birds of prey waited for the steppe animals. In the distance herdsmen, standing in their stirrups in the high Mongol saddle, appeared on the crest and ridges of the hills or circled grazing herds.

After a brief pause at the wild-west bar at Saynshand pullulating with soldiers and farmers bawling for Russian cognac, customs and immigration formalities were conducted at the Mongolian border station at Dzamin Uud. There Mongol officials searched not only the train roof through hatches in the ceiling, but also the samovars and the hot-water system, whether for people or goods. They seemed little interested in ourselves, remaining friendly, polite and incredulous.

After the stink and the cheerful, frequently drunken incompetence of Mongol railway stations, often patrolled by massive Soviet Military policemen, descent at the Chinese border station of Erh-lien, which was also the point at which the change is effected between Russian and Chinese gauges, created a different impression. (The place, in less happy days, was notorious to ill-used Queen's Messengers and other travellers.) The town lay in the Gobi Desert, roughly equidistant between Ulan Bator and Peking. The sprawling yellow station contained a comfortable lounge, bad restaurant, money changer and lavatories of unexampled squalor, its platform once hideous with bloodthirsty revolutionary posters. In the lounge People's Liberation Army genial officers interrogated passengers as to age, income and personal appearance, encounters lasting up to six hours and broken only by hilarious attempts at luncheon.

In late 1972, however, possibly to outface the Venetian campanile of Dzamin Uud, the Chinese were refurbishing Erh-lien. The station was in turmoil and closed to the public. Shaggy, fur-clad Chinese workers gaped industriously, while a large mobile crane repeatedly hauled to the roof one wheelbarrow containing coal or cement. (Full employment was assured.) The more aggressive posters had been removed post-Nixon-visit, the remainder peeling. Accommodation for passengers was confined to brick sheds lightly heated, in the savage Mongolian winter, by minute metal stoves.

Few members of the PLA were to be seen, formalities and contacts with passengers now in the hands of another department. Our 'guide', Mr Ho, a young man of bourgeois background employed by the Bank of China, invited us on a tour of the town, hitherto off limits. A wind of unprecedented velocity hurtled eastwards out of the Gobi, cramming the mouth with dust and sand. As we leaned laboriously into the storm, the achievements of Elias, Stein, Lattimore and Fleming became, for the first time, actual. 'Dear God,' as Scott observed elsewhere, 'this is an awful place.' The awful place at least contained a general shop selling bicycles, wireless sets and some fruit and vegetables, a department store and a bookshop, where, however, Chinese works greatly out-numbered Mongol. Among many institutions noted in the neat rows of two to three-storey brick buildings was a barracks for the PLA, 'responsible', according to Mr Ho, 'for checking foreigners'. A street to the south bore prohibitions in Chinese, English and Russian.

Mr Ho also told us that Erh-lien had a population of 10,000. A fertilizer factory lay a mile to the south. The town's water supply was pumped underground from thirty miles away, vegetables were, at least in summer, of local origin; in this arid region, with the limitless semi-desert bearing only isolated and scrawny scrub, it seemed implausible. In reply to my question, he said that Chinese only, not Mongol, was taught in the schools of Inner Mongolia. This categorically disposed of liberal arguments about Chinese policy towards this minority. (Equally, but incidentally, the effect of the gale on the desert invalidated Lattimore's contention that border security was guaranteed by sweeping with horse-drawn brooms. This, anyway, had seemed unsound, since the authorities could hardly investigate camel or horse tracks.) Mongols observed in the shops were cowed and frightened, lectured like children by the Han, without spirit or panache, their deels shabby and torn.

Two East German travellers were bundled out of our shed. A fair lunch was consumed before reboarding the train, to chug gently on through the terrible landscape of Inner Mongolia, unbroken by the mountains of Outer Mongolia, into the ochre beauty of the loess country, through the huge North China plain at dawn, the mists hanging about the walled villages, under the Wall and on to Peking.

The journey, in winter or in summer, was not the least enjoyable nor instructive of our tours in Inner Asia, its fascination matched by the evidence of Soviet hostility to her neighbour, and its attendant war-like preparations. Those included the facilities to move rapidly to the Sino/Mongolian border a much larger concentration of troops than the 30,000 stationed in the Mongolian People's Republic itself.

XI

MONGOLIA IN THE WORLD

IN 1973 THE LEADERS OF 'The First Satellite' still maintained the alliance with the U.S.S.R. and planning rigidities discarded elsewhere, while continuing to cram nomadic agriculture into the Procrustean bed of collectivism. The herd was no larger than in 1972 and as vulnerable to endemic natural disaster; no attempts at self-sufficiency in feed were made. The Five-year Plan for animal husbandry was unlikely to be fulfilled. Yet, as Lattimore once said, 'the world needed more and more her pasturelands, to supply civilization with wool and meat and hides.'

Meanwhile, rain, frost and hail rendered published grain statistics wholly misleading, in terms, at least, of quality. The figure of 100.4 per cent fulfilment of the Industrial Plan also looked fudged. Transport and building were slightly better, if not as good as claimed.

It was, however, clear from the 1971 Comecon programme that the partners could no longer tolerate the Mongolian disgrace, even if remedial methods involved large initial sums in Grant Aid. East Germany's agreement in the autumn to switch from loans, etc. to gifts was a consequence of this programme, as was the concurrent rescheduling of the Bulgarian debt. But the Soviet/Mongolian Agreement in February on the exploitation of copper and molybdenum at Erdenetin Oboo, claimed by Mongol and Soviet interlocutors to hold resources as great as Chile, was more likely to transform the M.P.R.'s long-term economy than any programme of light industry with its low quality and almost unsaleable products. (There were also unconfirmed rumours of revived crude oil extraction west of Saynshand.) The Japanese, too, seemed ready to consider disbursement of up to US$80 million on approved projects; but, even if Japan did not make agreement conditional on transit through China, lengthy bargaining lay ahead.

Thus, in the 1980s, if Socialist distribution systems allowed, one might perhaps be able to have a suit cleaned. The shops also might not then be restricted to pink berets, saucepans, and shelf upon unattended shelf of combs.

Communism in Mongolia was, nevertheless, an unnatural concept, originally not much more than an excuse for ridding the country of Chinese private traders. The excuse had now become ossified into doctrine, and its coincidence with Soviet objectives a source of feather-bedding for the Mongol. Although, for instance, the M.P.R.'s increased per capita income was presented as the result of Communist method, it was more precisely the result of Russian subsidy. The secret, independent, stubborn character of this Asian people, however regimented, and it was regimented, might thus just survive party and police-state pressures. Certainly the commitment of the leadership to narrow Marxism/Leninism and to Soviet power still evoked no obvious enthusiasm among the people, especially the younger generation. Neither were Mongols much more drawn to Siberian pretension and contempt than to Chinese.

The M.P.R. was now in diplomatic relations with over sixty countries and had mutual *Représentation sur place* with four non-Communist States (U.K., France (sometimes), India and Japan); negotiations over the establishment of relations between the U.S. and Mongolia were at a standstill, but Mongol/West German negotiations were at a more promising stage. In spite of this non-Communist presence, the M.P.R's foreign policy, whether in peddling the Asian Collective Security System in Iran, India, South-East Asia and elsewhere, or in direct defamation of China, followed her master's voice. (In this regard, and in her self-presentation as an under-developed nation regenerated by Socialism, she might not have been quite unsuccessful.) As in internal matters, any change of policy would depend on the development of the Sino/Soviet dispute and not, in the short-term, on non-Communist influence.

An Anglo-Mongolian Trade Agreement, under negotiation for eight years, was breathlessly concluded before the U.K.'s accession to the E.E.C. forbade further bilateral agreements. This Agreement eventually helped to expand the joint turnover beyond the 1973 figure. The renegotiation of the Cultural Agreement in 1973 led to a Programme of Exchanges wider in kind and degree than before, and the Mongols were pleased by its new Government to Government framework.

Indications of a Mongol taste for British qualities were again often observed more plainly in the provinces than in the capital, but, whether in the aimags or in Ulan Bator, a colder wind might blow for Mongols if the British Embassy, and those others named were not here at all. A more considerable presence, including a U.S. Embassy, might, however, be necessary before there could be effective counter-action to the increasingly interlocking structure of Soviet and Mongolian committees, ministries and other institutions. Nor might counteraction be effective without resumed carriage of Mongolian trade through China, that also dependent on a compromise in the Sino/Soviet dispute.

XII

FURTHER TRAVELS

IN 1973 MY FIRST TRAVEL DESTINATION was Bayan-Hongor aimag. The southern third of Bayan-Hongor aimag is Gobi, and the border runs with Inner Mongolia. The north is forested, and the centre, which I visited in June, is pasture. There had been no rain since September, 1972, and the Herd, except yak, were thin. Marmots, however, flourished in large numbers, up to 250,000 being hunted annually for the fur-clip.

For this pursuit, the stalker wears a white headdress in the form of two large ears and waves a white object on a stick, simulating a tail. The marmot, far from frightened by this impersonation of dog, fox or wolf, is enraged and, whistling, shows itself to the gun.

Bayanhongor city was destroyed by earthquake in 1961. (It is said that, on the preceding night, ibex, arghal, lynx and wolf from the mountains, 'forewarned' of the disaster, joined the herd on the steppe.) The new city, removed some miles from the old site, contains schools, a hospital, a hotel, offices and apartment blocks of Soviet design, but was only a quarter complete in 1973.

The aimag goldmine, prominent on Mongol maps, was said to be out of production and 'full of holes'. Basalt (for building materials) was exploited and the workings shown to me; the local administration temporarily refrained from mining most other minerals including copper. (The Soviets, in other words, had not provided finance.) Animal husbandry was the chief concern, and the 1972 census showed an increase in quantity, if not quality, over 1970. I saw few shelters, but efforts to improve the fodder crop and, under Soviet technicians, to bore wells, were evident.

The discovery of hot mineral springs at Shargaljort was recorded in 1907. They are now hard to miss, some 320 springs pouring or trickling down the rocks, whether cold, warm or at temperatures of up to 97°. The waters are piped into agreeable gers fitted with baths, or are drunk, or used to drench towels tied round the heads of patients who perambulate in that fashion about the upland village. High blood pressure, diseases of the liver, nervous complaints, kidney, stomach, eye and ear afflictions are treated at Shargaljort. The resident physician told me that one spring was of benefit to the left kidney and another to the right.

I also visited, on plateaux among the arid mountains, the somon of Erdenetsogt (Precious Flame), distinguished by a herd of 23,000 yak, and by a Yellow Faith Monastry in good preservation, with temple bells tinkling in the light air. We had that day eaten breakfast and three luncheons in various ornate gers between dawn and noon, with very large quantities of commercial (grain) and homemade (sheep, goat, yak or camel milk) arkhi and of airag. My concluding address made two Mongol officials weep, while the Chairman, when delaying our aircraft to suit his convenience, remarked, 'This province belongs to me. I do what I like'.

★ ★ ★

We visited Hovsgol aimag, the Switzerland of Mongolia, in the company of the equivocal Mr Loochin, pilloried viciously by René McColl in *The Land of Genghis Khan*, when Loochin was acting as his guide. Since that date (1962) he had seen service in the M.P.R. Embassies at Peking and Seoul, visited most countries of Africa and South-East Asia, and was, from 1969-72, Ambassador to the U.A.R., indeed to the whole of Africa, but neither his manners nor his English had in any way improved. Although more or less intoxicated throughout, Loochin yet retained (until rebuked) the instincts of lethargy and secrecy which ensured maximum discomfort and uncertainty. 'In my *negative* land', he shouted, 'Wine is made from *graves*', neatly examplifying characteristics of incomprehensibility and mendacity. At dinnertime, however, he would truthfully bawl, 'Mr. Ambassador, now is the time for *suffer*'.

Moron, the capital, with its older log buildings and shoddy modern concrete blocks, resembled a building lot where finance had been exhausted. Telegraph poles reeled through unpaved streets in which life had stopped. Features of the city included a statue of the aimag hero, Davaadorj, provided, as is the custom, with round eyes, staring out to the mountains where, in 1948, Chaing Kai-Shek's troops killed him. Beside him stood a vast marble Honour Board, usually employed to portray labour paragons, its niches empty save for the Mongol word for 'Daddy' scribbled in pencil with two question marks beside it. Water

192

(there was, of course, no hot water) and light in the hotel were irregular. The cook had been trained in Belgrade. Felt boots, one old flat iron, dolls, herbal medicines in paper spills, and Soviet face powder were to be obtained in the shop.

After a seventy-mile journey by jeep on steppe tracks, frequently interrupted for compulsory refreshment, we boarded the tug *Sukh Baatar* at Hatgal for a six-hour voyage on Lake Hovsgol. The command of this vessel had descended from father to son. Yarns were exchanged between old salts. The beauty of the vast blue lake, enclosed in its forested mountains, was undeniable. It was a pity, therefore, that the Captain should have told me that the boat was built on the Lake, when a plaque on the bridge housing showed the yard to have been at Perm. It was a pity that our hosts should have behaved as if we were, literally, in need of forced vodka feeding. It was a pity that they should have attempted to charge us for food and drink for the entire crew.

I understood that, in Switzerland, one pressed edelweiss could be sold for up to seven francs. In Mongolia, edelweiss (and delphiniums, iris, alpine asters, pinks, gentians, purple scabious) cover the steppe in banks. The plant is used for lighting fires and is also inserted in the boot as a specific against blood pressure. (Most Mongols, by Soviet example, are hypochondriacs.) In these great drifts of wild flowers, among the thick scent of worm-wood, we witnessed the next day, in Tunel somon, another demonstration of roping (with the pole lasso) and breaking, amongst a herd of about 200 horses, less exciting than that in Uvs the previous year, but as unchanged through the centuries as the bright deels and sashes of the horseman, and as the contempt for injury.

Also unchanged, no doubt, was the 'snack' presented in a ger after this performance. A saddle of lukewarm boiled mutton was laid before the guest of honour from which he was required to carve, starting at the right, one slice (not to be consumed) and, thereafter, for himself and all present. (Also displayed are all the intestines, *without exception*, of the animal.) This dish was accompanied by airag, tarag, urum, milk and grain arkhi (mare's milk, yoghurt, clotted cream, vodka), brick-like curds and boiled sweets. Three bowls of milk arkhi and three glasses of grain arkhi are obligatory upon the guest of honour; failure to comply causes grumbling, if not offence, as does inadequate consumption of mutton. (We considered a custom involving the intake by our hosts of tins of snails, or other substances repugnant to Mongols, brought by ourselves for that purpose.) This insistence, not to say nagging, sometimes did not seem like hospitality to me, rather the reverse. The Mon gol words for 'making war' and 'giving hospitality' are almost the same.) Replete then, a Mongol bard in an umber deel and a round purple felt hat recited a long poem to our address. The somon Chairman sang us a song. I replied, which gave pleasure, with our National Anthem. Mr Loochin then asked us at what time we wished to take luncheon; we must have disappointed them.

In downhill rushes at 55 mph in neutral with the motor off, enveloped in red dust, we descended the mountains toward the 'rest house', while the Khalkh driver, Baatar, in his figured blue silk Mongol waistcoat, sang the Long Song.

The province abounds in the Kherekhsur Turkic (Khirghis) burial circles, said to be 2000 years old. One of these circles enclosed a considerable semi-circular pile of stones, with a pit in the middle, about ten feet deep, alleged to have been the tomb itself, plundered in the 13th Century. Beside lay cylindrical granite stones, lightly and indecipherably etched. On one stone I thought to have traced the faint shape of a bird. Nearby stood the stump of a shattered red-stone monolith. Mr. Loochin informed us that, 'The Chinese, in order to destroy our culture, decapitated all our statues'. (We did not refer to Mongol destruction in 1932 of over 600 Yellow Faith Monasteries). But the origins and history, even the Khirghis provenance of these monuments and tumuli, are so controversial that almost any comment may be possible.

Accommodation at 'Rich Red' Rest House was in gers, unusually equipped with electric light, but with an exterior wash-can and sanitation. The fishing on the Eg River, due to recent flooding and to Mr. Loochin's incessant playing of a concertina, was poor. Dinner that evening was the most difficult we had yet endured. Dancing, theatricals and singing, preceded by a jovial address from myself, were staged by the administration and guests before we retired.

The highest point in the province was said to be Buruun Haan, 11,000 feet. I could not find this mountain on any map, but I was told, some 40 miles north of Moron, that I was standing on it. One third of the aimag consisted of forest, fir, pine, larch and some birch, without coherent cutting or planting pattern. The principle source of income was undoubtedly animal husbandry, although 100,000 acres were under cultivation, half to wheat, one third fallow and some to fodder. As elsewhere in Mongolia, severe, but not (by M.P.R. standards) disastrous drought had taken place in 1972. No rain fell before 24 June in that year, although there had been plenty subsequently. The steppe was very green.

The usual claims were made for local wild life, plus, this time, mink and white reindeer. There were also large quantities of 'white fish' from a salt lake in the province: I was unable to discover the eventual destination of the catch, but they were bony and not very agreeable. This province is also the home of the Tssatan, guardians high in the mountains of the white reindeer. This tiny minority, of Uighur stock, was still in the 1970s mostly nomadic, living not in gers but in wigwams.

★ ★ ★

My tour of Arkhangay province coincided with visits there by Soviet Trade Unionists and G.D.R. Youth officials, but excluded Mr. Loochin. One cannot have everything. The Soviet presence advantageously reduced both the attention paid to me and the number of hangers-on attached.

Arkhangay, in the cente of Mongolia and only 300 miles from Ulan Bator, although not a tourist resort, is conveniently placed to receive foreign delegations. No doubt for that reason, the capital, Tsetserleg (Flower Garden), in a bowl under harsh, granite mountains, contains paved streets lined with poplar and willow, while its white buildings with their green and red roofs and the remains of its Monastery are in immaculate condition, the surrounding ger encampments less so.

The Tsetserleg Museum is housed in the Zaya Pandita Khutukt Monastery, Tibetan in design, consisting of an arcade and two main oblong buildings, white but decorated and galleried, with flat roofs and slit windows. It contained a magnificent ger, previously the property of a High Lama, furnished with rich chests and religious incunabula, and a splendid collection of Mongol games, domestic implements etc., as well as the usual rubbish connected with Lenin and his cronies. The caretaker was a dish, with amazing eyes and a minute waist; my guide, Davaagiv, unfortunately, cut me out with her, but Ambassadors would be well advised either to steer clear or make hot-foot for the Museum immediately upon arrival.

The province contained more cattle than any other in Mongolia, more horses than any except Ovor-Hangay and the highest (human) rural population except Uvs. No time was therefore lost in proceeding, accompanied by Mr. Jaltsan, Head of Agriculture for the Province, glued into blue beret and plastic mac, to the steppe and mountains of Great Tamir County (Radiant Road cooperative). It differed little from others visited except in its capacity to receive visitors, in its museum and in the legend of the giant Buhbeligt, who crushed the head of a fire-breathing snake with a forty-foot-high rock (Tahir Rock), and then the tail seventy kilometres away. The rock stands nearby, covered with boastful Soviet and other graffiti.

That afternoon, the 'Zootechnican', using a small tree trunk and grasshoppers, and myself with wet-fly, caught fourteen fish closely resembling rainbow, but almost certainly char, with an average weight of 1¾ lbs. Mongols wrap the fish in an inner container of wet newspaper and an outer of wrapping paper, and cook them in the open over cinders, covered by more cinders for about ten minutes. Scotts could follow the example.

Meanwhile, Jaltsan had shot a marmot, skinned it, removed the bone, filled the skin with the meat and with hot coals, tied the neck and placed the animal on the cinders, periodically turning it by well directed kicks. 'This is illegal', said Mr. Davaagir, my Ministry of Foreign Affairs companion. 'If any responsible person were to know, Jaltsan would be fined fifty tugriks.' 'But is Mr. Jaltsan, as Head of Agriculture,' I enquired, 'not a responsible person?' I recalled John Gibbons' comment that the system of Government would be intolerable if it worked, but that fortunately it never did.

Heavy rains fell during our return journey and forest floods occurred. The steppe runway next day was soaking. We took off eastward in a forty-knot west wind, great waves of water enveloping the AN24.

★　★　★

Dundgovi (Middle Gobi) aimag, lacking the distant glamour of the Southern Gobi and Desert, is little visited by foreigners. Perhaps on this account, its people were of gentle charm and unaggressively hospitable.

Our journeys began from Mandlgovi, the capital, passing through thin Gobi (semi-fertile) land, with its scrub and bush suitable only for the Bactrian, to the northern steppe, a scenic amalgam of the Borders, Australia and the Berkshire Downs. As elsewhere in Mongolia that year, heavy rains had fallen, the pasture was relatively rich and the herd in fair condition. Although the 20-30% increase in weight during a good summer is usually lost in winter, the number of shelters for animals in this province may check this wastage; milk yields were given as: cattle, 300-350 litres per annum; mare, 130-150 litres; goat, 20-25 litres; sheep, 12 litres; camel, 90 litres. Not all these measures are capable of comparison in Britain.

Sum Huh Burd, where we spent the night in a ger, is a village and ger encampment with a small lake surrounded by reeds and rushes, golden in the early autumn, and busy with duck. On the northern shore stands a ruined castle built of the local flat red-stone, well-mortared but incomplete at the death of its builder, an 18th Century Mongol Prince. These great structures forty feet high, with walls four feet thick, are uncommon features of the Mongolian landscape; isolated in the vast plateau, in the howling Gobi winds, it recalled a stage-set for Macbeth.

Adaatsag County, (Life's Banner Cooperative), lies in the extreme north of the province. The Chairman of this somon, much resembling Humphrey Bogart, conferred on me Honorary Citizenship in reward for the consumption of three litres of airag, and invited me to shoot a wolf later in the year, for which I would be awarded a selected sheep. He also told me that overfulfilment of the Plan could carry salary increases of up to 70% and, secondly, that settlement − in buildings − of the rural population and the restriction to the summer of ger residence was long-term Government policy. I did not think that this would be popular, or efficient. What would happen to the grandmothers, on whom Mongol family life depended and what, indeed, would happen to the herd, distant from the somon, in hard winters?

Some twenty miles away, a ger in a Suuri (ger settlement of five to six families), contained not only silver harness bearing coins of the 34th year of the Emperor Kuang Shu, but a Yellow Faith Ochir (Thunderbolt) and three small Tankas. Although large portraits of President Tsedenbal and Marshal Choibalsan were also displayed, 'official' visits to gers do not often disclose religious objects. Their incidence generally, despite steady exhortation, seemed to be increasing.

The ruins of a solitary Lama's residence in a cleft in the red Delger Khangai mountains, lit by red and golden poplars had formed the site of an abortive attempt at a so-called 'Holiday Inn' for Young Pioneers, abandoned because of snakes and the absence of water. In the silence of this lonely and beautiful retreat, fit only for contemplation, one could but be relieved at the failure.

A 'concert' in Mandlgovi on our return, although initially somewhat Russified, included the curious Western Mongol dance with its shoulder and torso movement, deriving, although with Manchu and Shaman influence, via Tibet, from Northern India. In the museum were an undamaged 3-gallon Kiang Hsi blue-and-white bowl, some excellent mutton-fat jade ornaments, a collection of Stone and Bronze Age arrow heads and other artefacts, two 9th Century stone Turkic statues of a seated Prince and his Princess, and another, probably 7th Century, of a Turkic warrior with stylized moustache.

This town possessed a market, though it was not quite on the scale of the Ulan Bator Sunday Market, that vast, incoherent, stockaded gathering of townees and herdsmen in high leather, felt or dog-skin boots, of tankas and of celadon and blue-and-white china, silver koumiss bowls, bronzes, snuff-bottles, coral and silver hair ornaments, amulets and prayer boxes, chalices, bronze lamaist hand-bells, the 'thunder-bolt', silk and fur hats of breathtaking loveliness, purchased or sold in huddled, clandestine bargains.

Difficulty was experienced, owing to the flood of foreigners at the Southern Gobi tourist base, in persuading Mongolair to stop at Mandlgovi for our return journey to Ulan Bator. This was happily resolved on the telephone by Mr. Chuluudorj, our MFA companion: 'You cannot leave Ambassadors lying about the steppe like waste paper.'

XIII

THE LAST JOURNEYS

IN MY LAST YEAR, 1974, we first visited Töv (Central) aimag, which contains Ulan Bator. Our first destination was Dzuunmod (One Hundred Trees), the capital.

Rich as the aimag is in Hun, Uighur, Chinggisite and Manchu relics, we were invited to inspect only the ruins of the Yellow Faith Lamasery (1749) at Dzuunmod, burned down during the suppression of the Monasteries in the Thirties. A worker in the vicinity said that he had seen the bonfire of incunabula. One seldom, in Mongolia, received a prompt or coherent reply, but an instant negative answered my question about the survival of any monks then resident. Repellent accounts circulated about their fate. On the cliffs behind the shell of these Temples, with their four-foot thick walls, restorers had painted a head of Lenin to join the Buddhist iconography retraced in 1971. 'He ruined the place,' said Mr Davaagiv, our escort, 'so he should be there.'

Dzuunmod looks like a set for a B Western, hitching posts and all. It was the birthplace of the late President Sambuu, and of the national poet, Natsagdorj, who died, perhaps of drink, and perhaps by his own disillusioned hand in 1937. Posterity remembers him for:
'This is my homeland
Mongolia, a beautiful country.'
A photograph of his wife, like a Michael Arlen heroine, hung with his in the local museum.

We were despatched next day to shoot wolf and partridge at Ugtaal state farm, 120 miles north-west. On arrival, we were at once informed that all wolves had been shot the day before, and that partridges only migrated to the M.P.R. every third year. (The shortage of partridge was, in fact, due either to chemical fertilizers or to the summer floods of 1973). Our hosts spent the eventual return journey loosing off unsuccessfully, and blaming my rifles, at griffon vulture, and at bustard stalked on foot from behind ambulant cattle, thus presenting the ludicrous spectacle of a party of hunters walking across a water meadow in tenue de ville.

Ugtaal lurks in a fold of far-away encircling mountains at the site of an old Monastery. A small part is arable (wheat, barley and oats) and is rotated annually. Fires are lit around the crop when frost is expected and, in wet years with early frost, the grain is cut and left between the stubble for harvest. Erosion was prevented by alternately sown and unsown plots of fifty square metres, creating a surface of different levels. No foot and mouth had occurred among the herd at Ugtaal for thirty-three years, but the alleged remedy for brucellosis was to 'isolate the animal for six years, or until cured', not easy in an unfenced land. They were evasive, as well they might be on open prairies, about prophylactic measures to affected pastures.

The chatelaine of the guest ger had twelve children, mainly unattractive, between two and twenty-nine — a Hero Mother indeed. The cuisine, although lukewarm, was notably richer in milk and meat than that offered during summer journeys. (At one dinner we were served the same main course (boodz) twice running.) The Ugtaal staff, curious about British agriculture, yet showed a more than customarily Marxist rigidity. Ideas strange to them, or involving only technical discussion of the merits of different systems of resource distribution, fell on closed minds.

Hygiene in this province was not exemplary, but Mongols oscillate between total disregard for that concept, and a punctilious obligation to irrelevant minutiae. When my wife and children paid their farewell visit to a herdsman in the Tuul valley, the latter's wife poured milk into a Kumiss bowl, but then observed a piece of straw floating on the surface. When she sought to remove it with her fingers, herdsman Jig-jig slapped her crossly on the wrist before extracting the straw instead with an old match picked up from the filthy earth floor of the ger. Conversely, most Mongols not only refrain from fishing, but also from bathing, in part because of a belief that the souls of the dead are transformed into fish.

But this Province, from the great grain plateaux of the North to the extravagant mountains near Terlej, like Kwelin, or Ming scroll painting, is not the least beautiful of aimags, the hills and the wide Tuul and Kerulen Rivers affording space for relaxation at most seasons.

★ ★ ★

It falls to few to be drunk on the Mongolian steppe at nine o'clock in the morning. Such was my fortune, in a Landrover, after a gruelling Spring tour of Selenge province.

Selenge is the main granary of Mongolia, rudimentary agriculture having existed there since the 17th Century. (It also holds one of the three industrial centres of the M.P.R., Darhan, described above, which is administratively separate.) An asphalt road, badly damaged and in parts ungraded, runs across the steppe for at least 250 miles from Ulan Bator to Suhbataar and, beyond, to the Siberian frontier. Relatively considerable Soviet traffic was observed on this switch-back thorough-fare, while Darhan now increasingly resembled a Soviet industrial sett-lement. To either side of the road the rich dark earth, obscured by clouds of dust, was being sown to grain.

White, sprawling Suhbataar, although larger, does not much differ from other aimag capitals, a municipal tip of bungalows with green roofs, yurt settlements, factories and columned, classical Russian facades. (We did not, alas, visit Altanbulag or see, across the Soviet frontier, the spires and onion domes of Kyakhta.) At a luncheon given by the Province Chairman, his Deputy, Gombosuren, snored compla-cently, pursuing the practice in the cinema, and *on his feet* in the museum. This museum contained a brass ewer said to have been used by Genghis for the punishment of drunkards. One such actually drained it, earning from the Great Khan the remarkable tribute of 'Camel-Stal-lion'. A photograph of delegates to the 1915 Tripartite Agreement showed frock-coated Czarist officials with Chinese and Mongol digni-taries in their strange tasselled cocked-hats, robes like vast night-shirts and ponderous boots. Another group included 'Little Hsu' and his Chinese staff after their attempted abrogation of Mongolian autonomy in 1920. Their appearance goes far to account for qualified Mongol pref-erence for Russian, rather than Chinese, protectors.

Next day the Chairman of the wood-working combine said that his concern had, three years ago, adopted reforms aimed at greater planning autonomy, bonuses, incentives etc. He professed ignorance of Professor Liberman but, by this stage, our interpreter, Doljintseren, a shepherd-boy from Gobi Altai, was beginning to falter. He had showed his mettle from the start. 'They are doing physical labour,' he replied, when asked why some youths were digging up the roadside.

Our route to Tsagaan Tolgoi (White Head or Alphabet) began amongst conifers in sandy soil, not unlike a Surrey golf-course, soon changing to the mountain-ringed plateaux of Mongolia proper. An alfresco luncheon was consumed, according to custom, on the top of a wind-swept hill. Minutes away, near a sheltered river bank, Great Bustard, Ruddy Shell-Duck and Demoiselle Crane abounded. The Chairman of Tsagaan Tolgoi, had the face of a Stone Man, tiny eyes and mouth flickering malevolently in the flat, black, triangular surface. Mistrust confronted our simple interest. But the most distressing feature of travel in Mongolia, once again, remained the nomad requirement to eat a full and displeasing meal, not only between destinations, but also on departure from one 'centre' and arrival at the next. As the centres nowadays might be as little as two hours apart, and each repast involved a great deal of vodka, strain was imposed. Glorious Mongol days were clouded by thoughts of lunch, lies about one's liver, vegetarian habits and that; just no use. One recalled the Chinese complaint: 'Eating Bitterness'.

On 22 May, after inspecting an irrigation plant and being denied permission to photograph an ox-cart, we set off for Amarbayasgalant (Joyful Calm) Lamasery, in hills commanding a wide valley thirty miles from Tsagaan Tolgoi. Blue iris, yellow and violet Pasque anemone, peach and cherry blossom, purple azalea, trollius (like orange buttercups), columbine, wild pinks and carnations decorated the steppe.

The 17th Century (1635) Monastery lies in a vast pink-walled enclosure and consists of three courts containing temples in the Chinese, not Tibetan, tradition, with brown-glazed sloping roofs and Buddhist animals at their up-soaring eaves. The Great Seals in scarlet and gold swung from their frames in the entrance porch, while in the first court, small octagonal pavilions, like those at the North Gate of the Forbidden City, flank the temple. The second great temple is galleried, trellised and verandahed, its ceilings coffered with blue and gold Imperial Dragon medallions: within stand thirty-six crimson columns, some hollow and leading to conduits. The third main temple, approached by the Turquoise Steps, contains a ceiling medallioned in Manchu and Uighur script and a jumble of gilded lotus and broken statuary. (One of them is devoted to Maidar, the Buddha of the Future.) The Chinese lake and mountain frescoes painted over the roof beams and supports of all these temples, although faded, portray their lost, illusory and lovely world.

Behind, and to the east and west, lie many smaller, steep-roofed buildings, once libraries, seminaries, and dormitories for nine hundred Lamas. Stone and metal incense burners are frequent. Outside the west wall is the white, solitary stupa to Cardinal Duke Zasag, with white attendant yurts.

Amarbayasgalant, although dilapidated, survives. UNESCO, using Japanese technicians, planned to restore it, in order, according to Mongols, 'to provide Mongol youth with an idea of their past', but more probably to attract tourists. The exterior *and* interior columns, and the pavilions, bore the marks of attack by fire. It is strange that the attempt, unlike that on other Lamaseries, was not completed. A companion, Professor E. T. Hall, Director of the Archeological Research Laboratory at Oxford, whom I had not briefed on the Communist suppressions of Lamaism, asked for an explanation of this arson. The Mongols formed a huddle, Doljintseren emerging to inform us that the damage had been caused, not by fire, but by the sun. 'They are,' he asserted, giggling, 'sun-burned'. The ancient curator, who had joined the Lamasery as a novice when he was seven, paused from digging up shards to give us a detached regard.

Fishing on the little Even Gol, and a visit to a shepherd's ger took place. It was on the Even Gol that Teddy Hall remarked on the extraordinary drying property — 'like acetone' — of the dry Central Asian wind and atmosphere.) The ger was notable not only for modern statues of the Buddha and of Chinggisite warriors, but also for the presence of butter-lamps and of Tibetan (Mahayana) Yellow Faith sacred texts. (For the first time in our experience, these artefacts were not accompanied by portraits of Messrs Choibalsan and Tsedenbal.) Picking up a small wooden model of the owner's race-horse, I enquired if it was alive. The herdsman eyed me, and hesitated. 'No,' he said, 'but the horse is, on which it was modelled.' We had thus also met Shamanism. Dried mutton, three years old, was then boiled and reconstituted, a very unsavoury repast, even preceded by thick Mongol cream and sheep's-milk tea. My wife presented the chatelaine with a Wedgwood box of Huntley and Palmer biscuits, while her husband received three packets of Benson and Hedges Special Filter. The 'parting ceremony' from Tsagaan Tolgoi took place by the broad, blue Orhon.

The Orhon somon, (Choibalsan Cooperative), south of Bulgan, was largely devoted to sheep, mainly of its own breed of which each family might own thirty-seven head. The Chairman claimed a birth rate of eighty-nine lambs to one hundred ewes. The gross annual revenue was 5 million tugriks (£500,000), half of which went on salaries, one fifth on investment, and some 60,000 on repairs. Some land was down to wheat, very little to fodder and less to vegetables. The Cooperative had eighty mechanised vehicles, including tractors and combines. There were the moral school and First Aid post, with a medical point in the somon centre.

Under a portrait of Lenin, the Chairman spoke of his people's happiness and contentment due to Socialist Emulation and, in the case of pregnant women, State Care. It was all fairly awful. The most interesting objects in the museum were a maquette of Tsogt Taiji's castle, with Moorish arches and wholly un-Mongolian cupolas, and a model of a Divaazhin, or Paradise, a circular hill crowned by an octagonal Chinese pavilion, from the (destroyed) Buddhist monastery.

Events in the evening took a normal Mongol course. I cannot remember any statistics about this state farm, only song, his handsome mistress, tall tales about wolves, joviality, and the consumption of seven bottles of vodka between six people. Our departure at seven next morning by the new Soviet road between Darhan and the copper at Erdenet included three 'parting ceremonies' involving garlic, emotional embraces, arkhi and mutton.

It was thus that at nine a.m. on 23 May, on the Selenge steppe, I found myself in the condition described at the outset. It was a pity to have learned little about Orhon, but Orhon had not seemed to dislike what it learned about us.

* * *

Before 'glasnost' secrecy and indifference to the individual were as marked in Mongol Airlines as in other departments of that Asian Communist State. Flights, while frequently, and without warning to the traveller, *anticipating* schedules, under no circumstances arrived or departed at the designated hours. Information was regarded as the property of the airline, extracted only with persistence, even menaces, man being considered the passive agent of higher forces, religious or secular. These factors created for the impatient Westerner a mood of maddened uncertainty that did not induce harmonious relations with companions, still less with stolid hosts.

Thus, after waiting two hours for the scheduled flight to Bulgan on 1 July, we were instructed, without explanation, to return to the Embassy to await orders. On rearrival at the airport at noon, not only were no aircraft at all present, but our M.F.A. guide collapsed and was taken off in an ambulance. We boarded an aircraft at four, to be immediately disembarked on the pretext that 'rain' at Bulgan precluded flights that day. When we reached the aimag next morning, the authorities, who knew nothing of our arrival and failed to meet us on the strip, claimed perfect weather the preceding day. No aircraft arrived, in spite of a clear sky, on the day of our intended return owing, according to Bulgan and Ulan Bator respectively, to (non-existent) 'rain' at Ulan Bator and Bulgan. Menaces, for inactivity in a Mongolian provincial hotel is no joke, drew assurances of a special aircraft next morning from the Central Government itself.

Bulgan aimag is a typical, not to say boring aimag of steppe and forested mountain, distinguished mainly by the copper and molybdenum resources of Erdenetin Oboo, alleged to rival Chilean capacities. Since the mine, however, was in process of construction, and since it was Soviet-manned, the authorities claimed inability to provide statistics on the subject. The aimag, notably volcanic in nature, was mainly devoted to animal husbandry, although containing broad acres of cultivated land. The great rivers Orhon and Selenge, flowing between high cliffs, provide, as well as irrigation, the best fishing in Mongolia.

Bulgan was, in the 17th Century, the native land of Tsogt Taiji, perhaps the last Collaborator of the last Mongol (Chahar) Emperor, Ligden Khaan, who in his anti-Manchu, and ultimately internecine, struggles, succeeded only in damaging further the unity of Mongolia. In 1921 Bulgan city allegedly became the base of operations for a joint Soviet/ Mongol victory (the Battle of the Western Road) under Generals Schetinkin and Choibalsan, and including the native hero Hatanbaatar Magsarjav, over the White Russians. (This statement is not supported by historians.) The staff headquarters, in a small wooden house of Siberian design with a Chinese roof, is now a museum containing air-cooled belt-fed Maxim guns, revolutionary banners and proclamations in Uighur script. On a hill to the west of the town stands, modelled on a Mongol war-helmet, the tomb of Magsarjav. (An equestrian statue of Lhagvadorj, like Davaadorj in Moron killed when repelling the 'incursions' of Chiang Kaishek's troops from Chinese Turkestan in 1948, dominates the main square.) In one of the three town museums, each photograph of revolutionary leaders, Magsarjav, Tserendorj ('the old wolf'), Amor (liquidated in 1939), Elbegdo Natsagdorj (jailed 1931), contained also the coldly watching figure of the Soviet Comintern representative.

There is a monastery in Bulgan city, but here, unlike the great Gandan at Ulan Bator, the prayer-wheels did not turn; the flat chant of 'om mane padme hum' did not roll, like the sound from a bee-hive, from Lamas in golden robes albeit torn and often soiled; worshippers did not prostrate themselves on the prayer-boards. The ritual of the Faith, so similar to the Catholic order of service, was dead.

During a visit to a Cooperative, a herd of horses, three hundred strong, was seen nomadizing from Arhangay Province to Ulan Bator, where they subsequently entrained for North Vietnam as part of Mongolian aid to that country. Their fate, whether on North Vietnamese tables or working in the humidity of the Red River Delta, must certainly have been unhappy, paralleled by an earlier, unsuccessful attempt to acclimatize Southern Gobi Cattle in Vietnam.

★   ★   ★

The capital of Dzavhan province, Uliastay ('Aspens'), lies at about six thousand feet at the western edge of the Hangayn Range, a thousand kilometres west of Ulan Bator. The approach in our Ilyushin over mountains rising to thirteen thousand feet, and through narrow dog-leg gorges, was precipitous. In the snows and in summer, heavy rains frequently obtaining, visitors may wait up to ten days for egress.

In the absence of the Chairman and Deputy Chairman of the Executive Committee, we were received by a Department Head notable for his prevarication. The few statistics obtained stemmed mainly from sub-rosa conversations with a Praesidium member and ageing veteran of Khalkin Gol, closely resembling a retired, sunburned Indian Army Sapper Major, white-haired, dapper and white-moustached.

But the province, including Uliastay, a town in three separate encampments in an almost circular plateau amongst high peaks, is of staggering beauty. Our track to Otgon Tengriin ('Benjamin' Sky-God) Mountain lay for seventy miles and four hours along a boulder-strewn steppe ringed by mountains, snow-capped and touched in the evening sun by rose pink and the peculiar sunset maroon of Mongolia and Wyoming. On either side, also, shallow rivers hurried over the stones, bordered by larch, aspen, poplar, willow and pine, most in September turning to palest yellow. The track, now a hundred feet above the river, now across the plain, now forcing its way over intervening hills, was of excruciating discomfort. But great herds of yak and sheep filled the pasture, the white gers of their guardians pitched by the river banks or on sunlit valleys in the surrounding mountains. (At Otgon Tengriin Arshaan, we stayed in a 'prince's' ger, furnished for once with authentic Mongol wooden beds in their brightly-coloured traditional design (Buddha's bowels etc.), set along the sides of the ger around the huge central stove). The next morning we inspected, by an even more appalling track, the North Face of the mountain, and the hot sulphur springs, each named four hundred years ago in Tibetan after their Lamaist founders. Our Ölet (descended from Genghis' mother, and the ance-

206

stors of the whole Jungarian Empire) M.F.A. companion, at the Director's order, sprinted two hundred yards to instruct a herdsman to descend from his yak. Mongols like to be photographed on camels, but they are prejudiced about yaks.

Back in Uliastay, the hotel was under repair and we were accommodated in the headmaster's study of the new Soviet-built school, in which the plaster was already falling. This building was extremely cold, the dining-room being heated by two electric cookers. The cuisine was extempore. We were taken to the museum, the cinema, a motor repair factory and, in general, told a great number of lies. Later, at the vast, empty, walled site of the old Chinese Ambanate to the east of the city, surrendered almost without a fight in 1911 – but, according to our guides, 'taken against 10,000 Chinese by Hatanbaatar Magsarjab in 1921', – Yung Chieng and other shards littered the dry grasses. We were unable to visit the desert of the Great Mongol Sands, inaccessible by road, since the authorities demanded £150 for two hours in a helicopter (AN-2) and would not bargain on the subject, thus concluding our last journey in Mongolia.

In four years we stayed in one industrial city and in fifteen out of eighteen provinces, including two forbidden, in many the first British visitors and, in most, the first British officials. If there were occasions when we, and the Landrover, gave the impression of a County Class cruiser, or even a 74 of the line, the flag was still shown to fairly memorable effect.

The mountains and rivers of Mongolia remain, but no longer for us. 'And this really means,' I thought a little mournfully, 'that I am hardly any more a traveller. I have been a traveller.'

XIV

ENVOI

LIFE IN MONGOLIA BEFORE 1921 has been represented as solitary, poor and short. It does not seem to have been irredeemably brutish or nasty. Its culture was perfectly adapted to its purpose. The great social advances since imposed have been at the price of human and economic distortion, even destruction.

Although the régime that we knew was incompetent, hypocritical and illiberal, Mongols wish to survive as a people and these defects were thus less painful to them against the Statehood afforded through dependence on the U.S.S.R. Some observers, indeed, though their view is supported neither by the violent history of the Republic nor by the high incidence of psychiatric malady, even regard Mongolian Communism as no more than a cynical claim on Soviet finance and protection.

Such observers saw the deel, mini-skirts and jeans of the M.P.R. as evidence of relative liberty. Doubtless they are, and also indicators, if not effects, of the decline of the worst aspects of Soviet Imperialism. But political liberty is not less desirable for not having been a major component of Feudal Lamaism: assertions of the 'higher' necessity of economic equality mis-state the question. The question is not 'bread or liberty?' but how to acquire both. In that country, without political freedom, there was still not enough of either. The evil consequences were a herd lower than in 1929, an irrelevant light industry often at only 10 per cent of capacity, mortgaged mineral resources, food shortages, shoddy housing and consumer goods, a puppet culture, a totalitarian State, assimilation in the Soviet system and de-Mongolization.

Choibalsan's Stalinist excesses were no more, and some, not many, of the other doctrinaire features of party rule had also been modified. But although their passivity enabled Mongols to tolerate the dictatorship of the Few, or often to render it inoperable, the system remained.

The régime was wedded to it and had the power to enforce it on citizens, who, however reluctant, had nowhere else to go. Not many Mongols liked it, or the Soviet presence. They demonstrated their resentments by declining to make the System work, and by assaulting Europeans in the streets. (They also assault one another, but persons taken to be Russians were preferred targets.) So long, however, as the Sino/Soviet quarrel continued, the leadership may believe even now that Mongolia has only restricted choice in either matter. Should it end, and since China's performance in Inner Mongolia has not been magnetic, the choice would be disagreeable. Only a considerable Western and Japanese economic presence could then stiffen Mongols to rediscover enough Nationalism for limited independence of both sides. This concept may no longer be absent from Mongol planning and we should respond as best we can.

As for the economy, I was struck, in going through old Despatches, by all my predecessors' attitudes that the Mongolian People's Republic was viable under the present system, or that it would be if only people worked harder, the weather were better, China were more cooperative, the Russians gave more money etc. etc.

I thought, on the contrary, that Mongolia had for years been basically unviable, because of the futility of rigid Communist economic theories applied to a country in which they were irrelevant, and in which they had also been insanely misdirected. If study of this economy had value, it was not so much in itself, but as an awful general warning against involvement in Marxist/Leninist planning.

Anglo-Mongolian relations included growing exchanges of Trade and Culture which, necessarily without decisive political significance, did much less harm than good. Nor should we deprive ourselves of this window on Inner Asia, nor Mongols of our watching presence. And since it might now be no longer impossible for enterprising British businessmen at least to think about the exploitation of mineral resources here, the UK might have a future role, both profitable and political in terms of limited Mongolian independence, to play.

Life in Mongolia was often interesting and, because of the adaptability, patience and good humour of the other members of our Embassy, usually fun. Unofficial, and official, Mongols were people who, in the happier circumstances of today, have become our true friends. Nor have either Manchu or Russian corrupted the skies, rivers, plains and mountains, the space of Mongolia.

It was a difficult country to leave and, in rain, Tube, and rush-hour, difficult to forget. Our happiness there was deep, our longing for it is still acute, sharp nostalgia never far away. But because return, however brief, might bring either disappointment or, on the other hand, the terrible sadness of the first days after our departure, we will never go back.

Et in Arcadia ego.

INDEX

Reeves, Bishop of Chichester, 35
Roche, John; US Presidential Adviser, 93
"Rolling Thunder", 92, 107, 108
Rostow, Walt (U.S. National Security Council), 94
Rumbold, Sir Anthony. K.C.M.G., 15
Russian hypochondria and other habits in Mongolia, 183

Saiga (Antelope), 176
Salan, General, 51
Sambuu, President of M.P.R., 135, 137, 199
Savannakhet, 27-29
Selenge Province, visit to, 201-204
Shamanism, 177
Shargaljort Springs, 192
Shargyn Gobi, 175
Shaw, Philip, Head of Chancery, Ulan Bator, 131, 132
Shchetinin, Soviet Ambassador to Mongolia, 130, 141
Shchetinin, Soviet General in 1920s, 205
Shirendev (President of Mongolian Academy of Sciences), 182
Sihanouk, Norodom, Prince, 25-27
Shu Wen I, Chinese Ambassador to M.P.R., 138, 183
South Vietnamese Army, 15, 16, 92
South Vietnam, Republic of, 9-12, 19, 21, 90
South China Morning Post, 43
Souvanna Phouma (Lao Prince and politician), 28, 76
Soviets in D.R.V., 22, 52-55, 63, 75, 85, 88
Soviets in M.P.R., 141, 158-162, 174, 177-178, 185-7, 208-9
Stalin, J.V., 137, 177
Staples, Eric, Reverend: Chaplain to British Embassies Moscow and Ulan Bator, British Church, Helsinki, 166
"State Department" (Hanoi Department Store), 70
Stratoliner, 21-31
Suh' Baatar, capital of Selenge Province, 201
Suh' Baatar, revolutionary leader from 1921, 137
Sum Huh Burd: village and castle, 196-7
Suppression of Lamaseries, 1930's, 199-200
Suren, Mayor of Darhan, 151-153

Tassigny, de Lattre de, 51

Taylor, Maxwell: U.S. General and Ambassador to R.V.N., 91
Taylor, Mrs., the children's nanny, 181
Than Son Nhut Airport, Saigon, 15-76
Tien, Consul-General's chauffeur, 30-31, 53
Tov Province, visit to, 199-200
Transport in Hanoi, 68-69, 71-3
Trans-Mongolian Railway, 185-7
Tri Continental Commission, 39
Trombadori, Antonello; author and P.C.I. official, 35, 43
Truman, Harry: U.S. President, 89
Truong, Chinh, 75-87
Tsagaan Tolgoi county, 201-3
Tscherbakov, Soviet Ambassador at Hanoi, 53-5, 86
Tsedenbal, Jumjagyyn, President of M.D.R., 135, 182
Tsengel county, 171-2
Tsevgee, Secretary of Executive of Great People's Hural, 147
Tserendorj, Mongol Leader in 1921 Revolution, 205
Tsetserleg, capital of Arkhangai Province, 195
Tsgot Taiji, collaborator of Chahar Emperor, 205
Tsuge, Japanese Ambassador to Mongolia, 163-4
Tu Do (Rue Catinat), Saigon, 17-18
Tunel county, 193
Turkmen; Turkish General, Ambassador and later Foreign Minister, 167-8
Ugtal, state farm in Tov province, 199-200
Ulaangom, capital of Uvs Province, 173
Uliastay, capital of Dzavhan province, 206
Ulan Bator, capital of M.P.R., 127, 129, 131, 144-5 etc.
U.S. Military and air campaign against D.R.V., 52-55, 68, 80, 84-5, 96-7, 99-101, 103-7, 109, 113-4, 177
Vance, Cyrus, 95
Vientiane, 27, 76-7
Viet Cong, 12, 15, 114
Viet Minh, 8, 9

Warner, Sir Frederick, 76-7
Washington Post, 43
Wild flowers, 193, 202
Wilkinson, Sir Peter, 17, 76
Wren, Christopher and Marcianne, 6